LEARNING IDENTITIES IN A DIGITAL AGE

Digital media are increasingly interwoven into how we understand society and ourselves today. From lines of code to evolving forms of online conduct, they have become an ever-present layer of our age. The rethinking of education has now become the subject of intense global policy debates and academic research, paralleled by the invention and promotion of new learning identities, which are intended to incite teachers and students to think, feel and act as social operators in schools and beyond.

Learning Identities in a Digital Age provides a critical exploration of how education has been reimagined for the digital future. It argues that education is now the subject of a 'cybernetic' mode of thought: a contemporary style of thinking about society and identity that is saturated with metaphors of networks, flexibility, interactivity and connectedness. This book examines how shifts in thought have translated into fresh ideas about creative learning, interactive tools, curriculum reform and teacher identity. The text identifies how learning identities have been promoted and how they position young people as networked learners, equipped for political, economic and cultural participation in the digital age.

Included in the text:

- mapping the digital age
- reconstructing the future of education
- 'making up' digital learning identities
- assembling creative learning
- thinking with digital tools
- prototyping the curriculum of the future
- being a teacher in a digital age.

This book situates education and technology in an intergenerational and interdisciplinary conversation. It will be of interest to students, researchers and practising education professionals who want to understand the wider sociological and psychological significance of new technologies on education and learner identity.

Avril Loveless is Professor of Education and Head of Education Research at the University of Brighton, UK.

Ben Williamson is Lecturer of Education at the University of Stirling, UK.

Changing Times in Education

Series Editors: Ivor F. Goodson and Kristen L. Buras

Learning Identities in a Digital Age: Rethinking creativity, education and technology
Avril Loveless and Ben Williamson

LEARNING IDENTITIES IN A DIGITAL AGE

Rethinking creativity, education and technology

Avril Loveless and Ben Williamson

Routledge
Taylor & Francis Group

LONDON AND NEW YORK

First published 2013
by Routledge
2 Park Square, Milton Park, Abingdon, Oxon OX14 4RN

Simultaneously published in the USA and Canada
by Routledge
711 Third Avenue, New York, NY 10017

Routledge is an imprint of the Taylor & Francis Group, an informa business

British Library Cataloguing in Publication Data
A catalogue record for this book is available from the British Library

Library of Congress Cataloging in Publication Data
A catalog record for this book has been requested

ISBN: 978-0-415-67571-0 (hbk)
ISBN: 978-0-415-67572-7 (pbk)
ISBN: 978-0-203-59116-1 (ebk)

Typeset in Bembo
by Saxon Graphics Ltd, Derby

Printed and bound in Great Britain by
TJ International Ltd, Padstow, Cornwall

We thank our partners, Vanessa and Geoff, and dedicate this book to Cormac and Carys

CONTENTS

LIST OF ILLUSTRATIONS

Figures

Tables

SERIES EDITORS' FOREWORD

In one sense it is always 'changing times in education' – this is of its nature a milieu of transformation and change. There are though a number of reasons for believing this is a time of seismic social and economic change, not just in education specifically, but in the world generally.

Two aspects of these changes will be highlighted in this series. First the dramatic changes in the world economy. Comparisons with the Great Crash of 1929 have been widely commented upon. Significantly the Great Depression which ensued after 1929 and the American New Deal which followed and aided recovery led to broad-based changes in educational policies and practices. Broad changes in the economic landscape have, if history is any guide, led to considerable changes in the field of education.

Alongside these structural movements in the world economy there are the changes accompanying the changeover to the 'network society'. The digitalisation of interaction and, to a degree, of identity, is leading to a transformation of knowledge and subjectivity. To take one instance, our narrative character seems to be partly changing from a version of selfhood represented by a notion of 'inner conversation' towards a notion of selfhood represented by external interactive performance epitomised by 'Facebook identities'. If the subjective assimilation, processing and production of knowledge is changing so also is the means of production of knowledge. The current debate about the future of the book is just one instance of this. This is leading to a significant change in the sites and settings of knowledge production (M. Gibbons, 1999).

This series seeks to elucidate and explicate the significance of these changes in the external landscape of praxis and practice. It aims to do this by focussing on the different generational perspectives on change. The reason for the cross-generational focus is of course partly the seismic nature of the changes underway but also the speed with which these transformational changes are taking place. Such fundamental and rapid change is likely to reduce the common currency of cross-generational conversation and dialogue and make the transmission and production of knowledge much more perilous. For this reason above all, cross-generational perspectives need to be sponsored in the current epoch.

The age difference between the two writers is slightly more than two decades but because of the seismic nature and speed of change, in some ways they inhabit separate universes, as they rightly assert. They note that 'there are two voices in the book, in conversation across different stages of professional career, academic disciplines, research literatures and life stories'. As they explore the implications of this they come to the conclusion that: 'Our different perspectives, or our different *styles of thought*, have led us to address different kinds of questions, to frame and explore different kinds of problems in relation to very different research literatures, to mobilise different conceptual vocabularies drawing from different theoretical approaches, to make different arguments and to offer different kinds of explanation'. This articulate formulation of the cross-generational dilemma also, we think, pinpoints how important it is for us to attempt these cross-generational passages. For both sides of the seismic chasm have things to learn from each other. Some of the knowledge which preceded the digital revolution is of importance and some of it generated since that revolution has been of importance and the reciprocal crossover's in terms of knowledge transfers and knowledge contestations are vitally important.

The result is a book rich in questions and questing. The illuminations with regard to learning identities, the future of education, creative learning and the potential of digital tools are rich and profound. Moreover the cross-generational perspective allows the authors to think generatively and innovatively about future implications. Let us conclude with their words, 'In writing this book we have considered how our thinking for the future of education, technology and creativity is rooted in complex genealogies of past traditions and practices, yet sought to remain alert to emerging alternatives, counter-narratives, and different possible interpretations. This openness to alternative trajectories is important if … we want to insure that the thinking of our young is not fastened down, limited and fixed to our contemporary fantasies of certainty'.

Ivor F. Goodson, Professor of Learning Theory, University of Brighton
Kristen L. Buras, Assistant Professor of Culture, Curriculum,
and Urban Educational Policy, Emory University

PREFACE

This is a book about education, technology and creativity as *objects of thought*, as an array of problems, questions and forms of analysis. How do we think about and make sense of education, technology and creativity? How does our thinking about education, technology and creativity differ and change over time, and what difference does this make to how we act on that thinking? And how did we come to think like this anyway? In focusing on objects of thought, we are trying to provide ideas, concepts and tools for thinking about education, technology and creativity rather than stating what or how we think about them, still less what or how others should think about them.

The reasons for this emphasis on thought derive in part from the process of researching and writing the book itself. The book originated from an invitation by the 'Changing Times in Education' series editors to offer some different perspectives on education in the 'digital age.' As a result there are two voices in the book, in conversation across different stages of professional career, academic discipline, research literatures, and life stories. In particular, our different disciplinary outlooks, from one of us, sociocultural psychology and teacher education, and, from the other, educational sociology and social theory, have given shape to the arguments and the ideas that we pursue throughout. It has not always been easy to reconcile our very different ways of approaching things or to assimilate the very different things we have wanted to say about education, technology and creativity in the digital age. In writing the book, we have both had to try to make sense of how the other thinks, makes sense of, and tries to do things about education, technology and creativity. Our different perspectives, or our different *styles of thought*, have led us to address different kinds of questions, to frame and explore different kinds of problems in relation to very different research literatures, to mobilize different conceptual vocabularies drawing from different theoretical approaches, to make different arguments and to offer different kinds of explanations.

In pointing out these interdisciplinary difficulties, we are not trying to defend the adequacy of our account. Thought does more than direct analysis. It has *effects*. Shaped as we are by our disciplinary and conceptual perspectives and traditions, our styles of thought exert material effects on the very objects we are trying to explain. Through being made thinkable in certain kinds of terms, our objects of thought are made amenable to being changed. Things and thinking are practically inseparable; objects are not distinct from thought. Consequently, we are not presenting a book which details a kind of taken-for-granted reality, but a book which draws attention to education and technology as the effect of the work of thought. The ways in which socio-cultural psychology thinks about, makes sense of, and tries to explain education and technology are not the same as in sociology and social theory. Sometimes, as a result, an object of thought looks like many different objects, a plurality of things configured by different questions, problems and lines of analysis and interpretation. The book reflects these tensions. It seeks to show how, as objects of thought, education and technology in the digital age have been made thinkable in different ways in particular times and places; they have been made intelligible in relation to alternative conceptual directions of analysis; and they have been made legible through particular ways of writing them down, inscribing them as texts—packaging our thoughts up in pages of books—and passing them on as publications for readers to think about themselves.

Our names appear on the cover in alphabetical order, which does not quite reflect the dynamics and experiences of the conversations that have generated it. Avril initiated the invitation from the editors to reflect upon the digital age through her experiences of practice with educational technology in schools and teacher education over a period of 30 years. Ben took up the invitation and shaped the approach to interpreting the digital age as the product of 'styles of thinking' about technologies, pedagogic identities and practices. Without wishing to engage in too much autobiographical detail, it is worth noting that the origins of our respective ways of thinking about the issues here also lie in our own personal and professional histories. In describing her reaction to reading Seymour Papert's book *Mindstorms* (a constructionist approach to learning through active programming) in 1983, Avril reflected on the influence it had on her understandings of learning, practice and subsequent professional life as a teacher educator informed by sociocultural psychology: 'I'd never thought like that before.' A decade later, as a teacher educator, she was writing about 'ICT capability', trying to articulate the pedagogic moments when teachers understand the potential connections between learning purposes and the affordances of the technologies in context, and has subsequently worked extensively on encounters between learners and creative practitioners and educational technologies.

Ben, however, encountered the digital age while studying literature in the 1990s, amidst a swarm of literary, philosophical, cultural and social theories proclaiming the new techno-informatic conditions of postmodernism, the culture of media simulation, and the alleged disintegration of certainty in ideology, intellectual thought, historical narrative, and personal and collective identity.

Amidst such uncertainty and radical contingency, it became important to ask: 'How did we come to think as we do?' The way we have approached this book is an attempt to make sense of some of lines of thinking about education, creativity and technology from the 1980s through to our present, not in order to fabricate a historical timeline retrospectively, but in order to understand how education, creativity and technology have been made thinkable in different ways, through different genealogies of thought, at different points during this time. Our own historical experiences are reflected in this approach.

Perhaps above all, we have sought to show how alternative possible futures have been put together and promoted, and to consider how the things made intelligible in our present make them amenable to being thought, re-thought, and re-made for the future: 'How could we think *otherwise*?' We are, though, cautious of making normative prescriptions for apparently preferable futures. Maybe we can't even agree on one anyway. We seem to be at a moment when we are constantly being presented with images of possible futures for education, technology and creativity, whether represented in the glossy websites of commercial computing organizations, the conference presentations of educational technology gurus, in the field trials of new pedagogies and curricula for the future, or, more mundanely, in the routine appearance of 'next steps' chapters at the end of educational technology text books. These attempts to inscribe the future are all engaged in the shaping of seemingly unquestionable, common-sense narratives from the past into the future; narratives that this book sets out to interrupt. Rather than amplify this superabundance of futures, our aims in this book are more modest. Instead, we would hope it contributes in a small way to stimulating thinking in its own little field of operations – to focus on education, creativity and technology as objects of thought, as problems and questions, that have been thought differently in the past than they are thought now and that may be thought otherwise in the future, for better or worse, depending on your perspective. We hope that readers interested in education and technology will begin to ask themselves, as we have asked ourselves in writing it, 'How did we think about this before? How did we come to think about it the way we think about it now? And how are we to think about the future of education and technology?'

1

SHAPING SOCIETY, TECHNOLOGY AND LEARNING IDENTITY

Re-wiring and re-mixing education

Since the 1980s the educational uses of new information and communication technologies and digital media have been expanding. Whether in the form of computers in the classroom, as 'educational technologies' designed for explicit pedagogic purposes, or in the form of everyday new media being aligned with educational intentions, practices and activities, new technologies and media have become, it seems, almost naturalized as a common-sense feature of educational life. Schools are now seemingly built around a complex apparatus of electronic screens and surfaces, technical infrastructure, computing hardware, software and code, all hardwired to electronic communication networks.

Yet this has been no simple process of importing technological devices into classrooms and wiring them up to informational and communication networks. It has signalled the emergence of new ways of thinking about education, and about the future of education in an era that seems bound to become incessantly more digitalized. As a consequence of this massive rewiring of education itself, the ways in which many aspects of learning, the curriculum and pedagogy are *thought*, understood and practised have been gradually amalgamated with emerging ways of conceiving, understanding and practising with new technologies and media. In the process, new ways of imagining the future of education, schools, learning, pedagogy and curriculum have been generated. The future of education itself has been made thinkable, intelligible, and amenable to intervention in terms translated from the domain of new technologies and media. The outcome is the emergence of a new style of thinking that remixes and amalgamates educational concepts and ideals with technological concepts and ideals, along with wider social connections to political imaginaries like the 'knowledge economy' and intellectual constructs such as the 'network society.' In the chapters that follow, we explore education and technology as *objects of thought*, understood and shaped by different types of questions, problems and forms of analysis. And we suggest that education and technology are now being *re-thought*, re-imagined and reshaped according to a complex and heterogeneous mixture of social and material elements and conflicts and contests over their future.

As this book will show, education and technology are constituted by societal (economic, political and cultural) and technical components, and completed by the biological components of their embodied human users. That is, technology and education consist of a 'socio-technical' system. The term 'socio-technical' recognizes that technologies and society are mutually constitutive; technology influences social relations, while social relations influence the development and take-up of technologies. Technology and society are constantly interacting. Conceived as a socio-technical system, education and technology are therefore made up of interacting elements of educational practice and technical systems, as well as aspects of social policy, digital media culture, and economics, among other things. Education in the digital age is now becoming an increasingly hybrid domain comprising technological artefacts, physically embodied human action, social relations and institutions, and a range of new and emerging theories and practices of learning, curriculum and pedagogy all being assembled together. The future of education involves attempts to radically 'remix' these socio-technical elements, though the result, as we shall see, is to produce an inchoate, messy and sometimes incoherent vision of the future.

Such messy processes of socio-technical amalgamation have taken place over an extended historical duration often given the short-hand periodization of 'the digital age', which has given rise to all sorts of breathless techno-utopian claims that we are now on the cusp of new breakthroughs in learning, curriculum and pedagogy for the digital age. Grand historical claims about a digital age – or any of its temporal equivalents, the 'information age', the 'knowledge age', and so forth – as an epochal break with the past need to be treated extremely cautiously. The effects of new technology and media on education, for example, are highly (and often rightly) contested. Yet it is clear that new technologies and media are now a significant element of our age, as shown by high-profile events including the Wikileaks scandal, and the use of social media in the Middle East conflicts, uprisings and revolutions. In everyday life, millions of people sign in to their social networks in order to access social groups, and they take their social worlds and their preferred media with them in their pockets, contained in mobile, portable and pocketable devices. For some, work in the 'knowledge-based economy' is dominated by computing; wages are increasingly earned through informational labour. Moreover, our cities, towns and buildings are today extensively wired up to technical infrastructures and communication networks, their surfaces animated with pixellated informational displays and moving imagery. Less visibly or spectacularly, our finances and our personal data flow constantly as transactional traces through complex databases ... We could go on, but the point is clear. Today, new technologies appear to be everywhere. They are both spectacular and also invisible, sometimes appearing as a major force on the world's stage, but much more often working behind the scenes of society, shaping it in subtle ways through mundane everyday things like office software, web searches, templates, text messaging, GPS, email, photo manipulation, and databases. For that reason new technologies do need to be taken seriously as a component (albeit amongst other social, intellectual and material components) now exerting influence over the future of education. The key question is how such changes, collected under the periodization the 'digital age,' are being interpreted, thought, and translated into visions and prescriptions for the future of education.

Learning, curriculum and pedagogy have, in this period, been subject to a series of attempted reconfigurations. Beyond the mundane importation of computers into classrooms, new models of learning with digital tools have been put forward, curriculum reforms and other experiments in developing a curriculum for the digital age have been tried out, and diverse pedagogical innovations have been put into practice. Some enthusiasts see such developments as the breakers of great waves of educational transformation. We are far more circumspect, cautious and critical, motivated by a desire to begin to understand, interpret and explain the merger of new technology and media with education as a complex set of social processes with human consequences and effects. This is a highly messy merger, an ongoing process rather than a state of completion, and it is embedded in socio-economic, political, and cultural issues and problems in contemporary society. Ultimately, what is at stake here is the way in which young people are being sculpted and moulded in order to deal with social change. The future of education is being reimagined and young people's personal and social futures are being reimagined along with it.

This book is an attempt to untangle some of the consequences of the hybridization of new technology and media with education for young people's sense of identity. Who do young people today think they are? What futures do they imagine before them? What place does education have in shaping these identities? The book addresses three main questions.

1. How is the future of education being *thought and re-thought* in relation to new technology and media?
2. What kinds of learning identities are presupposed and promoted by the merger of new technologies and media with education?
3. How are these learning identities to be organized in emerging models of learning, curriculum and pedagogy?

We therefore stress 'learning identities' in order to emphasize how young people's identities are intricately connected to their ongoing learning, but also to indicate how identities themselves increasingly need to be learned through active, ongoing pedagogic opportunities both within the formal institutions of education and in the informal pedagogies accessed via new technology and media. Identities are not fixed forever, but are the subjects of constant lifelong learning.

Our central claim is that new technology and media are increasingly being articulated and constituted in various forms of knowledge, practical techniques, forms of expertise and authority within the educational domain, and organized in emerging models of learning, curriculum and pedagogy, in a variety of ways that are beginning to make it possible for children and young people to think and act in new ways. We are witnessing a rethinking of the future of education itself; a future already being anticipated, represented and 'made up' in our present. In the terms 'made up' and 'making up' we are indexing ideas about assembling, constructing, composing, creating and constituting the future of education, but we also recognize that 'make up' implies a cosmetics of appearance, as well as indicating an imaginative act, perhaps with the intent to deceive. What we take to be the archetypal institutions of education, schools, colleges and universities, are themselves under threat in educational futures where learning is now being 'made up' and imagined as being distributed via networked media into the textures of everyday life, aligned with and woven into the experiential worlds and personal aspirations of young people. In the background of our analysis, we have tried to remain alert to how such futures are now being constructed and 'made up' by a variety of new kinds of actors, organizations and influencers, not just from government education departments but from all manner of public and commercial sector positions. How are such actors working to reimagine and reassemble the future of education, according to what objectives and aspirations, on what authority and expertise, and how are these efforts intended to shape the actions, thoughts and identities of learners?

In addressing these questions it is important to remain cognizant of the fact that many of the claims made for new technology and media in education should not be viewed as statements of empirical fact or as straightforward accounts of an already-existing material reality in schools. Instead, what we are dealing with here are *objects of thought*, a complex entanglement of normative visions, ideals, imaginary futures, prototypical arrangements, objectives, aspirations, hopes and problematizations, all generated by particular social actors operating in the educational realm, that may or may not correspond with the material contexts in which educational processes take place. Rather than focusing on technical aspects of learning, curriculum and pedagogy with new technological devices and media platforms, here we are making a stronger argument that education and learner identities are being re-thought, reimagined and reshaped at a time when many aspects of socio-economic, political and cultural existence are themselves being influenced and reshaped in relation to technological change.

For those reasons, we are interested in how visions of the future of education are thought and 'made up,' and in how the identities of learners are 'made up' too. The reshaping of identities is no mere process of driving up educational standards, test scores, student motivation and so on. It involves the reshaping of the modes of living and the futures to which young people aspire. It reshapes and realigns their relations with socio-economic, political and cultural realities and makes certain futures seemingly plausible and thinkable. Certain presuppositions about learners' identities are built into emerging practices of learning, curriculum and pedagogy. The question of how learners' identities are being reimagined and reshaped is therefore embedded in social structures and power relations and in economic, political and cultural contingencies. Learners are being thought and shaped as certain kinds of persons who can think of themselves and feel and act in certain sorts of ways – as kinds of learners who, in a very real sense, did not exist before, equipped for futures still to come.

We concentrate on learning, curriculum and pedagogy because these constitute three 'master discourses' of education through which young people are offered specific positions of identity and agency from which to think, feel and act. We want to query, for example, how theories and approaches to learning are being reshaped according to new technological framings and new models of 'competence'; how the curriculum is being reimagined for the future; and how pedagogy is increasingly imagined to be taking place beyond the formal institutional boundaries of school, in informal and everyday contexts, especially those made available through new technologies and digital media.

These shifts in thinking about the future of learning, curriculum and pedagogy will affect the shaping of learner identities. Rather than operate from the pretext that learners possess particular fixed identities, we query how learners have been encouraged to think of themselves and their aspirations anew, and what the future repositioning of learning identities might mean for education. The amalgamation of new technologies and media with education has been made possible through a variety of discourses, institutions, materials and practices that, over time, have deposited and sedimented new possible forms of learning, curriculum and peda-gogy in schools in order to inculcate particular new learner identities. Consequently, young people have been encouraged to identify themselves in relation to new technologies and media, to think in terms of new technologies and media, to act in terms of new technologies and media, and to aspire to the future in terms of new technologies and media.

A corresponding array of technological reconfigurations of 'learning identity' have been promoted in different places, by different institutions and actors, through different approaches to new technology and learning. Young people themselves have increasingly been understood and encouraged to understand themselves in terms of their supposed 'digital learning identities' and even through collective identification with a 'digital generation'. The mixing of new technologies and media with learning, curriculum and pedagogy in much recent thought on the future of education, then, holds enormous significance for the shaping of who learners think they are and where they think they would like to be in the future, and this in turn has great potential consequences upon their socio-economic, political and cultural alignments and aspirations.

Technology in society/society in technology

What do we mean by 'technology'? When we talk of new technology we are usually referring to tools, hardware, devices and an assortment of material items, along with the operating systems, software, graphic interfaces and other sensorial displays which mediate the user's encounter with information and content. But this is a very innocent caricature of technology. It represents new technologies as simplified asocial containers of information, as artefacts without histories, as products without politics, and as objects seemingly without origins. But this is to neglect the complex social processes involved in the creation, design and development of any technological device, system, product or artefact. It locates technology as a separable and independent factor outside of society. Likewise it proposes a naïve technological determinism which holds that technological change is driven by its own internal dynamism and then that these technologies will have effects on society and the material, physical and biological conditions of our lives.

The opposite view, which we advocate, is that technology is inextricably a part of society. These arguments have been developed in the field of Science, Technology and Society (STS) studies (e.g. Bijker and Law 1992; Latour 1987). What STS research tells us is that all technological devices and systems are both *socially shaped* and *socially shaping*. As the products of intentional design processes, they are socially constructed and historically contingent, the outcomes of conflicts and compromises amongst designers, developers, programmers, funders and all kinds of other actors. One way of phrasing this is that technologies have 'social lives', as STS researcher Law (2010) puts it: they come into being with a purpose, through the efforts of sponsors, and through drawing upon previous resources. And just like most social lives, a lot of factors make them up. There is no single dominant shaping force which socially constructs technology but a multiplicity of heterogeneous shaping factors. There is plenty of mess, conflict, alliance, breaking up, making up and compromise between all the different social actors and groups involved in the development of a technology.

Reciprocally, however, technologies have a 'double social life' (Law 2010) because they also help to influence and shape human thought and action, even to influence the form and structure of society itself. This is no simple, causal and technologically deterministic process of technology imprinting itself upon human will and agency. Instead, STS claims that all technologies are 'interpretively flexible' (Woolgar 2002) at the point of use: whatever the intended purposes and objectives of their design, they can be interpreted and put to use in myriad other ways. This is why STS researchers talk of 'social shaping' and 'influencing' rather than either technological determinism, which privileges the supposed 'laws' of technology over human agency and social relations, or social constructionism, which can tend to over-privilege the dominance of human agency and social relations over technology. Rather, technology and society are in a reciprocal relationship. The emphasis on the social shaping of technology looks at 'the influence of social relations upon technologies', and also at 'the influence of technology upon social relations', so that it is 'mistaken to think of technology and society as separate spheres influencing each other: technology and society are mutually constitutive'— they are 'symmetrical' and 'made of the same "stuff" ' (Mackenzie and Wajcman 1999: 23–4). Societal values are embedded in technologies and reciprocally 'our technologies mirror our societies. They reproduce and embody the complex interplay of professional, technical, economic, and political factors,' and 'the processes that shape our technologies go right to the heart of the way in which we live and organize our societies' (Bijker and Law 1992: 3–4). Technologies, understood in this way, are things that humans have made which are then involved symmetrically in many of the ways that humans think and act – they help create society. This reciprocal relationship between the social and the technological is captured in the term 'socio-technical'.

In a powerful study taking up these socio-technical conceptual orientations to new technology and education in a sustained critical fashion, Monahan (2005: 9) deploys the concept 'built pedagogy' to refer to the 'lessons taught by technological systems'. Built pedagogy articulates how all technologies are inherently political, engendering power relations that are embedded in the same values and ideologies which catalyzed their invention. The implication is that the scripting of built pedagogies reshapes not only the practices and activities of pedagogy but learners' internalized sense of self and identity. In Monahan's detailed ethnography of new technology implementation in high schools in Los Angeles, technology includes more than just technical infrastructure, computers on desks, wiring and cabling, software and programmes – although it certainly does require those things too. It additionally requires the shaping and privileging of certain modes of human action, social activity, and states of being; new techniques for the body, new practices of the self, and new mental capacities; and the normalization of modes of conduct, behaviour and comportment that may be internalized in learners' identities and carried out of the classroom into the world. The uses of new technologies and media in education therefore need to be scrutinized for the pedagogies they constitute in material and virtual form, for the politics they embody, the experiences they generate, and the actions they make possible and foreclose.

Yet such studies perhaps neglect the very simple issue of how to classify and name the relations between education and new technology and media. Actor–network theorists Fenwick and Edwards (2010: 70), for example, usefully show how different terms deployed to frame our understanding of 'technologized learning', terms such as 'e-learning, networked learning, online learning, open learning, distributed learning, virtual education, digital media and technology for learning, technology-enhanced learning', all have their own genealogies of concepts, references, and vocabularies, usually linked to assumed affordances of particular devices, that characterize and privilege different relationships among electronic devices, teaching and learning.

From a similar perspective, Woolgar (2002: 3) refers to 'epithetized phenomena' where terms like virtual, interactive, digital, network, and so forth, are applied as an epithet to various existing activities and social institutions in order to 'conjure a future consequent upon the effects of electronic technologies.' The point made by such researchers is that the relations between technologies and education are extremely contingent, provisional, and prone to change over time. To take one very simple example, the popular term 'technology-enhanced learning' promotes a highly normative and positive view of technologies as an 'enhancement' to learning. Moreover, to focus on technology in terms of its effects on 'learning' also implies a certain kind of set of relations between tools and persons – a set of relations therefore amenable to certain kinds of psychological study – whereas focusing on technologies in terms of 'education' or 'schooling' would emphasize relations between devices and social institutions, making it the basis for more sociological investigations.

What we are getting at here, then, is not just the politics of built pedagogies embedded in technologies, but a more subtle politics of naming, the establishment of normative positions, and the role of our social scientific gazes in framing the objects we wish to study. At least in part the theories, concepts and vocabularies of social scientific disciplines such as psychology and sociology have played their own part in establishing the parameters and objects of study in the field of education and technology. Social science provides more than just explanatory resources; its dominant ways of representing education, technology, teachers, learners, and so on, have been enrolled and translated into a common-sense view of the roles and relations between education and technology. The very terms and theories we use to describe and explain technologies, devices, media, tools, and education, learning, teaching, and schooling, arrange and organize certain kinds of relations between them. This understanding makes it very important not only to identify the different technologies and practices that have been brought into education over time, but to trace the very different ways in which these historical developments have been paralleled by genealogies of concepts, frames, interpretations and knowledges that have been proffered by their advocates and enthusiasts as authoritative statements, whether from positions of social scientific authority or from other sites of expertise.

Authorities, experts and ensembles

To recognize the politics embedded in and catalyzed by new technologies and media, especially as they are transported as thought into schools and other pedagogic spaces, also requires us to identify some of the social and political actors involved in such shaping processes. Here we are influenced in our thinking by research on educational 'policy networks' (Ball and Junemann 2012) and 'policy enactment' (Ball, Maguire and Braun 2012). In ways that are similar to the perspective on technology and society derived from STS, these education policy studies emphasize the messy material and discursive reality of both policy creation and enactment. In particular, they focus on the variety of actors who participate in shaping educational policy. These actors come both from within the public sector education system and from the private sector, but also increasingly include a whole constellation of intermediaries and 'boundary spanners' who straddle sectoral divisions to form new cross-sectoral policy networks. Symmetrically, they examine the 'policy actors' within schools – teachers, school leaders, administrators – who, in different ways, are positioned to interpret, translate, and enact those policies as 'policy work'.

Such studies of policy thus seek to avoid a reductive form of policy determinism that assumes policies are set through bureaucratic institutions and administrative procedures and then implemented within schools and classrooms by educators. Instead it recognizes the diverse social, contextual and material circumstances and the complex networks of actors through which policies are made up, circulated and enacted in practice. Educational policy, like new technology, is interpretively flexible too. And it also recognizes that policies are constitutive of wider social processes of schooling in which the identities of both students and teachers may be remade as 'policy subjects', that is, as the subjects of policy inculcated with new ways of being. Ball, Maguire and Braun (2012: 141) deploy the thinking of Michel Foucault to explain educational policies as 'heterogeneous ensembles' of discourses, statements, propositions, institutions, social regularities, organisational vernaculars, pedagogical subjects, and much more besides. It is through policies understood as such heterogeneous ensembles that learning, curriculum and pedagogy are to be reimagined, not least through the deployment of new technologies, and learner identities are to be reconfigured.

Following this analytical perspective on policy networks and policy enactments, it is insufficient to seek to understand new technology uses within educational settings as a simple matter of technological implementation following policy mandate from the political centre of authority. Instead, increasingly it involves the participation of diverse actors and agencies from both official political positions and seemingly non-political areas of authority and expertise. This is not a phenomenon peculiar to education policy. Rather, it reflects changing understandings of the organization of society and the idea of the state. The theories of power associated with Michel Foucault have been particularly important to such understandings. For Foucault (1990: 92–3) 'power is not an institution, and not a structure'; it 'must not be sought in the primary existence of a central point', but rather should be traced in a multiplicity of mobile, heterogeneous, unstable and tense relations and confrontations that are present everywhere. Institutional and structural forms of power such as state apparatuses, sovereignty, social order, the form of the law, or any hegemonic system of domination, are understood by Foucault as crystallizations, terminal forms, outcomes and effects of this omnipresence of power rather than as being given at the outset. It is Foucault who has demonstrated the importance of being alert to the modes of thought and familiar assumptions upon which our day-to-day practices and actions rest.

Inspired by these theoretical cues, sociologists have begun to detail the limitations of the idea that society today is being programmed by the formal bureaucratic and administrative instruments and powers of state governments. Rather, modern societies make use of highly diverse forms of formally independent authority and autonomous expertise which connect the forces and institutions deemed 'political' with norms of individual and collective conduct that are considered 'non-political':

> One needs to ask how, and in what ways, have the rationales, devices and authorities for the government of conduct in the multitude of bedrooms, factories, shopping malls, children's homes, kitchens, cinemas,

operating theatres, classrooms, and so forth, become linked up to a 'political' apparatus.

(Miller and Rose 2008: 200)

The expertise of medicine, the law, finance, education, and the human sciences are amongst the varieties of forms of authority that diffuse as modes of thought throughout contemporary society. Each bears its own ideas, theories, vocabularies, practices and forms of knowledge, which mediate and translate the political and economic goals and visions of society through a multitude of mundane activities into the personal concerns and private mentalities of individuals. The professional expertise of psychology, medicine and economics, for example, is increasingly deployed at a distance through the everyday expertise of self-help 'experts', diet experts, money-saving experts. These little experts of everyday experience act as mediators who translate big ideas, powerful capacities and styles of thought such as those of governments into the mundane and distant concerns, aims, anxieties and aspirations of individuals (Dean 2010; Rose 1999a; 1999b). These arm's length relations are currently being exacerbated through the technologies of the internet. Increasingly, the internet promotes the 'experiential expertise' of a multitude of 'lay experts' (Rose 2007: 128) who mediate professional expertise at a distance and who are, reciprocally, involved in 'making up citizens' through reshaping the ways in which persons are understood and interpreted in the deliberations, calculations and strategies of experts and authorities (2007: 140).

Schools, too, now increasingly translate a multitude of voices of authority into programmes and practices which work upon the minds and mentalities of the young, which 'make up' learners as understood and interpreted as particular kinds of people. Particular kinds of policy specialists, entrepreneurs and 'intellectual workers' with good ideas, in addition to formal policymakers with big legislation, are becoming more and more involved in setting policy agendas, driving forward new initiatives, and propelling an educational culture of innovation (Ball and Exley 2010; McLellan 2004; Osborne 2004). Political parties and their associated think-tanks, commercial organizations, consultancies, non-governmental and semi-governmental organizations, non-profit start-ups, philanthropic and charitable operations, as well as academic research departments from a panoply of disciplinary positions within the social sciences, computer sciences and learning sciences, are all now involved in programmes concerned to shape the future of learning, curriculum and pedagogy in the digital age (Williamson 2012). They bring diverse forms of expertise and authoritative perspectives into the field of education. Many of them are non-political in the conventional sense; they lie outside the traditional organs and instruments of the education system. Moreover, many of them represent bodies of knowledge and expertise which are seen as depoliticized, innocent, and neutral. Theories and emerging sciences of human learning, for example, are proffered in place of overt analyses of the politics of educational institutions and structures.

New educational uses of technology and new technology-inspired visions of the future of education are now being assembled together through a composite of activities among all these political, semi-political and nonpolitical actors and agencies. The relatively brief history of technology in education epitomises new ways of working in public education, with a variety of authorities actually now doing parts of the work of the state on its behalf. All of these organizations, agencies and the individuals who people them, work as actors in an ongoing series of contests and alliances involving the invention of programmes and strategies whose object is the reshaping of learning, curriculum and pedagogy, and the sculpting and promotion of learners' future identities in a blurry hinterland of political, nonpolitical, and depoliticized forms of expert authority. If we are to get to grips with how new technologies and media have been articulated in education, and with the ways in which learner identities have been sculpted, shaped and promoted in the process, then we need to look at it as an ensemble of different authorities and expertise, a messy and heterogeneous network of actors, ideas and materials from across a spectrum of political and social positions, which has somehow come together to get things moving.

Styles of thinking

One way of conceiving of all the various activities and actors involved in this growing area is to see it as a 'thought community' with a distinctive 'style of thinking'. Rose (2007) articulates a style of thinking as a particular way of thinking, seeing and practising within a given field, based upon shared terms, concepts, assertions, references and relations that can be organized into arguments and explanations. Yet the style of thinking of a thought community does not merely explain the objects of its focus; it also shapes and establishes the objects of explanation, modifying them so that they appear in a new way, with new properties.

This idea needs to be set in a little context. By the late twentieth century, contemporary thought had become saturated with 'cybernetic' metaphors of information, networks, nodes, dynamics, flexibility, multiplicity, speed, virtuality and simulation (Osborne and Rose 1999a: 749). The contemporary cybernetic style of thinking, however, should not be seen as simply representing or explaining real concrete social changes. 'We do not live in cybernetic societies, but in societies that are increasingly understood and governed by means of a kind of cybernetic style of thought' (1999a: 750). The result is that the cybernetic style of thinking reshapes the ways in which various aspects of society are acted upon. Moreover, these cybernetic metaphors have been extended into how we think about human subjectivity and identity. Individuals and social collectivities are increasingly understood cybernetically, as, for example in the recent proliferation of 'social networks' and 'digital identities' as indices of human existence. What this means is that how we think about ourselves and our identities is twinned with how we think about technology, and these ways of thinking about ourselves have changed historically alongside technological change; genealogies of technological devices have been paralleled by genealogies of human identity (Osborne and Rose 1999b). Different identities have been 'made up' through technologies at different points in history, and people have come to identify with and fit those identities. We are increasingly encouraged to take ourselves to be certain kinds of persons, to adopt certain kinds of identities. Thus we are at a moment when human identity itself is to be made up through cybernetic metaphors, images and styles of thinking.

Such cybernetic styles of thinking have now been folded into education, not merely in the physical form of digital devices and technological infrastructure itself, but as part of a modern vision for the future of education. In the cybernetics of education, our familiar ways of conceiving learning, pedagogy and curriculum have been modified around metaphors such as virtuality and networks, although the use and meaning of the metaphors themselves keeps changing. The heterogeneous field of new technology and education thus operates as a loose kind of thought community whose objects and explanations and style of thinking have changed and been modified over recent decades. This is a cybernetic style of thinking with a complex genealogy rather than a rigid intellectual structure.

To give some sense of what this means, from our contemporary location in the twenty-first century, educational technology is not the same as it was in the 1980s when the field was concerned with Logo, programming, microworlds and so on. For the original entrepreneurs and innovators of educational technology in the 1980s, such as Seymour Papert, the prevalent style of thinking was 'constructionist'. By the late 1990s, however, constructionist styles of thinking had largely mutated into a concern with 'flexible interactive pedagogies' as a 'system of reasoning' with productive effects which construct learners as 'flexible subjects' (Fendler 2001: 133–4). More recently, the new style of thought that has taken shape in the twenty-first century is one of networked connectivity and 'connected learning', with learning increasingly being shaped around a constellation of web-like terms and concepts including social networks, networked publics, participatory media cultures, peer-based learning, systems thinking, cloud learning, DIY learning and so on (e.g. Ito et al. 2010; Jenkins et al. 2007; Salen et al. 2011).

Practices of learning, curriculum and pedagogy involving new technology and media are not, therefore, pre-given. They are lines of thought, embodied in various aspirations, programmes and strategies, traversed by social, economic, political and cultural debates and conflicts. How education and learning are to be understood is thus incessantly being reshaped, modified, and 'made up' anew through the creation and deployment of new explanations, arguments, terms, concepts, references, and new ways of thinking and acting. These shifting terms impact on the ways in which learners' identities are to be understood.

Prospective identities

Recent social theories about identity in the twenty-first century have been animated with ideas about digital and networked identities (Castells 1997). In discussions about the kind of learner identities that are considered desirable for the future, increasingly images of informal digital identities formed through interaction with digital culture and social networks are being amalgamated with images of the formal pedagogic identities inculcated through school. Yet the image of the youthful, technologically connected identity that has seemingly become so ubiquitous today itself needs to be understood as invented, assembled and composed of various operative elements rather than as something that is intrinsic to the body, mind or agency of the learner. Here we make use of Rose's (1996: 171) notion of humans as 'being-assembled-together'. Again, there is a conceptual resonance with the Science, Technology and Society perspective on technology and society as reciprocally constitutive. Only here we are dealing with the invention of humans instead of devices. Young people today are being 'addressed, represented and acted upon' as if they are people of a 'particular type' (Rose 1996: 169). This particular type of people possesses an identity – or rather a variety of identities – assumed to be technologically reticulated and extended through social networks. They appear to be motivated by aspirations and anxieties concerning their increasingly online and mobile lifestyles and social relations. Their very 'human agency' is itself fabricated and inscribed in terms of free choice and self-actualization. And it appears as though many young people are coming to recognize, identify and relate to themselves in such images and assumptions. They are being 'made up' as particular 'kinds' of people (Hacking 2006).

With the widespread prevalence of cybernetic, networked styles of thinking about education, it appears that the digital lives, experiences and identities of the young have been aligned and assembled together with an increasingly digital vision of education in the twenty-first century. Consequently, we are seeing the emergence of images of young people's digital identities that are simultaneously aligned and interwoven with the ideals, visions, politics and techno-euphoric beliefs and institutions of the web and its techno-fundamentalist correlates of global informationalist capitalism (Mager 2012). But we do not take a simple view that young people have naturally evolved new digital identities as a result of wider technological changes, nor in fact that we have witnessed anything so grand as an epochal transformation in which young people have been socialized by the effects of new technology. Instead, the emerging digital learning identity is an 'assemblage' formed of a multiplicity of parts. It is a construction formed out of complex contests and alliances over the future of education being acted out by the multitude of new authorities and experts on learning in the digital age.

These identificatory practices are mirrored in images of the 'schooled child' that are shaped by preferred ways of thinking about young people as members of a society and embodied in various functions of schooling (Austin, Dwyer and Freebody 2003). As Bernstein (2000) has noted, educational policy since the 1970s has been increasingly concerned with the formation of learners' 'prospective identities'. Prospective identities are pedagogic identities constructed by authorities and promoted in educational institutions to deal with cultural, economic and technological change. Prospective identities ground identity not in the past but in the future; they stand in contrast to the 'retrospective identities' promoted by a traditional curriculum of canonical texts, official knowledge, cultural heritage and so forth. The hope of government is that the inculcation of such identities will bring about new economic and cultural configurations and stabilities in the future.

Moreover, today more than ever, as Rose (1996) has shown, governments are concerned with the promotion of personal identities construed as active, creative, autonomous and self-responsible. Identities are the result of myriad techniques and norms which are implanted via the mundane routines and rituals of schooling into the lives and experiences of children. The active, autonomous, creative self that is promoted through new technological languages of schooling is no natural category but a new prospective pedagogic identity and a mode of life which is to be organized in pedagogy and curriculum. It is a way of understanding and acting upon the learner as a certain kind of person. Today, it seems, the ideas and images that are coming to shape young people's self-understandings and self-techniques are both disseminated through the authoritative channels of pedagogy and curriculum and through the heterogeneous lay expertise enabled by the internet.

The analysis we present is an attempt to trace some of the heterogeneous pathways in education, technology and creativity in the digital age that have led to the 'making up' of the prospective pedagogic identity associated with new technology – making up digital learning identities. In the face of all sorts of claims about the ameliorative potential of new technologies and media in education, and their role in expanding and enhancing the learning identities of the young, our aim is much more modestly to question how it is that educational technologies have been assembled in terms of particular sorts of problems and ambitions by a variety of authorities and experts. What we are trying to grasp is how learner identities have been made thinkable and intelligible by certain authorities for certain ends. What is it that these various authorities have wanted to happen? How have prospective digital learning identities been assembled? What objectives (of these authorities) have they been assembled to achieve? How have they sought to intervene in the management and shaping of learners' thoughts and actions, their conduct and identities? How is it that early in the twenty-first century learners have been positioned in terms of their supposed digital identities? How have such understandings of identity been assembled? How have they been promoted? Where have such assemblages travelled and settled? The prospective digital learning identity has not been formed through any single event or procession of events, or by political will from any single or central hegemonic or marginal position. It has been formed and shaped through a network of interconnections among a number of developments.

What we are dealing with here, then, is not a straightforward empirical record of technological implementation in schools followed by an assessment of its impacts on learning, or a study of the actual identity work done by young people and educators. Rather, it examines how ideas about learners and learning, teachers and pedagogy – about identities and about the acquisition of knowledge required for pedagogic identity formation – have been put together, promoted, circulated, and then picked up, translated and embedded in local and distant sites. What we are looking at, in short, is the making up of a prospective digital learning identity, or the assembling of a subject who is understood to be active, creative, autonomous and self-responsible. We are not putting this as a name to what we believe is an empirically observed kind of person who actually exists; we are trying to identify how ideas and ways of thinking about such a kind of person have been assembled and made plausible, how this kind of person has been made intelligible, how this kind of person is being made up in new approaches to learning, curriculum and pedagogy. The ambitions and objectives of the new authorities of education in the digital age have been aligned with the experiential worlds and personal aspirations of young people, nowhere more clearly than in the ongoing and incessant positioning of new technology and media in education.

Organization of the book

Throughout the book we trace and reflect on education in the digital age from different disciplinary perspectives, using conceptual tools and perspectives from sociology to comprehend these changing times, and tools and perspectives from sociocultural psychology as well as educational theories to understand the implications for learning and teaching. In Part I, four chapters focus on key social developments related to the amalgamation of new technologies and media with education.

2. *Mapping the digital age.* Chapter 2 explores a series of apparent changes in the social system linked to the proliferation of new technology and digital media in many cultural, political, and economic dimensions of social existence. We seek to understand a historical conjuncture which has now become known as 'the digital age', a period commencing roughly in the 1980s and continuing into the twenty-first century.

3. *Reconstructing the future of education.* In Chapter 3 our focus is on how educational research and practice has acted to translate claims about the digital age into concepts and theories for learning – that is, how social, economic, political and cultural problems have come to be redefined as problems to be addressed through technology and education and solved through pedagogic techniques in the classroom. The kind of questions we ask are concerned with how certain ideas and visions of the digital future have been enacted through a multiplicity of programmes, strategies, techniques and devices in schools. How has the digital age been studied and understood, and what specifically have been the educational developments which have taken place over this time? In other words, how has the digital age been constructed as a set of problems, opportunities and challenges in the educational domain? And how have these changed over time? Here, we'll be tracing how educational technologies have been framed in terms of emerging ideas and ideals such as constructionism and LOGO in the early 1980s through the emergence of 'network society' analyses and high-tech 'knowledge economy' policies in the 1990s to the explosion of educational interest in social networks and 'connected

learning' in the 2000s. We do not aspire to narrative historical completion but to explore important analytical insights from the 'memory' of education and technology.

4. *'Making up' digital learning identities*. Practice and research in education during the digital age has resulted in the creation and promotion of distinctive kinds of identities for learners. The period has seen the promotion, variously, of:

- a *construction-based identity* which emerges from a focus on the educational benefits of model construction, simulation building, and other forms of programming;
- an *'interactive' identity* emphasized by a more instrumentalist focus on the role of education in promoting the skills of 'human capital' for a future high-tech workforce; and
- a *'connected' identity* which is promoted by a 'Web 2.0' emphasis on learning through networked communities and interest-driven affiliations.

All three of these identities are historically particularistic creations which, at different times and in different places, have been promoted in the digital age. These are future-facing prospective identities constructed through particular pedagogic and curricular arrangements to promote particular kinds of 'desired' futures. They are constructed around a set of interlinked ideas about the digital age and education, ideas about ICT and media, innovation in the knowledge economy, and so forth. Learners, in short, are being positioned to adopt the identities required to create and maintain particular visions of the future, and educational institutions are being positioned to incubate these identities.

5. *Assembling creative learning*. We argue that a concern with creativity has become one of the most important, though highly contested, areas for the development of new practice and research in education in the digital age. Again, we trace creativity from different disciplinary perspectives and explore its shifting meanings. Creativity has been mobilized in different, conflicting, even paradoxical and contradictory ways as a political, social and economic project, particularly in the 'creative critique' of capitalist power structures from the late 1960s, and more lately in an explosion of creativity situated as an economically and commercially valuable set of personal dispositions and skills in using digital technologies. In the early twenty-first century, creativity has been associated closely with the latest internet developments as we have moved from a web based on user consumption of content, to a web based on user-created content. Responses to this digital 'democratisation' of creativity in the digital age in the educational domain have called for far more creative approaches to teaching and learning. The result of this emphasis on creativity has been the construction and promotion, of new prospective identities based on particular kinds of interpretations of creativity. We argue that understandings of creativity have been appropriated and hollowed out, yet there are still spaces for learners to encounter creative alternatives.

In Part II of the book we examine how such arguments about social and technological change, digital learning identity, and creativity have been mobilized and deployed in relation to theories and practices of learning, curriculum and pedagogy.

6. *Thinking with digital tools.* Digital learners are now organized in a pedagogy of action mediated by tools. Here we are looking at how digital technologies have been conceptualized as tools for learning with affordances to shape the nature of creative learning activities and environments. Our theories of learning in a 'digital age' are useful if they afford insights into the mutual interaction between people and the digital tools which are embedded in the contexts of our learning experience. We argue that the development of learning identities is underpinned by four characteristics: learner agency; the design and use of tools; the awareness of context; and openness to improvisation. *Agency* is the active participation in the social and cultural contexts in which we are learners. *Tools* express our relationship with technologies and the role they might play in our engagement in intelligent action. *Context* creates and shapes the learning environments that are appropriate for the demands of our lives and futures. *Improvisation* enables us to imagine and construct new contexts and communities to meet the challenges of our learning lives. Digital tools in physical, virtual and augmented environments can contain metaphors of learning as reproduction, synthesis and expression, and can generate new metaphors of production, performance and 'remix' in prospective learning identities.

7. *Prototyping the curriculum of the future.* This chapter follows developments in curriculum. The curriculum represents the knowledge that a society chooses to select from the past to bring into the present and from there project into the future. While mainstream developments in curriculum have tended to emphasize increased centralization, standardization of content, internationally comparable assessments, and so forth, a range of alternative curriculum visions has suggested different possible futures. The curriculum has been envisaged as a potentially connective apparatus that links knowledge domains, that may be constituted as a kind of non-linear, digitally hyperlinked text rather than embodied in the linear form of the textbook. Such curriculum visions reinscribe learner identities as active, connective identities.

8. *Being a teacher in a digital age.* Here we argue that teachers can be recognized in our society as those who engage in the design of learning for others, regardless of their formal or informal status, accreditation, or setting in society. Good educators demonstrate three dimensions in their practice: depth, scope and reach. They know their 'stuff', they know why it matters, and they can connect with people to help them to learn. The conceptual depth of educators' understanding relates to the questions of knowledge in subject domains that identify and debate disciplinary structures, conceptual organizations and principles of enquiry. An educator's 'contextual scope' is their awareness of their relationship to other people, ways of knowing, identity, culture, politics,

networks and power within wider contexts. Pedagogic reach describes the connection between educators and learners, where the purposeful designs of learning environments and experiences are successful in the transformation of understanding. The concept of 'didactic analysis' offers a useful framework for thinking about pedagogy that is grounded in a critical approach to the purposes of teaching, and presents a series of questions that help to link pedagogy with the wider context of being an educator in a digital age.

Throughout, the book is concerned with how a prospective digital learning identity has been assembled and promoted. Essentially what we are arguing, from a reflexive position, is that the shaping of digital learning identities has taken place through a dense, heterogeneous web of practical developments, political objectives, conceptual and theoretical advances related to the deployment, in various ways and through various programmes advanced by various authorities, of technologies in education. All these things must be thought in a particular way. The book represents an attempt to trace something of the genealogical developments and modes of thought which have brought new technology and education together in the ways that they have been, and to glimpse some of the ways they are being imagined into the future. We have tried to apply, as a loose kind of method, what Thrift (2005:2) calls a 'backward gaze,' to think 'rather as a historian from the future might, looking back at our present time and seeing vast numbers of unresolved issues, differences of interpretation and general confusions.' Looking with a backward gaze serves to remind us to be wary of the familiar and unchallenged assumptions and modes of thought upon which many educational practices and ideas in the digital age have been constructed and promoted. We want to avoid taking a hyperbolic view of the future, yet also to avoid falling into the opposite trap of dystopian despair. Rather, through a more limited form of critique we hope this book can make a modest contribution to interrupting some of the seemingly unquestioned modes of thought, presuppositions and assumptions about technology, creativity and the future of education.

PART I

Reconfiguring education and technology

PART I

Reconfiguring education and
technology

2

MAPPING THE DIGITAL AGE

Imagining a digital age

Are we living in a 'digital age'? In this chapter we explore a series of social, economic, political and cultural developments that together suggest we are now living in 'new times' in which technology and the prevalence of the 'digital' have become powerful influences on everyday thought and activity. The 'digital age' is one amongst a number of terms (including the 'information age' and the 'knowledge age') which have been used to define a period in contemporary history allegedly characterized by the proliferation of computing technologies, information processing, and electronic communication. These terms are the temporal equivalents to a range of other, related expressions which characterize modern society as 'post-industrial', 'post-Fordist', 'postmodern', 'informationalist', a 'network society', 'virtual society' and a 'knowledge economy' (Webster 2006; Woolgar 2002). Such terms sometimes appear to represent society and history as being at the mercy of an unstoppable force of technologically-determined progress. Indeed, they suggest that we have reached decisively 'new times' in history and a new kind of society with its own determinate features and cultural breaks.

Instead, in this chapter we examine the digital age itself as the social product of a 'cybernetic' style of thought which makes contemporary society intelligible through technological metaphors of information, communication, networks, decentralization, flexibility, speed, simulation, and so on (Osborne and Rose 1999a). But a style of thought does not just describe and explain things: 'it shapes and establishes the very object of explanation, the set of problems, issues, phenomena that an explanation is attempting to account for', so modifying 'each of its objects that they appear in a new way, with new properties, and new relations and distinctions with other objects' (Rose 2007: 12). Through cybernetic styles of thinking, metaphors and heuristics, more and more of organic and social life is now understood and treated, and thus modified, in terms of technological systems (Lash 2002; Thrift 2005).

People, even, are now being reconceptualized according to the latest cybernetic thinking (Bauman 2005). This is not to say that we now definitively understand the workings of the human body because of new technical procedures, but that we use the latest technical metaphors to comprehend and explain ourselves to ourselves, and to act upon ourselves in order to improve and modify ourselves. Inevitably, such thinking changes over time, so, for example, while the Victorian industrialist man understood himself in terms of the rhythms of clocks and the pressures of steam engines, today we are more likely to relate to ourselves as networked beings with social lives organized in social networks and mental lives organized in neural networks. How we think of ourselves as persons is thus historically intertwined with how we think about technologies (Osborne and Rose 1999b).

The recent history of the internet shows how twenty-first century developments in Web2.0 technologies have already given us a plethora of new terms by which our own new times have been made legible and intelligible. We live, so we are led to think, in a centrifugal world of networks, complexity, plastic information, disruptive distribution, extruded media, open source movements and campaigns, a user-driven and peer-driven world of mass participation (Ryan 2010). Such terms and metaphors, and the style of thinking they constitute, make it possible to think about and act in society, to think about one's own self, and to imagine the future in their terms. The digital age, and its cognates, may be largely imagined and constructed, a form of thought rather than an empirical reality, yet it has productive effects, the power to modify and reanimate the world in its own image.

We use the term 'digital age', then, as a convenient caricature or an artificial periodization that nonetheless usefully helps to define the cybernetic style of thinking that is characteristic of a particular moment in our times. The digital age is constituted by a series of historical conjunctures of long and slow waves of social, economic, political, and cultural changes intersecting with the more surface-level ripples of technological developments; less an epochal moment or a turning point in a single history than a series of ongoing continuities and contingent pathways from the past into the future (Goodson 2005). It is, like its other cognates, genealogically ambiguous, often ill-defined, selectively remembered, and historically illusive. As Kenway et al. (2006: 27) put it in relation to the knowledge economy in education policy, 'there is a politics to what it remembers and denies of its past' and yet it 'proffers its view of itself and its future trajectory as solid and certain.' The digital age is not merely a historical term. It comes preloaded with assumptions about futures that are proposed to be inevitably digitalized. It is a political simplification or an 'imaginary' (Rizvi and Lingard 2010) version of contemporary society, much simpler than the real one, that makes particular kinds of actions possible. To the extent that such terms have been taken up in policy they are already determinants of social and economic change and of consequence despite their ambiguity (Jessop 2002; Kenway et al. 2006).

So, the digital age is the result or effect of a combination of political, economic and cultural ideas and claims, rooted in distinctively cybernetic styles of thinking that have been articulated in order to define and periodize a particular interval in recent history and to fabricate visions of technologized futures. The digital age is, like all other 'new times' and their associated new terms, a chronological construction and also a cultural construction (Hartley 1997), but like all cultural constructs it has the potential to shape understandings and to mould action. As a result, when we talk of the digital age we are talking of the deployment of metaphors and ways of thinking that are now being built into pedagogies, curricula, and theories of learning, and that consequently have the capacity to shape human action.

In this chapter we articulate what we see as the 'big picture' of the digital age – a rough map of its contours and primary features – and then in the following chapter we examine how some specific features of the digital age have been represented and used to underpin educational policies and practices. Our approach is informed by a recognition that education is thoroughly heterogeneous; it is actively and continually being assembled, disassembled and reassembled in different ways as different people and groups get hold of it; as it is translated in different institutional structures; as it gets refracted through different ideologies and political attachments; as it is explained through different educational theories, policies, disciplinary discourses; and as it gets enacted through a whole panoply of learning theories, pedagogic procedures, curricular prescriptions, and so on (Fenwick and Edwards 2010).

Our account of the big picture of the digital age is an attempt to indicate something of the heterogeneity of resources, concepts, theories, politics and histories which have been translated into contemporary thought about education and learning, and to account for the educational futures they have seemingly made plausible. As Hartley (1997: 3) argues, education must always be understood 'within the realms of the cultural (which includes the intellectual), the economic and the political; it is never 'above' them, always *of* them.' Education, in whatever 'times' it takes place, cannot adequately be understood merely as an isolated institution but as one in relation to those other realms. The materials with which we must deal in our attempts to understand education, in other words, consist of ensembles of social, economic, political and cultural changes, along with the metaphors and ways of thinking they generate; specific kinds of technologies, and the affordances for certain kinds of action and interaction they appear to embody; and theories of learning which are used to legitimate the use of such technologies for educational purposes. The chapter is therefore our attempt to account for the social, economic, political and cultural changes shaping the future of education in the digital age. Our purpose is not to show direct historical continuity of ideas into the present, but to illustrate something of the complex of theories, concepts and vocabularies that have anticipated and been assembled into current reformatory efforts.

Next, we examine three particular configurations of thought in the digital age. First, we explore claims that constitute contemporary society as networked and connected; second, we examine the digital age as part of a 'cool' and 'smart' discourse which imagines the future in terms of high-tech knowledge work and collective intelligence; and third we consider the digital age in terms of how technological devices and digital data are understood as themselves reshaping society and human life itself.

Network thinking

Today, a significant body of social scientific research and theory refers to 'networks', and other horizontal, interdependent, rhizomatic, topological and transversal interconnections, as the basis of all social relations (Jessop, Brenner and Jones 2008). In this tradition of network-centric thinking, or an intellectual genre of networks, technical networks including the internet and virtual communication are said to surround us, businesses and corporations are said to have been restructured as network enterprises, networking has become a dominant metaphor for understanding and organizing political, economic, collective and individual life, and in academia research networks have been deployed in a variety of fields, disciplines and methods (Boltanski and Chiapello 2007; Knox, Savage and Harvey 2005; McCarthy, Miller and Skidmore 2004). The evidence for this profusion of network thinking can be found, for example, in a prestigious international 'networks network' of academic researchers dedicated to exploring and developing social network theory in the context of the rise of a network society based on information-based communication networks (http://ascnetworksnetwork.org/about; see also Castells 2011).

Much network thinking refers to complex processes of globalization, largely in economic, occupational and cultural terms, and to new forms of social interaction and socio-spatial relations in a world where the solidity of social structures seems to have been weakened. Such thinking conceives of society as a lateral society rather than a vertical society, 'increasingly viewed and treated as a "network" rather than a "structure" (let alone a solid "totality"): it is perceived and treated as a matrix of random connections and disconnections and of an essentially infinite volume of possible permutations' (Bauman 2007: 3). For Bauman we live in 'liquid times' where all social forms and institutions have become more fluid and unstable, where power has dispersed into the politically uncontrolled global space of digital information networks, and individual lives are experienced as collections of short-term projects rather than as long-term maturation or lifelong careers. Other critics, taking up similar issues, refer to related terms in this genre of networking thinking. Flows, movements, mobilities and hypermobility have all been used to refer to institutional processes of organizational remodelling, electronic offshoring, just-in-time production, as well as to the rise in individual 'fast-track mobile lives' experienced through mobile technologies, fragmented working practices and intensive consumerism (Elliott and Urry 2010).

Of course, networks are an old form of social organization, but the dominant point of reference in most emerging network theory is to new networked information-processing and communication technologies. The main reference for an account of networks in social scientific research and theory is Castells, whose theory of the rise of a 'networked society' is based on the argument that:

> while networks are an old form of organization in the human experience, digital networking technologies ... [have] powered social and organizational networks in ways that allowed their endless expansion and configuration, overcoming the traditional limitations of networking forms of organization ... Because networks do not stop at the border of the nation-state, the network society constituted itself as a global system, ushering in a new form of globalization characteristic of our times.
>
> (Castells 2010: xviii)

According to Castells' (1996) account of multi-dimensional structural change and globalization since the 1980s, the growth of networks based on digital information processing technologies has been intimately related to diverse processes of economic and cultural globalization. The emergence of a 'network society' is characterized by the growth of high-tech industries; flat rather than hierarchical organizations; multi-skilled and flexible workers; globalized, transnational corporations organized as decentralized 'network enterprises' rather than oligopolistic cartels; global movements of capital; the promotion of free trade through internationally agreed deregulation; and an emphasis on consumption and processes of individualization. The network society has taken form in the context of a major shift in western and northern capitalist economies and the alleged 'disorganization' of capitalism itself. Whereas the 'organized capitalism' of the twentieth century was characterized by money, production, consumer commodities and labour on a national scale, the 'world of a "disorganized capitalism" is one in which the "fixed, fast-frozen relations" or organized capitalist relations have been swept away' (Lash and Urry 1987: 313).

In tandem with this analysis of the economic, organizational and occupational restructuring in the network society, however, has come a cultural transformation. In a subsequent study, Castells (2009) argues that we now increasingly inhabit a convergent communicative universe that is multi-modal, multi-channel and multi-platform, involving participation in processes of production, editing, and distribution alongside the consumption of information and content. In the world of horizontal communication networks organized around the internet, 'virtuality' has become an essential dimension of reality. Rather than mere recipients of standardized and centrally organized 'mass communication', in the culture of 'real virtuality' media, audiences have become increasingly participative 'creative audiences' which interact among themselves by forming networks of 'mass self-communication'. However, this potential for creative autonomy is shaped, controlled, and curtailed by a concentration of interlocking corporate multimedia, financial trade, and government strategies which have permitted the expansion of for-profit entertainment and the commodification of personal freedom. Rather than a utopian vision, as Castells (2010) has recently reflected, the network society is now the site of agony, uncertainty and disorientation, brought about by global financial crisis, upheaval in business and labour markets, cultural exclusion and disaffection, global criminality and fundamentalism, environmental crisis and the growing incapacity of political institutions to handle global problems and local demands.

The network society thesis is perhaps the most influential and well-known of the networked style of thinking in social science, though it is certainly not without critics, some of whom view it as a transferral of a 'techno-economic paradigm' which is in thrall to 'the miracle of ICT-enabled global networking' (Jessop 2002: 237). This 'connexionist genre' and reticular mode of thinking is, as Boltanski and Chiapello (2007: 104) explain, the result of a particular historical conjunction characterized by the development of communication networks and by the search in the social sciences for concepts to identify emerging social structures that are flexible and minimally hierarchical. Such concepts, as those authors show, now flow between social scientific analysis, political discourse, journalism and the world of commerce and business as a generalized form of representation. The keywords of such a connexionist genre are adaptability, alliance, association, autonomy, communication, connection, coordination, creativity, decentralization, flexibility, integration, mediation, mobility, reactivity, self-organization, and versatility. It is characterized by interpersonal 'electronic relations at a distance', 'more sincere and freer than face-to-face relations' (90), whereby 'connections with various groups [are] activated at potentially considerable social, professional, geographical and cultural distance' (104).

Taking the network concept even further, Latour (2011: 799) has proposed some novel applications of networks in social theory, referring to the 'complex ecology of tributaries, allies, accomplices, and helpers' that make up any form of action, or to the attributes that constitute any object. This form of 'actor-network theory' recognizes that any action or object is not self-contained but the result of a network of social and material attributes being brought together into association with one another (Latour 2005; Law 1992; Law and Hassard 1999), a theory that Latour *et al.* (2012) have now begun to extend to an analysis of Web 2.0. The logical endpoint of such an approach to social theory is that society itself needs to be understood as made up of networks of social actors and material things constantly forming and reforming dynamic associations. In the 'network revolution' accelerated by digital technologies, therefore, Latour (2011: 802) insists on recognizing that all the things we tend to see as 'virtual' actually depend on increasing the 'material dimensions of networks'. For example, GPS relies on complex satellites; web searches require servers; online videogames require fast bandwidth, and so on. Woolgar (2002), likewise, argues that virtual technologies 'supplement rather than substitute' for real activities; and, in fact, that virtual activities stimulate *more* of their correspondingly real activities. From the perspectives put forward by Latour, Woolgar and other researchers working with similar 'socio-technical' and 'socio-material' approaches in education (Fenwick, Edwards and Sawchuk 2011), digital technologies and communication networks of all kinds need to be understood as themselves linked to complex networks of non-technical circumstances, human actors, and material artefacts.

Other critics have queried the extent to which the concept of networks accurately captures the dynamic social and technical textures of the twenty-first century. As Mackenzie (2010: 9) argues, 'after a decade of heavily network-centric social, cultural, organizational and mathematical network theory', it has begun to seem as though networks are 'the epitome of the contemporary real', though this disguises how networks are part of a 'typically modern political fantasy' which glosses over the specificities and inconsistencies of society itself. Mackenzie (2010: 29) offers the alternative term 'wirelessness' to refer to social changes resulting from the proliferation of wirelessly connected devices, services and products. The effects of the 'air interfaces' of such wireless technologies are felt in everyday life, such as how people interact with gadgets, objects, infrastructures and services, how they arrive, depart and inhabit places, how they work, study and socialize, how they get together as communities, and how they communicate and relate to others. Wirelessness is related to the network character of contemporary society, including commercial, political and economic ambitions, such as the marketing of global wireless cities, the generation of new consumer products, and the enhancement of the capacity of knowledge economies. But it also refers to more disordered, qualitative, 'post-network' processes of moving, making, changing, altering, and connecting feelings, things, events, images, textures, ideas and places, and to a heightened sense of incompletion and openness in the flow of experience. Wirelessness implies greater fluidity than the formal rigidity of networks, with their nodes and hubs, will permit.

Such analysis shows how networks and other technological metaphors are deployed as explanatory devices in almost all dimensions of existence, whether economically, occupationally, politically, culturally, experientially, and even, increasingly, organically. Lash (2002: 15), for example, argues that 'we make sense of the world through technological systems' which themselves 'work on a cybernetic model.' In such a world, Lash argues, social life, culture, and even nature itself are all experienced 'at a distance'. 'Social life-at-a-distance' refers to sociality achieved through technological systems, interfaces, communication and transportation devices; 'culture-at-a-distance' is culture experienced technologically, for example through cultural resources accessed vicariously online; and 'nature-at-a-distance' refers, for instance, to the storage of organic DNA and genomic data in external and distant databases as genetic information. The network genre and style of thinking, then, is the connective tissue that links everything from communication and culture, and economics and enterprise, to mind and matter.

Cool culture

The connected world of network-centric thinking has been accompanied by a 'creativity explosion' which has transformed many aspects of business culture, education, and psychological discourse (Osborne 2003). Boltanski and Chiapello (2007) have persuasively documented the emergence in France of a 'new spirit of capitalism' from a very real explosion of creative passions. For them, a creative style of thinking had been born amidst the tear gas of the student protests in Paris in 1968. Whereas the old spirit of capitalism was based on a set of shared beliefs in the large, centrally organized industrial firm, professional vocations, structured tasks, product standardization and mass production, the new spirit of capitalism has been made intelligible through a discourse of creativity, flexibility, 'being smart', dynamism, freedom, openness, autonomy, spontaneity, rhizomorphous capacity, multi-tasking, conviviality, informality and the search for interpersonal contacts and networks. This discourse is 'taken directly from the repertoire of May 1968' but has come to permeate a whole set of mental representations and discourses running across politics, commerce, media and culture (Boltanski and Chiapello 2007: 97; see also Žižek 2008).

Boltanski and Chiapello (2007) specifically show how the creative repertoire of 1968 has entered into, and been circulated around in business management texts. In the corpus of management texts they study, it is clear how the main concerns of 1960s businesses were with hierarchies of management, formal authority, planning, organized bureaucracy, job security, and careers for life. By contrast, by the 1990s, the faceless bureaucracies, massive conglomerates, corporate-entertainment complexes and their shady cousins in the military-industrial complex seemed increasingly like outdated relics of a patriarchal, masculinized era of uncaring producer capitalism. Inbetween, two things had happened. First, the 'spirit' of 1968 had given rise to an 'artistic critique' of capitalism rooted in the invention of a bohemian lifestyle and an indignation towards the oppressive bureaucracy and disenchantment and inauthenticity of capitalism. The artistic critique foregrounded the freedom, autonomy and creativity of leftist intellectuals and artists against the exploitative bourgeoisie, with their land, factories, possessions, and obsession with meticulous forethought and rational management.

The second thing that happened was that during the 1970s a number of writers began to show how the centrally organized industrial firm was no longer 'fit-for-purpose' for a computerized future that was increasingly going to be based on information rather than manufacturing. As a result of the explosion in technology from the 1960s, then the 'micro-electronics revolution' of the 1970s and 1980s, and the birth of the internet in the 1990s, plus an increasing 'Japanization' of 'just-in-time and 'lean production' processes, ideas such as 'post-industrial society', 'post-Fordism', 'the information age' and 'cybersociety' proliferated, largely based on the speculative extrapolation of current trends into the future (Cohen and Kennedy 2007; Jessop 2002; Webster 2006). In order to compete, organizations would need 'informational labour' and brainpower rather than the musclepower required for manufacturing. And the key qualities of informational labour, it seemed, were exactly those qualities identified by the artistic critique. It is important to note, however, as Thrift (2005) points out, that this new discourse is not just an ideology reflecting pre-formed economic interests or needs. Rather, it is actively constitutive of a social reality that does not really exist; it 'makes up' a new social world and new ways for people to be in it. This new creative discourse is now part of the 'background hum' (Thrift 2005: 31) of the digital age, increasingly used to bring ideas into being.

The artistic critique and the informationalist argument reached a historical conjunction in the 1990s in the making up of a revived form of capitalism, as corporations such as Apple, Google, the Body Shop, Nike, Pepsi and Virgin all sought to position themselves as 'different' from more traditional corporations. Consequently, a new 'reflexive' capitalist conscience, self-consciousness, and creative spirit has now arrived, a form of 'nice', 'smart' and 'fast' 'knowing capitalism' (Thrift 2005). This was particularly the case in the creative and culture industries, where knowledge work and the commercialization of expressive value are said to be the fundamental sources of material wealth, as well as the sources of all that is 'funky' and 'cool' in the new creative neo-liberal capitalism (Peck 2010: 192). For consumers, the new 'neat capitalism' of the twenty-first century is now more self-consciously socially responsive, ethical, compassionate, fun and informal (Rojek 2006).

But for workers, too, the emphasis is less on hierarchical and organizational rigidities, and more on permanently expandable portfolio careers, constant re-training and re-skilling, and working on projects within lean, streamlined firms whose slim core is surrounded by a network of temporary suppliers, subcontractors, and just-in-time providers. Organizations have become – or been exhorted to become by the new funky management literature – flexible and innovative, staffed by people who are creative and self-organized. A 'new image of the worker' has been invented in parallel with a new image of the company that values autonomy, creativity, flexibility, adaptability, initiative, innovation, ad hoc groupings, cross-divisional collaboration, experimentation, and informality (Rose 1999a: 115). The new image of the creative company is characterized by its non-conformist countercultural 'cool,' its narcissism and hedonism (Liu 2004; McGuigan 2009), and by the 'compulsorization' and 'capitalization' of creativity (Osborne 2003; Peck 2010).

The creative makeover of neoliberal capitalism requires new kinds of citizens and workers. Relentless innovation, and 24/7 productivity are now the chief characteristics of the 'techno-bohemian' creative types who seek 'free-market self-actualization' through self-indulgent overwork, expressive play and conspicuous consumption habits, and who yearn to 'validate their identities' in heterogeneous 'plug and play' communities (Peck, 2007: 5). In this creative universe, immaterial 'affective labour' takes place 'in-person', engenders 'feelings' such as ease, well-being, satisfaction, excitement, passion and so forth, and distinctions between leisure, labour, domesticity, sociability, production and consumption are becoming blurry (Hardt 2008). Immaterial labour refers to work involving information and communication and the production of informational, cultural and affective commodities, but also to the processes involved in managing the workplaces that produce them and in appealing to the consumers who buy them (Dyer-Witheford and de Peuter 2009). The affective, immaterial form of capitalism is no longer to be associated with the 9 to 5 businessman in the dark suit but with the restless creative entrepreneur dressed in black (Peck 2007), and the 'young nerds', 'former hackers' and 'countercultural geeks who take over big corporations' (Žižek 2008: 15). Affective labour and creativity in the digital economy displace the faceless bureaucracies of the twentieth century with what Thrift (2005: 11) calls 'soft capitalism' with a 'caring and sharing ethos', or business with a reflexive personality. In other words, we have now been 'taught that corporations have a soul' (Deleuze 1992: 6). The breathless dynamism of the cool cultural argument, though, needs to be treated cautiously, not least in the light of the economic crisis (Gamble 2009; Harvey 2010; Jones 2010).

Biopolitics, devices and data

Less widely discussed than the network thinking and cool neoliberalism of the digital age, particularly in relation to education, is a third approach which seeks to describe the ways in which specific digital devices, digital data, and the computer code working behind them are involved in reshaping modes of life and reshaping society. One element of such arguments is cast in terms of 'biopolitics' (Lemke 2011). This focuses on the ways that life processes and the concept of natural and organic human life itself seem to be being transformed or 'reinvented' by the development of biotechnologies, artificial prosthetics and other bodily enhancements, leading to new 'post-human' forms of life (Haraway 1991; Hayles 1999). 'Life itself' has become the object for 'political struggles', and the capabilities of the human body the object for intervention, control, disciplining and optimization (Foucault 1990: 143). Through technologies such as brain scans, DNA analysis, transplant medicines and reproductive technologies, life is increasingly being redefined in terms of an:

> ... artificial plurality of life forms, which resemble technical artefacts more than they do natural entities. ... The body is increasingly seen not as an organic substratum but as molecular software that can be read and rewritten.
> (Lemke 2011: 93)

These developments have made the body and life processes into objects for technological and political intervention, allowing for the body's deconstruction, compartmentalization, recombination and reconstruction, whether for medical or aesthetic purposes. Life itself has become more 'flexible' (Lemke 2011: 95). As a result, individuals are increasingly able to view their own bodies as malleable, correctable and improvable, and to employ 'self-techniques' to 'experiment' and 'act upon themselves to make themselves better than they are' (Rose 2007: 27). This form of biopolitics as the 'enhancement' and 'optimization' of life changes the ways in which people think about themselves, but its political importance lies partly in the fact that biotechnology and biomedicine are big business. The proliferation of biotech corporations in the digital age has given rise to forms of 'bio-capital' and 'bio-economics' within 'a new political economy of life' (Rose 2007: 32).

Indeed, for Rose (2007: 258), biopolitics brings about a transformation in the very nature of capitalism itself, another 'new spirit of capitalism', the 'spirit of biocapitalism', which can be characterized by the relation between bioeconomics and individuals' 'unease and discontents' and their 'hope and potential overcoming'. In this new spirit of bio-capitalism, the 'praxeomorphic' symmetry detected by Bauman (2005) between humans and technologies is literally embodied in the bio-technologies of optimization. Moreover, as Lemke (2011) has shown, bio-capitalism both reproduces existing forms of inequality and exploitation, and serves as the counterpart to economic neo-liberalism, which now increasingly views the optimization of the human body as overcoming existing ecological and economic limits to growth. The new biotechnological flexibility of the body and life itself is mirrored in the flexibility required for labour in the creative working culture of soft capitalism.

In addition, biopolitics has important educational dimensions. One implication is the attempt to educate the public about science and technology and in enhancing their biomedical and biotechnological literacy. Another, though closely related, educational dimension is the fact that through the internet individuals are now able to access biotechnological and biomedical information easily, and to engage with online communities of 'lay experts', in order to engage in the process of 'bio-medical self-shaping' (Rose 2007: 141). Here we can see how biopolitics has a part to play in education in the digital age, both as a formal pedagogy for the public understanding of science and technology, and as an informal pedagogy of self-directed learning and self-improvement. Again, the self-shaping biological citizen empowered by bio-science is the mirror image of the self-shaping worker fabricated in much management literature.

Biopolitics is concerned with the biological reshaping of people and life itself, and with the wider social and political implications of biotechnology and biomedicine. But other new and emerging twenty-first century digital technologies and devices can have a much more mundane role to play in society. Research on the sociology of 'digital devices' by Savage, Ruppert and Law (2010) has shown how specific devices are themselves productive of new social and material arrangements. Technologies are far from mere innocent devices which exist neutrally outside of the social world. Instead, they constitute and are 'composed of many different kinds of elements, ranging from computer networks, scanners, algorithms, software and applications to different actors, institutions, regulations and controversies' (Savage, Ruppert and Law 2010: 7). That is to say that technologies are through-and-through social, and vice versa – technological devices and society are mutually constitutive. One useful historical example they provide is the national census survey. Rather than being understood as a simple container of national data, they argue, the census survey is itself a device which produces certain new sorts of social categories, classifications, and organizational forms. Likewise, Osborne and Rose (1999b) describe opinion polls as a historical example of a data collection technique that has not just captured public opinion, but actually worked to produce public opinion. Public opinion is an artefact of the technical procedures and devices that are designed to elicit and capture it. As a result, people have *learned* to have opinions, with ways of thinking that fit their expectations and understandings of the techniques, devices and purposes of public opinion research, and society has become opinionated.

Moving back into the digital domain, similarly, Latour (2011) has argued that society is itself an artefact of the ways in which digital data itself is accumulated and aggregated. What we take to be society is itself shaped by the tools and instruments used to record it. In the new 'datascapes on the screen' (2011: 804) made possible by Web 2.0 technologies and media, therefore, what we take to be society can be viewed, analyzed and in fact defined in completely novel ways. This has the potential to change not just the ways that we read data but the ways in which we view society itself. Another way of putting this is that new technologies such as Web 2.0 platforms and social networking sites, however crude their definition of society, are becoming increasingly constitutive of it. In the vocabulary of actor–network theory, social networking sites are giving us new ways of viewing ourselves as actors in connection to networks and aggregates, but also new ways of understanding ourselves *as* networks made up of all of our various connections. We are only actors because of our networks of attachments, as amply demonstrated, for example, by our personal social network profiles, which are essentially representations of all the aggregates that make up our individual online selves (Latour *et al.* 2012). Perhaps, then, we can say that just as people learned to have opinions because of public opinion research techniques, today people are learning to live as networks because of their enmeshment in social networking sites.

Thus devices are themselves implicated in the production and performance of contemporary society – they help create society. Thrift (2005: 16) has argued that software now exists in such profusion, 'plaster[ing] the everyday world with a new and active surface', that it is increasingly changing the character of the everyday world and redefining what it means to be a person. The proliferation of software, according to Thrift (2005: 173), produces 'highly coded domains' in which sets of rules and standards of conduct are written down in the underlying computer code. He uses the mundane example of spreadsheets. Spreadsheets are a form of software that have provided a new language for everyday business lives by generating new forms of information, presentation. interaction, and new forms of persuasion. This has enabled new forms of business based on a shift in the presentation of quantitative data, twinned with a qualitative change in how people work with that data and thus a redefinition of what it means to be a person in business. That is to say that spreadsheets promote capacities, standards of conduct, and qualities – forms of identity fashioned in the techniques, practices and knowledges of the work of business. But spreadsheets have migrated out from business to fabricate new social realities in all areas of social existence. Even in the humdrum detail of software applications like spreadsheets, word processors and videogames, code is 'changing the nature of human subjects by producing enhanced capabilities'; it consists of 'rules of conduct' which 'operate at a distance' to 'constantly direct how citizens act' (Thrift 2005: 172–3). Code is programming and writing the world itself, along with new and redefined forms of humanity, into existence. To use Woolgar's (1991) expression, software is 'configuring the user', or, as Thrift puts it, software constitutes a 'mass produced series of instructions that lie in the interstices of everyday life, pocket dictators that are constantly expressing themselves' (Thrift 2005: 156).

A particular implication raised by seeing technologies, devices and software as 'pocket dictators', as 'mass produced instructions' which are themselves 'productive', regards the ways in which digital devices increasingly collect data and aggregate individuals into vast databases. Personal digital data created by and about people has become a major issue in both policy and research on digital technologies. The World Economic Forum (2011:5) has suggested that personal digital data should now be classified as a 'new asset class', the 'new oil of the internet', that will generate 'a new wave of opportunity for economic and societal value creation':

> The types, quantity and value of personal data being collected are vast: our profiles and demographic data from bank accounts to medical records to employment data. Our Web searches and sites visited, including our likes and dislikes and purchase histories. Our tweets, texts, emails, phone calls, photos and videos as well as the coordinates of our realworld locations. The list continues to grow. Firms collect and use this data to support individualised service-delivery business models that can be monetised. Governments employ personal data to provide critical public services more efficiently and effectively. Researchers accelerate the development of new drugs and treatment protocols. End users benefit from free, personalised consumer experiences such as Internet search, social networking or buying recommendations.

This suggests major societal ramifications, as every digital transactions and personal data trace becomes webbed to enormous interconnected networks of databases which may be analyzed for all sorts of political, commercial and research purposes.

As Mackenzie (2012: 337) puts it in his account of 'database-oriented social theory', there is a 'recognized centrality of databases in information societies, networked cultures, and so on', and thus a 'generally acknowledged shift in new economy and new media to "database-driven" processes.' Such database-driven processes and architectures structure and organize social networking sites, customer profiling systems, and search engines (amongst many others). Amazon, Google, Facebook and all the rest are continually generating and aggregating data as byproducts of many millions of human interactions and transactions. As a consequence, the 'sociotechnical instantiation of many aspects of the contemporary world depend on database architectures and database management techniques' (Mackenzie 2012: 335). Indeed, for Mackenzie (2006), databases and their underlying computer codes and mathematical procedures are to be found almost everywhere in a globalized world, and may therefore now be understood to structure and organize human agency, behaviour, and intention. Despite appearing as mundane technical objects, Mackenzie (2006: 4) argues, all software applications 'overlap and enmesh with imaginings of sociality, individual identity, community, collectivity, organization and enterprise.' That is to say that software applications, databases and code interlace with and actually constitute many aspects of contemporary social, cultural, political and economic life – there is sociality in software. Many of the relations that make up material and social life are now organized, stored, configured and performed through the aggregation technologies and architectures of databases. Rather than looking at individuals and collectivities as social actors, they are re-positioned in terms of the traces of their transactions.

Perhaps the key point to be made about many such digital devices and technologies is that they have made individuals into 'transactional actors' within dynamic flows of data exchange and interaction processes (Savage, Ruppert and Law 2010). There are political and ethical consequences based on the collection and aggregation of people's web transactions, data trails and traces, and on what they do online rather than on what they actually say. 'Transactional politics' (Ruppert and Savage 2012), describes how new kinds of informational experts and gatekeepers, largely from the commercial sector, are now involved in the collection and analysis of transactional data, and how Web 2.0 platforms are also increasingly allowing the public to access various forms of data, such as politicians' expenses claims. Database-driven technologies therefore imbue contemporary society, and contemporary forms of human subjectivity, with particular technological textures and architectures – they shape aspects of society, invent new kinds of social identities, and shape new ways of acting.

The focus on productive technologies, productive software, and productive code raises some important insights for the analysis of digital technologies and education. It suggests that the use of technologies in educational contexts is actually changing the way in which education and pedagogy are done, and in the process changing the kind of subjects – teachers and learners – that are doing it. It suggests tending to the ways in which pedagogies involving database-driven technologies may be understood as transactional pedagogies. Emerging devices and technologies like track-and-trace technologies, digital mapping, software visualization, transactional data, data mining, social network analysis, digital databases, wikis, Web 2.0 and open source social analytics are all beginning to change the ways in which learning can be tracked, recorded, visualized, patterned, documented and presented. Digitally networked learning is being inseparably shaped through new transactional methods that are genealogically rooted in commercial interests and non-humanist transactional politics. These are implications as yet little explored.

What we have seen in this discussion of biopolitics, devices and data is how many of the technologies emerging in the digital age – from the spectacular examples of biotech to the mundane and invisible databases that organize and structure everyday tools like web searching and social networking – are themselves productive of new forms of human action and thus new organizational forms of society. These, like the cybernetic imagery of networks and the cool capitalist ethos that have animated much recent social thought, pose some substantial challenges for education.

Conclusion: 'Making up' new realities

This sketch of some of the key contours of thinking in the cartography of the digital age, then, has attempted to indicate something of the complexity and heterogeneity of perspectives on digital, technical and related social developments. What we have revealed is a series of variations on a cybernetic style of thinking, a way of understanding the social, economic, political and cultural landscape of the present in terms of a genre of technical metaphors with a complex genealogy. In focusing on styles of thinking and metaphors, as expressions of a background hum in the social realities of the present, we are seeking to distance ourselves from grand epochal claims about a digital transformation of the present era, whilst also recognizing the potential for productivity built into such claims and the metaphors they recruit. Today, metaphors, theories and images of networks have attained particular importance. From the perspective of the present, the future looks very much to be a networked future, all flows, connections, reticulations, extensions and so on. Networks are found not just in the connections between informational and communication technologies, but in the circulation of finance and debt in economics, in the new governance techniques of contemporary politics, in the communication circuits of culture, and in the very weave of sociality and society.

These ways of thinking and these metaphors have become shared in society as a kind of common sense or taken-for-granted reality in the making. These ways of thinking do not so much *frame* a whole bundle of social and technological changes that have actually occurred or exist in social reality, as work to *force* them into existence, to make up new social realities that did not formerly exist; they work not so much to explain the objects they describe but to reshape the very objects for which an explanation is required (Thrift 2005; Rose 2007). In the next chapter, we show how some of these ideas and explanations have been translated and rearticulated in terms of their educational implications, and been used as the impetus and the force to catalyze a whole arsenal of reformatory strategies and techniques.

3

RECONSTRUCTING THE FUTURE OF EDUCATION

Thinking the future

How do we *think about* technology and education? In the last chapter we explored how the digital age has been made intelligible through a variety of conceptual discourses, such as those of networks, cool cultural capitalism, and the social and biopolitical influences of devices themselves. Some of these discourses and the ideas and visions they carry have been translated into the education and technology field. But the ways in which education and technology are made 'thinkable' and are 'thought' are not historically immutable. Styles of thinking change over time. In this chapter we want to trace some of the ways in which the styles of thinking associated with the digital age have been developed and deployed in the normative ideals of policy texts and in the specification of new classroom practices and programmes. We are especially interested in how the thought underpinning such imaginaries and objectives has changed and mutated over time. In singling out thought we are drawing on Dean's (2010: 31) description of 'fairly coherent sets of ways of going about doing things' and the more or less organized ways, at any given time and place, that practices can be thought, made into objects of knowledge, turned into problems, and solved through the specification of new reformatory programmes.

Following this framework, we can say that at different times, various ideas about the technologized futures of the digital age, articulated through its characteristic cybernetic styles of thinking, have been redeployed through educational policy and practice as a way of representing possible futures, encouraging or conditioning what it is possible to think and say about the future, and 'making futures apparently present' (Kinsley 2010: 2779). As Rosenberg and Harding (2005:9) argue, 'we live in a world saturated by future-consciousness as rich and as full as our consciousness of the past', each of those futures 'haunting their presents' and carrying their own 'histories of the future.' The futures of the digital age have their own histories of thinking, and the ways in which we think about technology and education are therefore related to these genealogies of thought and the practices and programmes they make possible.

Looking at things this way, our approach is to recover something of the memory politics of the digital age which is so often erased from enthusiastic accounts of the potential of technology for educational improvement and transformation. By foregrounding the memory politics associated with education and technology, we seek to show which digital age arguments, explanations, terms, references and so on have been articulated, reimagined and translated in education, and which have been excluded, downplayed and repressed, in different places and times. This general form of genealogical investigation – a history of the present – seeks to destabilize and denaturalize taken-for-grated assumptions and certainties by querying how the present has been constituted by complex couplings and continuities, as well as by unexpected disjunctures and discontinuities (Dean 2010; Rose 1999b). There is no simple lineage, linear line of descent, or single point of origin in a genealogical investigation, but multiple divergences and diversifications.

Perhaps, then, we can conceive of this chapter as a first effort in a genealogy of educational futures. In the networked, cool, cybernetic future we are told that we are now entering, the function of education is being transformed. Liu (2004: 3) phrases this brilliantly in his cultural study of a knowledge economy in which everything is 'only cool or not cool':

> In the 'knowledge economy', education occurs across a whole lifetime in an unprecedented variety of social sectors, institutions and media: not just schools, community colleges, and universities, but also businesses, broadcast media, [and] the Internet… Education, in other words, is now a decentralized field where no one institution individually corners the market and where we encounter a dizzying dispersion of the kinds and scales of learning… [H]ow can society create the most inclusive, flexible, and intelligently interrelated mix of educational options to take care of its citizens hungry to 'know'?
> (Liu 2004: 22)

This excerpt is significant because it identifies three significant educational outgrowths of the digital age style of thinking. In this chapter we will start with arguments about the existence of a knowledge economy, perhaps the dominant policy narrative of the digital age and showing little sign of going away any time soon. We then look at the implications of commercial media, privatization, and consumerism for education. And finally we look at claims that learning is now a lifelong pursuit among citizens and indeed that in the digital age learning is dispersed throughout the informal pedagogies of the networked society. Using these major discourses as a basis for the rest of the chapter, we then go on to examine how educational practices with technologies have been made intelligible. Without claiming exhaustivity, what we suggest is that there are at least three key mutations in thinking about technology and education: 'constructionism', 'interactionism', and 'connectionism'.

In the 1980s, at a time when major policy statements were beginning to reflect the potential importance of technologies and knowledge to future economic development in a 'learning society', the youthful field of educational technology led by people like Seymour Papert, was focused on 'constructionism'. Later, as the 1990s gave way to utopian fantasies about the twenty-first century of a 'knowledge economy' and 'informational capitalism', education and technology were increasingly yoked to key concepts like creativity and flexibility, and to socio-cultural theories of situated learning and communities of practice, that gave rise to the development of new pedagogic innovations characterized by 'interactionism'. And our final mutation is from interactionism to 'connectionism', a thoroughly twenty-first century spin on the digital style of thinking which is saturated with ideas and ideals from Web 2.0 and puts the emphasis on networks of connections, connected learning, connected communities, connected learning institutions and so on. These three variations give us some sense of a genealogy of contemporary ways of thinking on education and technology in the digital age. Demarcating them with three different labels, and periodizing them by decades, risks suggesting that each represents a self-contained period and a clean break from what came before. But we see them as contrapuntal continuities and overlapping combinations. Much of what was advanced under a banner of constructionism is continued in twenty-first century versions of connected learning, not least in talk of 'DIY learning' and 'knowledge construction,' for example. But the dominant ways of thinking about education and technology have subtly changed over the last three decades, and the categories of 'constructionism' 'interactionism', and 'connectionism' capture those genealogical mutations in thinking.

What we demonstrate is how long waves of social change (Goodson 2005), intersecting with ripples of technological development, have come together at particular historical conjunctures with particular kinds of learning theories. Bauman (2005) uses the term 'praxeomorphic' to refer to the historical tendency for humans to understand themselves, their consciousness and minds, in terms of metaphors derived from the latest cutting-edge technologies, whether mechanical, chemical, electric, or cybernetic. Scientific models of the human mind have tended to run parallel with the progress of technology, followed closely by new technological framings of human action and practice (Osborne and Rose 1999b). Adapting this slightly for our purposes, technologies and learning are being thought praxeomorphically, whereby the practices of learning are perceived to run parallel in history with technological progress. The genealogies of learning are paralleled by the genealogies of technologies. Consequently, in the digital age contemporary educational thought is saturated with cybernetic metaphors which assume learning to be praxeomorphic with the very latest technological developments and breakthroughs. Or, perhaps more accurately, in the futures imagined in the discourses of the digital age, humans are to be *made* praxeomorphic with new technology; it is through metaphors of networks, connectedness, flow and so on that learning is to be reconceived and translated into pedagogic practice. The rest of this chapter now attempts to unpack something of this praxeomorphic thinking about learning and new technology, and it does so through examining education and technology in the digital age as an ensemble of discourses, imaginaries, institutions, social actors, technologies, theories, claims, conceptual content, politics and historical associations.

Knowledge economy

The dominant policy narrative underpinning educational reform and the reimagining of the future of education for the twenty-first century is that of the emergence of the knowledge economy (Robertson 2005). Lauder *et al.* (2012) call the knowledge economy a 'social imaginary', following the definition set out by Rizvi and Lingard (2010: 34). Those authors define social imaginary as a 'way of thinking shared in a society by ordinary people', that carries with it normative notions, narratives and images that are constitutive of a society. In the contemporary era, a social imaginary is carried in images and narratives and increasingly in the mass media and popular culture. The notion of an 'imaginary' also implies, as Jessop (2008) points out, that the knowledge economy is a simplification and reduction of 'hypercomplexity' in the actually existing economy. The social imaginary of the knowledge economy repositions schools as providers of 'post-industrial training'. Post-industrial training is focused on increasing efficiency, productivity and worker investment, and on ensuring the adequate supply and quality of human capital – the development of skills and dispositions required by nation-states in a globally competitive economy dominated by the technology industries (Brown and Lauder 2001; Lauder *et al.* 2012).

In a post-industrial or post-Fordist world where knowledge and creativity have higher economic and cultural value than physical products or manufacturing and where economic restructuring depends on high-tech innovations in new technology and media, greater emphasis is put on education to teach the skills associated with knowledge work, on producing ideas, knowledge and information rather than the production of material 'stuff' (Ball 2008). Production increasingly requires workers to be 'flexible specialists' who can adapt to fluctuations and changes in the demands of markets. A high-tech, high-skills, high-wage future is promoted as being simultaneously good for the economy and good for individuals and good for social equality overall (Brown, Lauder and Ashton 2011). Individuals who invest in education can become knowledge workers, and will be rewarded financially as well as with power, greater autonomy, and creativity (Allais 2010). This makes quite new social, intellectual and educational demands of employees. What is required of education for the future, then, is flexible learning for flexible specialists (Young 1998). It is in the context of these new flexible correspondences that schools are understood less as specific institutions and more closely resemble and operate like businesses (Stevenson 2010). In such institutions the emphasis is put on individuals perpetually re-training and adapting to a continuous multi-tasking environment, being self-enterprising and self-regulating. That is to say that both schools and businesses now speak the same language of flexibility, modularization, componentization, competences profiles, soft performance, brainpower, problem-solving and so on.

Although critics have queried the conceptual clarity and empirical reality of the knowledge economy, it is clear that as a policy idea and a social imaginary it has exerted material effects on schooling (Kenway *et al.* 2006). As Jensen and Lauritsen (2005: 365) have argued, policy ideas may be understood as 'active travelers' that move and settle in new places, and that function by constructing links between their visions and a diversity of local practices – they work 'as a relay between certain administrative and political practices and a diversity of local initiatives'. As the idea and the imaginary vision of the knowledge economy has been shuffled around and settled, the result has been a proliferation of programmes and initiatives intended to equip young people as the flexible and adaptable 'human capital' required by network-based enterprises and more widely by knowledge capitalism itself. In the information-rich, knowledge-based network society almost every government policy is now made with reference to the 'realities' of the global economy. Owing to the needs of the knowledge economy and its correlates of international trade and global competition, schools, colleges, universities are required to supply 'smart', highly-skilled 'collective intelligence' embodied in flexibility, creativity, problem-solving, innovation, collaboration, continuous improvement, risk-taking, entrepreneurship, and social responsibility (Brown and Lauder 2001). Here it is possible to detect the new spirit of cool, creative capitalism being carried in the social imaginary of the knowledge economy and settling down in new educational practices everywhere.

However, the fallout from the explosion in education is a new global struggle for middle-class jobs. The global jobs market is already congested with well-educated and high-skills young people all seeking 'boundaryless careers,' and this is leading to a competition for 'cut-price brainpower' that forces 'students, workers, and families into a bare-knuckle fight for those jobs that continue to offer a good standard of living' (Brown, Lauder and Ashton 2011, 7). The cultivation of a small élite of creative star producers in the knowledge economy is at the expense of the 'children of neo-liberalism' who now represent an 'abandoned generation' (Little 2010) or a 'cognitariat' with an uncertain and anxious future as skilled 'perma-temps' (Newfield 2010). Despite these flaws in the ways in which the knowledge economy has represented itself, and in spite of its very obvious part in the boom-years economic narrative that has since 2007 or so looked increasingly untenable, 'there are good reasons for thinking that this ideology will persist, despite significant fraying at the edges, because there is no viable alternative on the horizon' (Lauder *et al.* 2012: 5). While we understand the 'knowledge economy' as an imaginary, then, we must also note that it has been 'conjured into existence' in such a way that it 'has the power to make its theories and descriptions of the world come alive in new built forms, new machines and new bodies' (Thrift 2005: 11). We cannot dismiss the knowledge economy as an imagined policy mythology but should instead view it as an agency, carried in a variety of policy texts, programmes and practices, that has continued to exert productive material effects on education in the recession.

Privatization, commercialism and consumerism

The flexible future envisioned in the knowledge economy is in some ways linked with a parallel development of greater commercial activities in schools. Commercial activities include sponsorship of programs, sponsoring materials, promotion and marketing of software and technology infrastructure, exclusive agreements such as those made with textbook publishers, electronic marketing, incentive programs such as store vouchers, school facilities reconstruction programs, plus the full privatization and management of schools – and as a result commercial activities 'now shape the structure of the school day, influence the content of the school curriculum, and determine whether children have access to a variety of technologies' (Molnar 2005: 84). Commercialization represents an array of practices which contribute to a complex series of ever-shifting alignments between commercial organizations and education, or the 'entanglement' of politics, education and private finance in 'the new world of global for-profit education and knowledge industries' (Spring 2009: 88).

The massive increase in educational services industries, corporate involvement in public education, and the rise of private companies in the creation and marketing of for-profit online learning are all evidence of how public education is fast being transformed by (and in some cases into) big business, and many critics find this alarming. 'Edu-business' and privatization bring the normative assumptions of global market competitiveness into public education, arguably leading to a narrowing of what is seen to count as students' learning (Ball 2007). Notably, such processes of commercialism and privatization are now increasingly massaged by the involvement of new philanthropists and social enterprises which have 'provided a kind of rehabilitation for forms of capital that were subject to 'ill repute' in the public imagination' (Ball and Junemann 2012: 32).

While commercialization takes place within education systems and institutions, a no less significant transformation has been occurring outside of the school gates, where children are increasingly understood as 'born into' cultures and practices of consumerism (Cook 2008; Martens 2005). The so-called 'post-industrial conundrum' of schooling describes the mismatch between the dominant bureaucratic mode of schooling, a model developed in the nineteenth and early twentieth centuries, and the experiences of children and adults in other sectors of highly mediated twenty-first century society (Carolan, Natriello and Rennick 2003). Putting it simply, many organizations have been better than education systems at aligning themselves with the lifestyles, identities and ego-projects of young people who seek to identify themselves as autonomous, pleasure-seeking consumers (Kenway and Bullen 2005). By shifting learning into a cultural landscape rich with multimedia, learners are now increasingly exposed to the hidden curriculum of commercial culture, a culture which for some educational commentators is participatory and sophisticated yet for others ideologically aggressive and 'miseducative' (Seiter 2005), as shown in Molnar's (2005: 81) argument that the miseducative 'curriculum of our culture, 24 hours a day, 7 days a week, 365 days a year, is advertising.'

In a globalized media culture, a competition has been established between the 'competing resources for youthful identity building offered by the global corporate curriculum of consumer-media culture and that of schooling in corporatized education systems' (Kenway and Bullen 2005: 31). The 'corporate curriculum' and 'voluptuous' commercial pedagogies of consumer media culture have 'become postmodern society's most successful teachers,' and through them 'young people are offered identities as pleasure-seeking, self-indulgent, autonomous, rational decision-makers' (Kenway and Bullen 2005: 36). A series of erosions, effacements and elisions of established divisions between children's media cultures and their education has been the consequence of this hybridization of education with advertising and entertainment, resulting in the emergence of new ideas about identity and subjectivity. School commercialism can be understood as 'a vehicle through which corporations can deliver a broader ideological message promoting consumption as the primary source of well-being and happiness' and positioning young people less as 'active citizens-to-be' and more as 'passive consumers-to-be' (Molnar 2005: 44–5). As Buckingham (2011: 217) concludes in his extensive assessment of materialism and childhood in consumer culture, 'the "logic" of the market appears to require both teachers and learners to behave in ever more individualistic, competitive ways, and yet also to engage in more intensive forms of self-regulation and self-surveillance.' Within this commercial consumerist logic, schools are repositioned as 'vendors in the educational hypermarket', and as digital media have become more sophisticated and increasingly accessible, learning activities have become 'consumer goods in themselves, purchased as the result of choice within a marketplaces where learning products compete with those of leisure and entertainment and are often indistinguishable from these' (Usher 2009: 42).

Lifelong learning

An important educational discourse through which developments and arguments concerning commercialism and consumerism have been rehearsed is that of 'lifelong learning'. The idea of lifelong learning, as Nikolas Rose (1999b: 161) has surveyed, goes back to the 1970s and to concerns with ensuring that individuals were capable of adapting to the pace of technological change. This concern was articulated simultaneously in terms of re-skilling the redundant and unemployed, and also in terms of the industrial and economic consequences of rapid technological change. Thus lifelong learning has appeared equally as a psychological state of constant re-learning and as an economic imperative for perpetual labour-force adjustment, as evidenced by the involvement of international economic organizations such as the OECD in lifelong learning policies. Lifelong learning has therefore been interpreted as hybridizing humanist ideals and practical market demands, and has transformed society itself into school (Fejes and Nicholl 2008). The requirement for lifelong learning in a 'learning society' or a 'totally pedagogized society' has shifted pedagogy away from the formally canalized institution of schooling and interwoven it into the informal textures of the contemporary social world, while perpetual retraining and constant change-readiness have replaced the idea of fixed curricula and the idea of a complete course of study (Bernstein 2000; Bonal and Rambla 2003; Pykett 2007).

As a result, lifelong learning has been understood as part of the creation of new ideas about the 'active citizen':

> Education is no longer confined to 'schooling', with its specialised institutional sites and discrete biographical locus. The disciplinary individualisation and normalisation of the school sought to install, once and for all, the capacities and competencies for social citizenship. But a new set of educational obligations are emerging that are not confined in space and time in the same ways. The new citizen is required to engage in a ceaseless work of training and retraining, skilling and reskilling, enhancement of credentials and preparation for a life of incessant job seeking: life is to become a continuous economic capitalisation of the self.
>
> (Rose 1999b: 160–1)

Policies concerned with lifelong learning – understood in this way as a lifelong project, in which national and international competitiveness has been re-coded in terms of the psychological capacities, attitudes and aspirations of individuals – have put the emphasis on individuals who can continually improve themselves, upskilling and retraining as changing job descriptions require. The active citizen promoted by lifelong learning policy is therefore 'an entrepreneur of him- or her- self' who is to conduct his or her life 'as a kind of enterprise, seeking to enhance and capitalize on existence itself', through 'new forms of consumption' in identity and lifestyle formation and through 'contractual relations' in new marketplaces of education (Rose 1999b: 164–5).

Put more specifically in terms of learning with new technologies and media, the 'enterprising selves' of 'permanently unfinished', reflexive, self-adjusting, lifelong learners are essential as the 'human capital' required by the knowledge economy (Popkewitz 2008):

> Children are not being taught ICT competences so that they can stop learning when they have finished the curriculum. There is no state of 'completion' or 'journey's end' in view. Rather children are being taught so that they can continue to learn and change after school, so that they are ready to adapt to future unpredictable demands and circumstances. ... The habits of staying in touch with a changing world, of wrapping that world around

one's plans and interests, and of continuing to do so as one's plans and interests change, will be vital to future economic success.

(Lee 2001: 84)

All manner of forms of learning with new technologies and media are now increasingly understood in relation to lifelong learning, with learning viewed as dispersed in time and space, horizontally structured, networked and connected together, and convergent across many different media. Here, lifelong learning is articulated as a particular capacity to be acquired in order to cope with technological change, and once again the enterprise of the learner is linked up to the changing requirements of labour in a digital age.

So far we have begun to see how developments in the digital age have been translated as high-level policy discourses in education. It is important to reiterate that we are not talking about the digital age as a definite era with definable developments based on the properties of particular devices, but about ways of thinking about and making the digital age intelligible, and similarly that we are concerned with the invention and promotion of new ideas, normative visions, and objectives for the re-imagining of the future of schooling. The knowledge economy, as well as lifelong learning and many accounts of private sector innovation in public education, are imaginaries based on particular policy interpretations of social and technological change in the digital age. The digital age is the background hum with which schooling is being set into resonance. The discourses of the knowledge economy, increased commercialism and privatization, and lifelong learning are all developments that in various ways have adjusted or re-positioned the work of schools and the identities and subjectivities of learners and teachers that they promote. In the knowledge economy, we see the construction of flexible workers through new educational skills programmes. In school commercialism and privatization we see learners made up in the logic of the market. And in lifelong learning we see learners repositioned as active citizens who are to make their own selves into lifelong projects, self-enterprise, and continual entrepreneurial self-fulfilment. In sum, as Ball (2007) articulates it, students are being reconceived and repositioned, through a 'new technology-based child-centredness' of personalization, individualization and responsibilization (2007: 141), as 'responsible for their own learning and for making a planning office for themselves' (2007: 182).

The social developments articulated through the cybernetic style of thinking of the historical conjuncture now known as the 'digital age' have led to several waves of attempts to link up the digital more closely with processes of schooling and learning. Caught in the long, slow tidal surge of the digital age, it is possible to identify at least three smaller waves of development around technology and education. We now turn our attention to a constructionist wave of developments originating in the 1980s, an interactionist set of developments that accompanied the growth of ideas and policies concerning the 'global economy' at the end of the 1990s, and finally the development of a connectionist style of thinking about learning in a highly mobile and networked twenty-first century. Carried on these three waves of change, particular kinds of technologies have been related to particular kinds of theories about learning, particular approaches to pedagogy, and particular forms of curriculum organization. We can say that the various histories or genealogies of technologies in the digital age have been paralleled by genealogies of pedagogic reform, curriculum development, and learning theory. Of course, these are not entirely separate developments or historically clean breaks, but gradual mutations brought about through the formation of new alliances between technologies, theories and the actors who advocate for them.

Constructionism: cybernetics for children

Constructionism is perhaps the archetypal conceptual model for the educational use of technology. With Seymour Papert, Lego Professor of Learning Research at MIT as its long-term figurehead, constructionism extends psychological theories of constructivism into the technological domain. Constructivism is itself chiefly associated with the work of the developmental psychologists including Jean Piaget and Jerome Bruner. The emphasis in constructivist accounts is on learning as an iterative process of active and spontaneous problem-solving that is based on and builds upon learners' previous experience and knowledge, rather than on predetermined sequences of instruction. Learning is understood as knowledge production rather than knowledge reproduction. In constructivist pedagogies, teachers are encouraged to act as facilitators of learners' own self-directed processes of exploration, inquiry, interpretation and individual meaning-making, with learners filtering and constructing new knowledge for themselves upon a foundation of prior learning. Through such processes, learners need to be able to assimilate, alter and modify incoming information to fit with what they already know; and to accommodate and alter what is already known on the basis of new knowledge.

Seymour Papert was a student of Piaget's, and his basic argument is that the use of computers can accelerate constructivist forms of learning. In his well-known 1980 book Mindstorms, Papert adapted aspects of constructivism into the model of constructionism. Constructionism blends constructivist pedagogy with the idea of construction kits and toys like Lego. Papert (1993: 182) called it 'cybernetics for children'. Constructionism focuses on learning through making and building. On one level, this refers to the construction of physical objects or electronic artefacts, such as building a model or doing some computer programming. Papert's original research was on children learning to program computers using the LOGO programming language, a simplified programming environment that allowed children to see a visual representation of their programming. Using LOGO, children could control the 'turtle', either as a small motorised robot or an onscreen cursor, to move and create line graphics and complex geometric patterns.

On another level, however, Papert saw the construction process as more generally transferable, allowing learners to understand more about their own thinking and learning processes. More recently, the legacy of LOGO has been extended to the Lego Mindstorms robotics kits; an online Net-Logo programming environment for exploring emergent phenomena and complex adaptive systems; MicroWorlds, a multimedia authoring programme, and Scratch, a tool for programming simple videogames and animations (see Bogost 2007; Buckingham 2007; Ito 2009; Selwyn 2011b). Simulation videogames like the SimCity and The Sims franchises and other 'empire-building' games have also been positioned as part of a broadly constructionist genre. With the proliferation of social media and user-generated content in the Web 2.0 environment, these arguments have taken on an enhanced educational significance (Bruns 2008; Burn 2009; Davies and Merchant 2010; Knobel and Lankshear 2010). Activities such as digital media authoring and social networking are now extending the constructionist genre into a world where young people are making, messing around with and sharing digital media as part of learning in everyday life in participatory networked cultures (Ito *et al.* 2009).

Symbiotic with the constructivist philosophy, constructionist approaches are characterized by an emphasis on building, testing and refining models, on user authoring, personal production (rather than consumption) of content, autonomy and ownership, creative accomplishment, self-directed learning rooted in personal experience, and on giving the child the subject position of agency and authorship. As Ito (2009: 146) argues, in constructionist approaches the computer's interactive qualities enable 'users to embody their agency computationally: as Papert states, users programming the computer rather than the computer programming them.' The constructionist narrative is one of self-actualization in which learners appear to be making their own choices about their learning, to be building, authoring and exercising their own agency (Ito 2009: 183), through 'thinking like a computer' (Papert 1980: 155).

Of course these claims are vulnerable to critique. For a start, Bryson and de Castell (1998: 74), influenced by Foucault, have argued that 'the epistemological underpinnings of Papert's LOGO culture':

> ... serve to lend an aura of scientificity or systematic rationality to models of human thinking that place the ability to reason, or to make use of inductive/ deductive logical operations, at the highest level of human intellectual achievements. ... Critical theory stresses that covertly entrenched in the technicists' processes of categorizing, and thus hierarchizing, different types of software or different types of learning are existing social norms and relations of power.

From this critical perspective, LOGO must be viewed as a 'technology of normalization' that serves to regulate what is considered normal behaviour. Constructionist arguments are also open to the critique that computers too are social constructions which configure their users. Users of constructionist tools and programmes are not simply able to build agency for themselves. Agency is built and shaped for them by those tools. In part at least the computer is also programming them through re-coding standards of conduct and directing how to think, act and interact. Through the 'cybernetics for children' of constructionist tools and programming environments, users are subtly configured with new cybernetic ways of thinking and new forms of collective intelligence, or thought mediated through interaction with a complex ecology of devices (Thrift 2005).

Moreover, it ought to be clear that the discourse of constructionism shares many similarities with the imaginary of the knowledge economy and the ideals of lifelong learning surveyed previously. The normalized ideal-typical constructionist learner is an active and creative co-constructor of knowledge, an autonomous self-directed learner and a self-actualizing actor with a reflexive knowledge and self-understanding – a 'self-constructionist' constantly assimilating and accommodating new knowledge into its own life projects. As Rose (1996: 169) has shown, this image of the autonomous actor with an 'individualized subjectivity' and 'aspirations and anxieties concerning their self-fulfilment', is now being animated equally in political life, in working life, and in everyday life. Such an autonomous subject has been made up as the ideal figure to inhabit a world in which lifestyles are lifelong projects to be continuously constructed and in which more and more work involves the construction of knowledge for its economic value. Legitimated through such ideals, constructionism, and the theory of constructivist, self-directed exploratory learning that it is built upon and extends, has retained considerable influence in ongoing attempts to advocate the positive effects of the educational use of technologies, especially as technologies have been advanced to become more interactive and responsive.

Interactionism: flexible pedagogy at a distance

We use the term 'interactionism' to refer to the mutation of constructionism that took place in the 1990s as new discourses and policies such as the 'network society' and the 'knowledge age' were popularized. Interactionism continues to emphasize the broadly constructivist theory of learners constructing their own knowledge and understanding. It additionally emphasizes how this process of knowledge construction happens through interaction with others located within authentic sociocultural environments. These authentic interactions may take place through the tools and resources of interactive technologies and the increasingly virtual environments that are now available through the internet. Interactive sociocultural theories of learning and technology stress collaborative and socially situated processes that take place in 'communities of practice', with the addition of interacting with tools and devices as augmentations of human capacity or as extensions of collaboration and 'learning at a distance' (Selwyn 2011b: 77). Although this form of social constructivism is largely based on theories of social psychology associated with, for example, Lev Vygotsky, it has also been traced to the epistemology of the American progressivist educator and pragmatist philosopher John Dewey and to the child-centred Italian educator Maria Montessori (Bogost 2007). As Hultqvist and Dahlberg (2001: 5) have shown, the work of progressive educators such as Montessori have combined psychological thought with pedagogy to make up 'the image of a self-regulating child', who, 'when set free would regulate or steer him or herself with the slight guidance of the professional pedagogue.' These are genealogical antecedents to the mode of thought underpinning the more recent development of interactionist pedagogies.

As Fendler (2001: 120) has explained, interactive pedagogy is a 'recent pedagogical innovation ... promoted as a solution to the problems associated with previous 'teacher-centred' and 'child-centered' pedagogies'. For Fendler, interactionism is constituted in three ways. First, it is based on assumptions about the 'learner' who is to be educated. Following constructivist principles, this learner is often thought as an 'active learner', a 'constructivist learner' or an 'autonomous learner' and is assembled through pedagogies which emphasize constructivism, metacognition, and motivation. This active and autonomous learner has elsewhere been termed a 'constructivistically-oriented learner' who is engaged in active, self-directed and lifelong learning empowered by the internet and portable digital media to engage in self-motivated learning in authentic contexts and in augmented realities, anywhere and anytime (Weigel, James and Gardner 2009).

Second, interactionism is based on a disciplinary discourse of developmental appropriateness which correlates teaching objectives and outcomes with a sequence of capabilities based on the scientific findings of developmental psychology, found first in the work of Jean Piaget and then Lev Vygotsky. Whereas Piagetian developmental psychology stressed child development as an 'intrapsychic' process that was largely independent of social interaction and socio-cultural context, in Vygotskian discourse social interaction itself constitutes the basis for an individual's knowledge and for the social construction of development.

And third, interactionism is constituted as an 'open-ended' pedagogy in which teachers are supposed to be responsive to the learners' words and actions, although the objectives are usually specified in advance and justified through developmental psychology. As Fendler (2001: 132–3) further articulates, in interactive pedagogy 'the teacher teaches by adapting the material to the child's momentary interests and imparts information that is set by the children's questions. This pedagogy requires the teacher to respond flexibly to the child's feelings, words, and actions.' This is close to what Bernstein (2004) articulated as an 'ideal–typical invisible pedagogy', rather than an 'obvious' or 'visible pedagogy', in which there is a reduced emphasis upon the transmission and acquisition of specific skills, the teacher retains implicit, not explicit, control over the child, and structures the learning context which the child is expected to re-arrange and explore, while the child apparently has wide powers over the selection, structuring, sequence and pace of learning and appears to regulate his or her own movements and social relationships.

The invisible pedagogies of interactionism, then, are based on an understanding of child development and the acquisition of knowledge to be the result of social interaction, or 'interactive development' (Fendler 2001: 132). Interactive pedagogy is combined with developmentally appropriate learning objectives because the course of development in both is determined by social interaction, and 'interactionism and developmentality both imply continuous and never-ending responsive change' (2001: 138). In tandem, developmentally appropriate objectives and interactive pedagogies work together to construct the subject of the active, autonomous and constructivist learner. Fendler views these pedagogies as idealized approaches for promoting learning through online interaction and other interrelated pedagogies 'characterized as fluid, dynamic, situation responsive, pragmatic and virtual' (2001: 133). In such responsive pedagogies, students and teachers are both supposed to act 'flexibly' which Fendler regards as 'the cutting-edge solution to the challenges of productivity in a fast-moving global economy' (2001: 119). As Fendler explains, 'interactionism constructs both a response-able/-ready child and a response-able/-ready teacher' (2001: 132). In the British context, interactionism may be understood as the intellectual mode of thought underpinning the policy discourse of 'personalization', with its uneasy commingling of 1960s child-centred progressivism and the marketing discourse of the twenty-first century knowledge economy – indeed, it was Bernstein who first coined the term 'personalization' in his depiction of the invisible pedagogies of child-centredness (Hartley 2009).

Within this ensemble of psychological theories of development and human-computer interactions, a new subject position is created, that which Hartley (2010) has called an 'interactive social identity', characterized by its interaction in networks, its ease with interdependence, flexibility, responsiveness, shared learning, collective collaboration, distributed intelligence, and its hybridity. Interactive theories of developmental psychology, interactive pedagogy, and interactive identities, are constitutive of a particular historical moment discursively characterized by flexibility, connectivity, dynamism, fluidity, and interactivity. These are discursive correlates with the proliferation of cybernetic metaphors in the digital age and are clearly continuous with the re-enchanting discourse of cool cultural creativity that animates the knowledge economy.

But perhaps these are more than just metaphors. Interactive pedagogy also needs to be understood in relation to changes in the nature of human–computer interactivity. Thrift (2005) has detailed several new patterns of interactivity. For example, with more and more wireless and mobile devices, interaction with computers has now migrated out to everyday environments. As a result, computing has become more context-sensitive, so that devices know where they are in relation to other devices and users and are thus able to interact and communicate with and adapt to other users and devices. Since computing is 'always on' and constantly connected it has become a constant 'cloud' of possible interactivity augmenting many different practices. But perhaps most significantly, with the development of 'soft' computing, devices increasingly have their own capacity to 'learn' through interaction with other devices and users, and 'will increasingly second-guess the user, becoming a part of how they decide to decide' (2005: 184). Soft computation is a form of augmented cognition. Soft computing is based on the role model of the human mind, and soft computing techniques incorporate a wide variety of applications including artificial intelligence, artificial life, robotics, recognition technologies, data mining, expert systems and intelligent agents. These examples of smart, 'self-learning software' have 'begun to breathe new life into a multitude of everyday things' and 'helped software begin to take on many of the characteristics normally associated with biological life' (2005: 167–8). Indeed, 'bio-mimicry' is now an important field for computational development.

Altogether, these soft computational developments appear to be bringing about the development of more 'intelligent environments' and 'smart spaces' in which two-way human–computer interactivity is increasingly blurring the distinction between animate and inanimate beings. Increasingly, things can be said to be able to think, to possess personalities, and to have psychologies. In terms of educational implications, the appearance of smart interactive toys such as the Furby, MicroPets and Lego Mindstorms in the 1990s have already shown how machines can interact with their environments and their users to bring about new forms of play and games, new ranges of affects and emotions, and new modes of learning. These devices are illustrative of the real possibility of future classrooms that themselves seem to think and speak back to learners – 'thinking classrooms', animated by soft computational software in which chalkboards and static display boards function more like massive circuit boards. While remaining cautious of overblown claims about the future of such technologies, it is important to take seriously the shifts in interaction ushered in by such devices. These devices are now able, like the ideal interactive pedagogue, to respond and react to their users; they have sufficient reactive intelligence to interact on the basis of what they have 'learned'. This not 'educational technology' but 'educated technology.' To interactionist pedagogy we must now add the element of two-way responsive human–computer interaction, and recognize that through interaction with smart devices, learners' own development is increasingly being catalyzed and shaped by machines.

In sum, interactionism is constituted by the establishment of a praxeomorphic relationship between the conception of human development as an interactive and relational process and the affordances of smart, responsive and networked technologies. Interactionism is a form of pedagogical 'praxeomorphic thinking' within which both the human mind and network technologies are articulated in terms of their capacity for dynamic interactivity, continuous change, self-organization and the values of flexibility (Bauman 2005). For Thrift (2005), again, we are beginning to experience a new 'technological unconscious', a background sense of life that is structured by highly complex systems of communication, networking, and adaptation. That is to say, we are becoming more like 'technological forms of life', reconfigured in databases, networks and other informational platforms as 'self-regulating man–machine systems' (Lash 2002: 199), but without even thinking about it.

Connectionism: networks as schools

What we term 'connectionism' resonates very strongly with the flexible interactive pedagogies and human–computer interactions detailed above. But connectionism goes a step further by more fully aligning educational matters with the rise of networked technologies – particularly social media and technologies of 'mass self-communication' (Castells 2009). Connectionism is constituted in a pervasive network logic of Web 2.0, 24/7 learning, nomadic learning networks, transmedia convergence, smart mobs, crowdsourcing, user-generated content, open source, DIY media, and cloud culture, and so forth, much of it distributed in publications by think-tanks and by academics involved in researching digital media and learning (e.g. Bentley and Gillinson 2008; Davidson and Goldberg 2009; Jenkins *et al.* 2007; Leadbeater 2010; McCarthy, Miller and Skidmore 2004; Mulgan and Steinberg 2005; Rheingold 2003). These future ideals have been articulated most strongly in a major US programme of educational research and development called 'Connected Learning' funded by the MacArthur Foundation. According to the vision underpinning this programme, 'connected learning':

> ... harnesses the powerful new connection to ideas, knowledge, expertise, culture, friends, peers and mentors we have through the internet, digital media and social networking ... . Connected learning is an answer to three key shifts as society evolves from the industrial age of the 20th century and its one-size-fits-all factory approach to educating youth to a 21st century networked society:
> 1. *A shift from education to learning.* Education is what institutions do, learning is what people do. Digital media enable learning anywhere, anytime; formal learning must also be mobile and just-in-time.
> 2. *A shift from consumption of information to participatory learning.* Learning happens best when it is rich in social connections, especially when it is peer-based and organized around learners' interests, enabling them to create as well as consume information.
> 3. *A shift from institutions to networks.* In the digital age, the fundamental operating and delivery systems are networks, not institutions such as schools, which are one node of many in a young person's network of learning opportunities. People learn across institutions, so an entire learning network must be supported.
>
> (Yowell 2012, np)

The model of connected learning is based on an epochal narrative that a systemic trajectory of change – the formation of a networked society – has brought about a wholesale imperative for educational reform. Notably, education and educational institutions are marginalized in this vision with the learning that 'people do' and a 'person's network' instead positioned as the main centre(s) of operation. Scholz (2010: xi) argues, 'Digital learning not only takes place online, but is also situated in high schools, museums, after school programs, home schoolers' living rooms, public libraries, and peer-to-peer universities.' Learning is dispersed into the very atmosphere of culture through a vast range of techno-educational services, thus requiring a new 'attitude' to learning:

> The most burning problem for digital learning is technological obsolescence and the attendant need to learn and readapt to new technological milieus and cycles of transformation. Openness, flexibility, playfulness, persistence, and the ability to work well with others on-the-fly are at the heart of an attitude that allows learners to cope with the unrelenting velocity of technological change in the 21st century.
>
> (Scholz 2010a: x)

Within the overall vision of connected learning, new methods of learning based on peer-to-peer distributed systems of collaborative work, open source and mobile networks, de-centred pedagogies, and self-driven learning have been articulated as characteristic of the new network-based age (Davidson and Goldberg 2009). In such visions, networks themselves are recast as ideal–typical learning institutions. There is a seemingly natural affinity between networks and the ways in which learning ideally takes place – a highly symbiotic, praxeomorphic form of thinking which understands the psychological aspects of learning as essentially networked, and the mind of the learner as itself a network connected to networks.

Rather than emphasizing core knowledge and teacher-organized pedagogies, a future, connected, network-based image of learning is to be accessible beyond school; learning is envisaged as nonlinear and navigable like new media rather than transmitted like conventional mass media; it is imagined as being editable like a wiki instead of hierarchical and authorial. Twenty-first century learning is to be characterized by 'cyberpedagogy', 'network flows' and 'lifelong self-education', hyperlinked with everyday participatory media cultures and networked publics (Francis 2010; Hanke 2011; Jenkins *et al.* 2007). 'Networked publics' are:

> ... publics that are restructured by networked technologies. As such they are simultaneously (1) the space constructed through networked technologies and (2) the imagined collective that emerges as a result of the intersection of people, technology and practice. Networked publics serve many of the same functions as other types of publics – they allow people to gather for social, cultural, and civic purposes, and they help people connect with a world beyond their close friends and families.
>
> (boyd 2011: 39)

However, networked publics are differentiated from other publics because the properties of network-based technologies introduce new possibilities for interaction, common dynamics and participation. Networked publics refer to the intersections of domestic life, nation-state, mass-culture and commercial media, and everyday life in the context of a convergence of mass media with online communication. As a result, the 'growing salience of networked publics in young people's daily lives is part of important changes in what constitutes the relevant social groups and publics that structure young people's learning and identity' (Ito *et al.* 2009: 19). Within such networked publics, many social and learning practices may be reproduced and even replicated, but online communications also reshape such practices and create new opportunities for the development of public identities, as well as opportunities for engagement in hobby-based or 'interest-driven' publics that exist outside of formal institutions such as school or which are independent of existing friendship networks. Networked publics are thus technologically mediated spaces and collections of people. Increasingly, young people are able to move across multiple different publics, including those that are friendship-based and those that are more interest-driven, with the result that many young people now 'maintain a dual identity structure' whereby they possess 'multiple online profiles' (Ito *et al.* 2009: 20).

A key aspect of the connectionist style of thinking is that it makes learner identities intelligible in new ways. Rather than understanding and promoting learners as behaviourally conditioned by specific stimuli, the connectionist perspective sees learners as actively and autonomously identifying and retrieving data and information from a variety of mediated environments, and creatively recomposing and transforming those bits and pieces into coherent learner-created knowledge. Such a shift implies a move away from understanding the learner in terms of individual intelligence to a new ideal of learners in terms of collective intelligence. The new identity of the learner is to be made up and organized in a pedagogy of connection-making and collective intelligence, through a curriculum that is imagined as a dense web of connections between knowledges, epistemologies, and media, within an ecology of learning in which schools are not centres of education but networked nodes of learning among many other formal and informal, institutional and non-institutional nodes of learning.

These arguments may even cast the very idea of school into doubt. For advocates of connected learning, it has become increasingly desirable to see 'something as dispersed, decentralized, and virtual as the Internet being a learning institution' which provides 'a greater degree of fluidity and access to participation than at traditional educational institutions' (Davidson and Goldberg 2009: 10). In this decentralized ecology of do-it-yourself learning options and DIY media (Knobel and Lanskhear 2010), the 'radical' idea of 'learning webs' imagined by de-schoolers in the 1970s now appears more realistic as 'learning networks' are made possible through the internet, with learning 'both individuating and fragmenting to society as a whole' (Jarvis 2004: 79). A much more 'convivial' new 'hidden curriculum' generated and extended through these learning networks appears to facilitate communication, cooperation, caring and sharing between free agents and distributes learning into a nomadic network of authentic practices, cultural locations, and online spaces (Suoranta and Vadén 2010). These claims for a more connectionist and networked outlook are set against a caricature of schools as innately conservative institutions which continue to rely on structured hierarchical relationships, a static print culture, and old-style transmission and broadcast pedagogies which are at odds with the networked era of interactivity and hypertextuality (Selwyn 2011a).

These connectionist claims are strengthened by existing attempts to make education more openly accessible. In an open access system, educational materials may be digitized and offered freely and openly for educators and learners to use, customize, improve and redistribute in their own teaching, learning and research. 'Open education' is an educational paradigm for a seemingly 'open era' based not only a technological discourse (open source, open systems, open standards, open archives, and so forth) but also on a new collection of values of openness, an ethic of participation, an emphasis on peer-to-peer collaboration, and even a change of philosophy which emphasizes ideals of freedom, civil society and the public sphere (Peters 2012). Indeed, the ideal of connected networks have become an institutionalized utopia with seemingly unlimited ameliorative potential for education, despite concerns about negative social effects such as aggravating disunity, disconnection, and dysfunctionality, and reducing educational knowledge to marketable commodities, 'soundbites' and populist user-generated knowledge (Ferguson and Seddon 2007; Frankham 2006; de Lima 2010).

In sum, as the dominant style of thinking about new technology, media and education at the current conjuncture, connectionism is more than a technical issue. It also has epistemological dimensions, with knowledges to be connected in novel ways through interdisciplinary blends and cross-curricular hybridizations, and so forth; it has organizational dimensions, with new connections configured between public sector, private sector, and cross-sectoral intermediary organizations; institutional dimensions, with learning reimagined to be taking place in a seamlessly connected and borderless ecology of formal and informal learning opportunities that smash down school walls and stretch right through the lifecourse; and it is also an issue of identity formation, with learners' identities increasingly understood to be cultivated by the public pedagogies and commercial curricula of digital media culture. In this connectionist style of thinking, a whole new ecology of learning is being fabricated.

Conclusion: Re-coding education

In this chapter we have sought to show that whenever we talk of 'educational technology,' or 'education in the digital age', or any other of the myriad different terns used to frame our understanding of technologies in education, we are talking not just about computing devices, nor just about 'enhanced' pedagogies. Rather, the relations between education and technology are formed out of a dense ensemble of devices, tools, pedagogies, practices, theories and concepts; organic, textual and technical materials; and the webs of ideological and political connections and histories with which they are each connected and from which they draw force (Fenwick and Edwards 2010). These things constitute the ways in which thought becomes possible – they make things thinkable, intelligible, and thus practicable as problems seemingly requiring solutions. We need, amongst other things, to consider the societal implications of networks, the cultural makeover of capitalism, the politics of biotechnology and the performative effects of devices, software and code on even mundane everyday activities.

Education today is increasingly being shaped and influenced by such developments and by the debates and controversies and problems they have generated. In relation to educational policy, the advocacy and deployment of new technologies needs to be understood in relation to the politics of the 'knowledge economy', increased commercialism, privatization and consumerism and 'lifelong learning'. And we need to note, too, how the relations between education and technology have been organized and shaped through key discourses of constructionism, interactionism and connectionism, which each express a praxeomorphic link between the mind of the learner and technologies, mediated through theories of learning which emphasize constructivist learning, sociocultural theories of interactive learning, and connected forms of learning situated in networks respectively. Indeed, as the chapter has attempted to show, new technologies increasingly shape learning, 'configure' learners, and structure life itself, and this is achieved in part through the strength and force of claims made through the various discourses of learning theory.

Perhaps the most significant, and most overlooked, of all these elements is the productivity and performativity of code and software itself. Even the humble and humdrum technologies of the spreadsheet and the word processor should be understood as a new digital underlay to the contemporary classroom, as a software subtly shaping pedagogies. Edwards and Carmichael (2012) talk of the 'hidden curriculum' of computer code in educational technology. Moreover, education today is increasingly organized in a world in which more and more technologies have the capacity to 'learn' about, adapt and respond to their users. The effects of soft computation, wirelessness and databases on learning, and on the shaping of the conduct, thoughts, actions and feelings of learners, are little studied and weakly understood. Through this digital layer of the classroom and its 'hidden curriculum', education is being shaped and re-coded around new standards of conduct, new images of learning, and new images of the learner. The future of education is being made thinkable and intelligible as a set of problems to which a variety of programmes, technologies and other practices have been offered as solutions, whether framed in constructionist, interactionist or connectionist styles of thought. Through such thought, new types of learners are being fabricated; learners seemingly enhanced and extended with constructive, interactive, and connective capacities that are praxeomorphic, respectively, with constructionist tools and resources, responsive and adaptive interactive devices, and connected, networked environments; learners with new pedagogic identities for emerging futures.

4

'MAKING UP' DIGITAL LEARNING IDENTITIES

Technologies of the self

What kinds of people do we take ourselves to be in this digital age? In this chapter we want to explore how the cybernetic style of thinking which is characteristic of the digital age manifests itself in the ways we address, represent and identify ourselves. What do we think our identities are in these cybernetic times? And how are such identities defined, projected and distributed through education? In order to unpack these questions, we first provide a partial overview of recent approaches to the issue of 'identity' in social theory, particularly accounts of 'digital identity.' We then articulate the formation of a particular kind of 'pedagogic identity' associated with the use of new technologies for learning, and show how the construct of a 'digital learning identity' has much in common with notions of an 'enterprising self' in recent social theory, an identity understood in terms of its capacity for self-regulation, self-fulfilment, and self-realization. And finally we explore how such self-realizing digital learning identities have been promoted through one particular prototypical area of educational technology development: the use of videogames as a medium for learning.

While much has been written on the positive pedagogic potential of new technologies and digital media to allow young people to experience alternative identities, less has been written on how such media might operate pedagogically to configure the identities of their users as subjects who can deal with the new digital age. As Buckingham (2008: 11) argues, 'there is often a shared assumption that the ways in which identity is defined (and hence what *counts* as identity) are undergoing far-reaching changes in the contemporary world.' Focusing on identity therefore 'enables us to connect the study of technology with broader questions about modernity and social change' as well as to understand 'the role of digital media in the formation of youthful identities' (2008: 19).

As a theoretical framework to explore the cybernetic style of thinking about pedagogic identity, we make use of three sets of resources. The first is from Michel Foucault (2007) and others writing on identity from a 'governmentality' perspective (Deacon 2006; Dean 2010; Rose 1996). These approaches focus on the kinds of identities which are presupposed by particular social practices, such as the forms of learner identity presupposed by particular pedagogic practices or by particular software programmes, and on the processes through which these identities are defined, assembled, and promoted to persons. The object of investigation for such an approach, as Hultqvist and Dahlberg (2001: 2) phrase it, is to ask 'how historical discourses and practices that are mobilized today in education, popular culture, the media, and social policy construct the child differently from the past.' We view the technological transformation of education as an important historical discourse that traverses all these areas (education, popular culture, media and social policy) to construct new identities for learners. From this perspective, identities are understood not as pre-given but 'made up' as 'subject positions'.

The work of Nikolas Rose is especially important to this argument. According to Rose (1996) subject positions – or, as he terms them, 'subjectifications' – have their own genealogies, or histories of intellectual and practical techniques which have sought to constitute people as selves of particular kinds. Rose (1996: 24–5) does not view 'changing forms of subjectivity or identity as the consequence of wider social and cultural transformations', but rather as the result of techniques and vocabularies that 'have to be invented, refined and stabilized, to be disseminated and implanted in different ways in different practices' in places like schools, workplaces and communities. From this perspective, terms like identity itself (or its historical correlates of character, citizen, individual, personality, and so on), are themselves inventions that encode the particular kinds of aims, ideals and exemplars through which people are supposed to understand and identify themselves and others.

The ideal subject position in today's advanced, liberal societies is that of the free, autonomous individual. As autonomous individuals we are 'free subjects' entitled to our own views, values and choices, but only so long as we subject ourselves to certain culturally accepted norms, representations, terms, meanings and categories (Belsey 2002). This means that we need to conduct ourselves according to existing acceptable modes of comportment. Much research in this direction draws on Foucault's idea of 'technologies of the self' (Dervin and Abbas 2009). Technologies of the self are the proposed techniques and models by which individuals may act upon their own thoughts, conduct, and ways of being, through self-reflection, self-knowledge and self-examination, so as to fashion and transform themselves. Picking up on these activities of self-fashioning, Rose (1996: 157) emphasizes the invention of particular kinds of 'entrepreneurial' and 'enterprising selves' who are 'incited to live as if making a project of themselves', to project themselves a future and shape themselves to become what they want to be, which we see as symmetrical with many arguments about education and technology.

The second set of resources includes what Bernstein (2000: 67-68) termed 'prospective pedagogic identities.' These identities are crafted through pedagogy to acquire particular competencies, attitudes and dispositions to deal with changing social and technological futures. A key element of this process is the projection and distribution of identities through educational reforms. For example, New Labour's Third Way project in the UK, with its attempted reconciliation of entrepreneurial capitalism with the social purpose and community commitment of socialism, was paralleled by the creation of new curriculum approaches within which appropriate prospective pedagogic identities were promoted. These identities were 'made up' and promoted through schools to be self-enterprising, entrepreneurial, and ethical. Bernstein (2000: 205) also emphasizes the importance given to 'projects of the self' and to 'Foucault's technologies of normalization, disciplines and the construction of the subject.' Taking up this moment of symmetry in the work of Foucault and Bernstein, we explore how new prospective pedagogic identities have been invented, normalized and promoted as appropriate ways of thinking, acting and feeling in the digital age. For Bernstein, prospective pedagogic identities were usually to be formed and controlled by the state, but our argument, closer to Foucault, is that an alternative prospective identity, that of the enterprising, lifelong digital learner, is being formed through the participation and intervention of myriad organizations and actors from across the public and private sectors, not least from those involved in the technology industries.

The third set of resources is from Thrift (2005: 223) who emphasizes how digital technologies 'structure life,' or rather 'socio-technical life.' By providing a new underlay to everyday existence, an 'extra layer of thinking,' technologies are now part of a contemporary form of 'semi-artificial life' or 'the extended organism of a new form of humanity' (2005: 178–179). Technologies now form a kind of background hum to even the most mundane everyday activities, thus subtly and almost unnoticeably shaping the organization and juxtaposition of human life and machine artefacts. Many technologies, argues Thrift (2005: 213), have become part of society's 'unconscious,' sitting 'quietly in the background,' and shaping everyday thinking, knowledges and competencies.

Taking these three sets of resources together, our argument is that a particular kind of prospective pedagogic identity has been formed and promoted to young people, though the extent to which such an identity has been enacted is a matter for further empirical research. The prospective identity characteristic of the digital age is a digital learning identity, a self-enterprising, entrepreneurial and ethical learner equipped with the relevant digital competencies, knowledges, attitudes and dispositions to deal with social and technological change. This is an identity configured for the new cybernetic order of the digital age. This identity is the product, therefore, of a cybernetic style of thinking which has become so normalized that it now forms a kind of background unconscious to our current milieu.

Our argument is not that such an identity pre-exists as a real subject. Rather, it is that such a socio-technical digital learning identity is now being fabricated, elicited and promoted through various activities and interventions, such as the promotion of videogames and other forms of entertainment software in education.

The success of these interventions will depend on the extent to which young people come to identify themselves, understand themselves, experience themselves, and relate to themselves through such an identity. In other words, are young people coming to position and address themselves as digital learners configured with the 'appropriate' ways of thinking, knowledges, competencies, attitudes, dispositions and capacities? Are they enacting digital learning identities rather than 'schooled' identities? Are new ways of thinking, acting and feeling being configured and packaged in emerging cyberpedagogies? In this cybernetics of identity, we are witnessing the emergence of new pedagogical technologies of the self through which young people are to be inculcated as enterprising, networked, digital lifelong learners – the appropriate subjects of the digital age.

In the following sections we provide an exploration of some key arguments in recent writing on identity, social and technological change. What we want to show is that a number of ideas about identity emerging from social theory – that it is hybrid and multiple, and increasingly understood in terms of individualized, do-it-yourself life projects – are paralleled by accounts of digital identities which posit identities as re-mixable and networked projects of the self. In addition, a number of claims have been made about how new understandings about the workings of the brain itself, but particularly new technological methods and devices for intervening in the brain's functions, may be challenging conventional understandings of human identity, whether for better or worse. We thus want to stress how new kinds of cybernetic identities are being assembled and promoted, identities seemingly empowered by new technologies as themselves autonomously self-fashioning, self-fulfilling, and self-regulating.

Identity crisis?

Identity is the answer to questions such as 'Who do I think I am?', 'What do I think is my place in the world?', and 'Who do I want to become?'. Bauman (2000) explains that in the classic account of Erik H. Erikson in *Identity: Youth and Crisis*, identity means a personal sense of invigorating sameness and historical continuity. Our identities can be individual and personal, or have a collective aspect related to a group with which we think we are identified. Identities correspond to beliefs, values and commitments, whether spiritual or ideological or related to lifestyles and consumption patterns. However, identity is now understood as a far more complex concept than that. According to Bauman, in a 'globalizing world' the sense of sameness and continuity articulated by Erikson are now seldom felt either by the young or by adults. Instead, 'identity crisis' has become widespread in a seemingly kaleidoscopic world of mutating values, melting frames and perpetual liquidity.

For example, from a legal and criminal perspective concerns about identity theft and online anonymity have exploded, along with contentious 'solutions' such as ID cards, deregulation and the privatization of free virtual space. The politics and ideologies of neoliberalism have been blamed for creating a society of short-termism and economic individualism in which personal identity and life narrative is reduced to fragments and episodes, a particular problem for young people who are now described as a 'jilted generation' (Howker and Malik 2010), or 'the children of neo-liberalism' (Little 2010). Recent developments in internet technologies and social media seem to indicate the shift to a new kind of 'identity capitalism' where individual and collective identities are constructed and managed for their potential value in different kinds of markets. A 'transnational public pedagogy' seeks to produce identities exclusively through the values, ideologies and social relations of economic transactions (Giroux 2005).

Likewise, consumerism, it is claimed, now plays a part in forging identities that are reflections of lifestyles associated with commercial brands, and which have the potential to become 'substitute identities' (Barber 2007: 167). Digital media culture operates as a powerful cultural force which shapes public consciousness and private identities through 'hypercapitalist' commercial and consumerist ideologies (Sandlin and McLaren 2010). In the domain of work, employees are discouraged from expressing personal identities online that might compromise the integrity or image of their employers, although increasingly web platforms such as Twitter are being recognized as key sites for 'professional identity construction' (Gilpin 2011). The 'Facebook generation' is now obliged to 'manage their online reputations constantly', 'create successful online fictions about themselves', and 'tend their *Doppelgängers* fastidiously', with the result that identities are being 'locked-in' to computerized templates, algorithms and databases (Lanier 2010a: 70–1).

And lastly, according to research in neuroscience, developments such as information technology, nanotechnology and biotechnology are now leading to a new condition in which humans are being defined by a 'nobody identity' characterized by an emphasis on sensation, momentary experience, and on constant reactivity to incoming stimuli, rather than emotion, meaning or longer-term implications and significance of personal actions (Greenfield 2008). In this version of identity crisis, technologies exist predatorily, threatening to 'penetrate' the human body and along with it to perforate the ostensible division between human identity and its exterior.

No doubt there is credibility to these claims, however gloomy. Beyond their scepticism about the outlook for identity, and their implicitly nostalgic longing for an ostensibly better time in which developing a stable and historically continuous personal and collective identity was possible, though, these accounts all demonstrate how questions about identity, and concern about how we might identify ourselves in these increasingly digital times, have moved from the psychologist's couch to mainstream consciousness.

Hybrid DIY identities

The common-sense idea that we all possess a unique and stable self has been subjected to sustained scrutiny, especially as digital media and technologies such as the internet have allowed each individual to express a range of different online versions of themselves. To what extent is your ostensibly 'real world' identity continuous with your online identity? Identities are socially and politically constructed categories which both shape access to and are shaped by social, material and economic resources. It is not possible to simply read a person's identity, how they identify themselves, and what they think and believe, from surface features. The concept of identity does not signify a stable core of the individual self which remains the same across the lifespan. Nor does it signal the existence of stable collective belonging or 'cultural identity' based, for example, on nation, shared history and ancestry, or, for that matter, on supposed technological mastery. Instead, the 'construction of identities uses building materials from history, from geography, from biology, from productive and reproductive institutions, from collective memory and from personal fantasies, [and] from power apparatuses' (Castells 1997: 7). In this sense, identities now appear to be much more historically contingent, heterogeneous and culturally relative than the idea that we all possess a stable self would have us believe (Rose 1996).

The influence of poststructuralist theory has been particularly powerful in generating such understandings, and has anticipated theoretically the apparent fragmentation of identity in the digital age. Poststructuralism proceeds through processes of 'disintegration,' 'deconstruction', and by 'dismantling' or 'disrupting' stable concepts of identity and meaning; it is the 'enemy of identity' (Dews 1987: 26). From a poststructuralist analysis, it is accepted that 'identities are never unified and, in late modern times, increasingly fragmented and fractured; never singular but multiply constructed … and are constantly in the process of change and transformation' (Hall 2000: 17). A useful distinction is between the 'assumed identity' or social traits and group affiliations we attribute to ourselves, and the 'ascribed identity' which is attributed to us by others (McDonald 2009). That is to say, certain identities are constituted and imputed to us; these may be accommodated or resisted; they may be in conflict with other assumed and ascribed identities; while still other identities may be proffered in the future. Poststructuralist accounts emphasize how:

> … identities are neither fixed nor one-dimensional. Rather they are fluid, contingent, plural and hybrid. That is to say, in actively constructing our identities, we draw on a range of representations, and the way that we combine these representations is different in different contexts and at different times.
>
> (Gewirtz and Cribb 2009: 139)

These things 'change our relationships with other people and ourselves and require continual reassessment of who we are and who we want to be' (Gewirtz and Cribb 2009: 141).

The main consequence of seeing identity as a hybrid, constantly changing form which we are actively involved in constructing (as well as deconstructing and reconstructing), rather than a stable unity with historical continuity across the lifecourse, has been to see identity as a lifelong, active learning project – a do-it-yourself project for life:

As Michael Foucault suggested, only one conclusion follows from the proposition that 'identity is not given': our identities (that is, the answers to questions like 'Who am I?', 'What is my place in the world?', 'What am I here for?') need to be *created*, just as *works of art* are created.

(Bauman 2008: 54)

Giddens (1991) has referred to a 'post-traditional' world in which we are all responsible for taking charge of our own lives, developing our own self-identity through a plurality of choices about how to act and who to be and engaging in ceaseless strategic life-planning, while for Bauman (2004: 15) identity is now 'an objective' 'to be invented rather than discovered'. Such individuals are incited to be responsible for their own 'experimental' identities and 'do-it-yourself biographies' in what is known as a 'self-driven culture' which puts the emphasis on an ethic of individual self-fulfilment (Beck and Beck-Gernsheim 2002). As Bauman (2008: 13) summarizes, while identity was once considered a project for our whole lives, it is 'no longer "built to last forever", but needs to be continuously assembled and disassembled'. Identities are 'presumed to be do-it-yourself jobs, even if they consist only in selecting and assembling the right type of flat-packed IKEA-style kit' (2008: 56). Similarly, Beck (2006: 5) describes how 'one constructs a model of one's identity by dipping freely into the Lego set of globally available identities'. According to such views, a DIY identity is an extremely time-consuming and demanding task requiring constant active management. Life-planning, lifestyle creation, active self-management, self-responsibility, self-realization, self-determination and free choice are all features involved in the crafting of self-identity. Yet this freedom comes at a cost, as Rose (1999b: 66) shows: 'maximum individualization and maximum "freedom" is developed only at the price of maximum fragmentation, maximum uncertainty, maximum estrangement of individual from fellow individual'. The kind of personal freedom to stage-manage one's own biography is obligatory and compulsory.

Moreover, with such rapid change comes a collapse in long-term thinking and the need for different skills and assets. Perpetual retraining and constant change-readiness have replaced the idea of anything ever being finished (Deleuze 1992), and forgetfulness therefore becomes a prerequisite for successful identity-building, as Bauman (2007: 3) argues: 'A swift and thorough *forgetting* of outdated information and fast ageing habits can be more important for the next success than the memorization of past moves and the building of strategies on a foundation laid by previous *learning*.' And above all, maintaining a DIY identity should be understood as an 'enterprise.' As Rose (1996) has elaborated, 'enterprise' describes a certain image of the human being that has been accorded political value since the 1980s. The 'enterprising self' is an ideal of the individual as an autonomous, choosing, free self:

The enterprising self will make an enterprise of its life, seek to maximize its own human capital, project itself a future, and seek to shape itself in order to become that which it wishes to be. The enterprising self is thus both an active self and a calculating self, a self that calculates *about* itself and that acts *upon* itself in order to better itself.

(Rose 1996:154)

The increasing globalization of media is important in this post-traditional world of lifestyle choice, constant personal reflexivity and self-making. The 'fast, short-term techy culture of globalization ... puts pressure on people to "improve", "transform" and "reinvent" themselves ... to "refashion" themselves as more efficient, fast, lean, inventive and self-actualizing than they were previously' (Elliott and Lemert 2009: 60). In a networked, multi-directional 'Wikiworld,' Suoranta and Vadén (2010, 32) articulate the reflexive identity as an 'ad hoc project': 'no longer the autonomous subject of the enlightenment, but rather a heteronomous postmodern chameleon and nomad, rearranging him- or herself and his or her identity according to the situation.' In sum, the identity fabricated in the global information society is an active, autonomous, agential, self-responsible and empowered lifelong learner who solves problems, has a voice, makes choices, and collaborates in communities of self-determining learners through the computer and the internet (Popkewitz 2008). The 'enterprising self,' increasingly empowered by new technologies and media, is the ideal figure of our age.

Re-mix identities

Many of these themes of enterprise, self-making, DIY identity, and personal projects resonate strongly in the globally networked culture of the internet, where questions of identity have taken on renewed importance (Castells 1997). With the proliferation of digital media and networked communications technologies in many aspects of public and private life, our identity questions today may be recast as 'Who do I think I am, when I'm on Facebook?'. 'What do I think is my place in the world, in World of Warcraft?'. And 'Who do I want to become, in my Second Life?'. Do we possess one kind of identity in the analogue world, and yet another in the digital world – a kind of 'Identity 2.0'? Are identities possible when they have been detached from their bodies? (Baym 2010).

Lanier (2011a: 4) conceives of technologies as 'extensions of ourselves' and argues that 'identities can be shifted by the quirks of gadgets.' He asks how online practices such as 'blogging', 'twittering', and 'wiki-ing' might change our answers to key identity questions like 'Who do I think I am?' and suggests that much human potential has been reduced to 'multiple-choice identities' (2011: 48) and atomized into 'bits' by 'the latest techno-political-cultural orthodoxy' (2011: 22). Latour (2011: 801), too, has argued that: '"To have" (friends, relations, profiles...) is quickly becoming a stronger definition of oneself than "to be".' While Bauman (2004: 93) has claimed that electronic networks of 'tiny attachments' and interactions now stand in place of the '"real stuff" – the closely knit networks, firm and secure connections, fully-fledged relationships – [which] have all but fallen apart.'

Furthermore, the proliferation of technologies such as social networking, data mining, track and trace, and other database-driven devices is increasingly distributing personal information as transactional data (Savage, Ruppert and Law 2010). The result is to see a digital identity as an assortment of disorganized data traces constantly being sorted, calculated, mined and aggregated in databases. Cheney-Lippold (2011: 165) refers to 'a "new algorithmic identity", an identity formation that works through mathematical algorithms to infer categories of identity on otherwise anonymous beings'. A digital, algorithmic identity is no mere performance or expression of the self, but a mathematical aggregate of data traces that is too complex for any individual to manage. Grant (2011, np) explains:

> As the use of … data mining techniques by employers, credit and security agencies becomes increasingly mainstream, digital identity management businesses are likely to develop services similar to those of search engine optimization consultants, advising clients how to 'game' the algorithms to tell the right kinds of stories.

In such contexts, human identity is no longer thought about in terms of its unity, but in terms of a multiplicity, heterogeneity, and fragmentation of 'cyberselves' and by seeing ourselves as 'plugged-in technobodies' that are flexible and multiple and decentered in different roles in different settings at different times (Turkle 1995: 177).

The multiplicity of identity in digital media and new technology may be interpreted positively or negatively (see Buckingham 2008). The virtual dimensions of social networks allow for the fluidity and multiplicity of identity as an ongoing creative process of constructing 'identities-in-action' and 'work-in-progress' (Weber and Mitchell 2008; also Boyd 2008) but also permits the construction of fractured, confused and 'half-real' reflections of a person (Boon and Sinclair 2009). Moreover, the potential of 'DIY media' is understood to 'empower' young people in a do-it-yourself ethic of creative collaboration, production and participation which puts the emphasis on the autonomy, agency and creativity of users (Knobel and Lankshear 2010), or, as they have been fondly neologized, 'pro-sumers' and 'prod-users' (Bruns 2008).

However, this pleasurable and playful multiplication of identities is also intensely political, not least as personal data is increasingly mined and harvested as a cybernetic commodity, and online communications and social networks are subjected to increased commercial, political and economic pressures (Andrejevic 2011; Castells 2009). As Papacharissi (2011) has argued, a 'networked identity' traverses a constellation of social, cultural, economic and political realities against which it must be continually presented, compared, adjusted or defended. Individuals are encouraged to become perpetually involved in optimizing their preferred identities through DIY processes of accessorization and upgrading, enhancing their social reach through network extensions, and ensuring the credibility, trustworthiness and reputation of their profiles through constant processes of consumption and self-censoring (Dervin and Abbas 2009). Consequently, self-editing, self-censorship and digital identity management have become key lifelong skills as individuals are required to self-adjust or constantly update and upgrade their identities. Put in these terms, identity is a process of self-presentation and performance that is 'remixed and remixable' (Papacharissi 2011: 305).

In sum, the self-remixing DIY discourse stems from the promotion of a specific new kind of ideally reflexive and enterprising identity that is active in practices of self-responsibility, self-shaping, and self-mastery. New hybrid identities are produced actively and reflexively as persons negotiate worlds that are both tangibly nearto-hand and virtually dispersed. They are not given at birth but are the effect of constantly juggling multiple real-world and virtual identities, and working upon one's self as a personal project. For Castells (2009), the identity proffered in the new culture of the internet, wireless communication, online games, and digital networks of cultural production, re-mixing and distribution, is 'networked individualism.' Networked individualism puts personal preferences and projects first. It is characterized by 'autonomy, horizontal networking, interactivity, and the recombination of content under the initiative of the individual and his/her networks,' and it resonates with the 'culture of freedom,' autonomy and experimentation associated with the Silicon Valley 'culture of hackers' and the 'culture of the designers of the internet' itself (2009: 125).

As an identity concept, networked individualism extends upon Castells' (1997: 8) earlier work on 'project identities,' understood as the project of building of a new identity, based on 'the desire of being an individual,' in the context of the dissolution of shared social identities. In networked individualism, we find perhaps the clearest articulation of a new kind of identity, or a subject which is positioned by the cultural norms, values and representations of internet culture. The networked individualist identity associated with the internet is based on the apparent importance of seeing one's own life as a constant do-it-yourself project, as an experimental life, and on being self-actualizing and self-improving. The identity of the networked individualist is an idealized image that, exactly like the ideal of the 'enterprising self', has been accorded a particularly political significance.

'Making up' identities

The image of the networked individualist identity, with its personal projects and its web of technological connections and extensions, needs to be understood as itself a social invention composed of various elements rather than merely as a seemingly natural outgrowth of web culture or as something intrinsic to the human actor. That is to say that concepts such as digital identities, enterprising selves and so forth are ways of making people intelligible, or thinkable, in new ways. Rose's (1996) concept of humans as 'being-assembled-together' is important. According to this view, what we take to be our essential human qualities and features – our bodies, our minds, our individualities, our identities, our agency – are all historically contingent inventions, ways of understanding and enacting our selves. The process is captured in Hacking's (2006) phrase 'making up people.' According to Hacking, different 'kinds' of people can come into being through procedures such as the creation of new bureaucratic categories, new regulative norms of behaviour, new medical and biological descriptions, and so on, which change the characteristics of the kinds of people to whom they are applied. In these dynamic making-up and assembling-together processes, ideals and images of 'kinds of person' or 'human kinds' are fabricated and promoted. Such images of human kinds make it possible to think about and act upon the thoughts and actions of one's self and other people, with the result that actual persons may ascribe personal meaning and their sense of identity to them. This puts in motion events that result in the creation of a type of person who did not exist beforehand – a kind of person who has learned to think, act and interact in new ways.

What needs to be brought into focus here are the links between new technology and media as part of the objectives of government and as part of the thoughts, actions and identity of the young person. These links between government and the subject were the focus for Foucault's (2007) analyses of 'governmentality'. Governmentality articulates the links between forms of governing, and forms or modes of thought, or mentalities. For Foucault, governmentality worked as a guideline to understand the interdependence of the modern state and the modern autonomous individual, a relationship mediated by multitudes of mundane little experts of everyday life and normal conduct (Miller and Rose 2008). School was to be one of these mundane sites and one amongst a heterogeneity of authorities for the promotion of conduct. Indeed, for Foucault (1990: 92-93) the modern state, its institutions and its powers were to be understood as the 'terminal form' and 'over-all effect' of innumerable relations and a multiplicity of 'unbalanced, heterogeneous, unstable and tense' forces and strategies, rather than 'given at the outset'. This brings the conduct of people into the field of government at the same time as it recognizes the plurality of governing agencies and authorities. Governing is no longer accomplished by mere implementation of schemes or by direct extension of ruling power into daily existence. Instead, it is a matter of shaping, regulating and controlling human conduct in order to turn it to specific ends, or, as Dean (2010: 18) puts it:

> Government is any more or less calculated and rational activity, undertaken by a multiplicity of authorities and agencies, employing a variety of techniques and forms of knowledge, that seeks to shape conduct by working through the desires, aspirations, interests and beliefs of various actors, for definite but shifting ends and with a diverse set of relatively unpredictable consequences, effects and outcomes.

From this perspective, modern societies are not just made up of institutions of big government, authority and politics, but are constituted in the space of human lives, personalities, bodies, and identities. As Dean (2010: 20) elaborates, the task for government is to 'try to shape, sculpt, mobilize and work through the choices, desires, aspirations, needs, wants and lifestyles or individuals and groups' in order to 'affect and shape in some way who and what individuals and collectives are and should be.'

These relations between 'political' objectives and the 'non-political' minutiae of everyday identity formation is increasingly mediated by the rise of 'experts' who can translate big ideas such as those of governments into the mundane and distant concerns, aims, anxieties and aspirations of individuals. The traditional expert figures of the scientist, engineer, civil servant and bureaucrat, with their claims to expertise based in the disciplines of economics, statistics, medicine, the law and the social sciences (Miller and Rose 2008), are nowadays increasingly being replaced by 'mediators,' 'creative catalysts' and 'intellectual workers' who work at places like think-tanks, consultancies, and nonprofit organizations to generate new and marketable ideas and to propel innovations that are capable of arousing attention (Osborne 2004). Through the intermediary intervention of such experts, the objectives of government are now increasingly achieved at arm's length through individuals' own 'projects for themselves' and their '"responsibilized" and "educated" anxieties and aspirations' (Rose 1999b: 88). As a result, 'we have come to relate to ourselves as creatures of self-responsibility and self-mastery, with the capacity to transform ourselves and make our own lives the object of practices of self-shaping' (1996b: 95). It is through the freedoms of such self-identified individuals that modern governmental rule now appears to operate. In other words, governing is made possible by subtly shaping identities or mentalities. It is achieved not through force or coercion but through the choices of individual citizens acting out of their own freedom and aspirations to self-fulfilment.

What we can see now is that the ideal image of the networked DIY identity, with its projects and its web of connections, looks increasingly like the kind of ideal 'enterprising' subject of modern governmentality. The networked identity and the enterprising self are treated in exactly the same way. Through the culture of the internet, individuals are increasingly able to identify themselves as a certain kind of person, more active, more autonomous, more freely choosing, with greater capacities to know, to gain experiences, to access expertise of many kinds, and to communicate and interact (Miller and Rose 2008; Rose 2007). New technology is not simply a matter of computer hardware, cables, software and so on, but of the shaping of identities. Rose (1999b) links the 'mentalities' of governing to sociological studies of technology, showing how new technologies themselves are involved in the shaping of conduct:

> Every technology also requires the inculcation of a form of life, the reshaping of various roles for humans ... techniques required to use the devices, ... the mental techniques required to think in terms of certain practices of communication, the practices of the self oriented around the mobile telephone, the word processor, the World Wide Web and so forth.
>
> (Rose 1999b: 52)

The notion here that new technologies imply new 'practices of the self' is important. Technologies require a certain shaping of conduct, certain new ways of acting and interacting upon one's own self that did not exist before. That is to say that technologies are involved in the assembling-together of new kinds of human subjects, with newly fashioned identities, new kinds of skills, dispositions, capacities and knowledges, and new ways of thinking about, understanding, addressing and representing themselves.

Taking up similar arguments, Thrift (2005: 172) argues that technologies are 'changing the nature of human subjects by producing enhanced capabilities' and by modifying their 'techniques of the self.' In other words, technologies consist of highly coded rules of conduct which, like lines of computer code, provide a 'set of modulations which constantly direct how citizens act' (2005: 173). That is to say that more and more new technologies are being designed to be 'capable of conducting "thought"; thought is increasingly packaged in things' (2005: 7). Software 'consists of rules of conduct' which 'operate at a distance' so that its effects on the real lives of people, its human consequences, are often invisible (2005: 172).

These are indeed new technologies of the self, devices and techniques with human consequences, which provide rules of conduct that operate at a distance to subtly shape individuals' thoughts, conduct and actions, and produce new characteristic configurations of identity (Dean 2010). Lash (2002: 192) talks of new forms of 'technological life' in which more and more areas of everyday life are treated as if they are to be worked upon in high R&D laboratories. The ideal identities to express technological life are 'R&D laboratory identities' constantly engaged in research, using new digital and networked technologies, to develop themselves. R&D lab identities, and the new technologies and practices of the self they constitute, are sculpted in terms of technological systems. The significance of such arguments is to see how technologies themselves are now implicated in assembling together, shaping and governing how individuals think, act, interact, and identify themselves. And this in turn appears to strengthen and extend the image of the free subject, the autonomous, choosing enterprising self, as the ideal citizen of the digital age.

Prospective pedagogic identities

Processes of education such as pedagogy invent and promote preferred kinds of identities and mentalities which, through ongoing study, students are encouraged to adopt as their own schooled identities (Austin, Dwyer and Freebody 2003). The making up of enterprising, DIY identities and the idealized networked identities characteristic of the digital age have been extended into the pedagogic sphere as particular constructions of pedagogic identities.

The educational sociologist Basil Bernstein (2000) described 'prospective identities' which ground identity not in the past but in the future. Prospective identities stand in contrast to the 'retrospective identities' promoted by a traditional curriculum and pedagogies of canonical texts, official knowledge, cultural heritage, and grand narratives of the past. What is at stake with retrospective pedagogic identities is the stabilization and preservation of the past and its conservation into the future. But with prospective identities what is important is the construction of appropriate attitudes, dispositions and performances for preferred futures. They are constructed and promoted in educational institutions in order to:

> ... *deal with cultural, economic and technological change*. Prospective identities are shaped by *selective* recontextualising of features of the past to defend or raise economic performance ... to stabilise the future through *engaging with contemporary change*. ... [W]ith prospective identities it is careers (that is dispositions and economic performances) which are foregrounded and *embedded in an especially selected past*.
>
> (Bernstein, 2000: 68; *original emphases*)

Prospective identities are future-oriented identities constructed through particular pedagogic and curricular arrangements to promote particular kinds of 'desired' futures. In Bernstein's analysis, both the New Right of Thatcherism and Blair's New Labour offered up new prospective identities based on an amalgam of resources from different pasts. Thatcherism selected features which would legitimate, motivate and construct prospective identities appropriate to the creation of a market culture and reduced state welfare; New Labour recontextualised aspects of market culture with a 'third way' of community, local responsibility and participatory responsibility in the economic sphere.

Bernstein intended the model of prospective identities to describe the resources and practices of the state. But we make rather more flexible use of the concept in the context of the decentralization of government articulated by Foucault. This interpretive flexibility allows us to consider the role of non-state actors in the formation of prospective pedagogic identities, such as, for example, hightech industries. Bernstein (2000: 68) himself referred to 'decentred pedagogic identities' which were shaped by 'local' resources. Our own interpretation of prospective pedagogic identities also draws from the decentring of pedagogic identities to refer to identities which possess 'flexible transferable potential', the capacity to be 'appropriately formed and re-formed according to technological, organizational and market contingencies', and the ability to be taught, continuously and lifelong, in order to project him/herself meaningfully into a 'pedagogised future' (Bernstein 2000: 59). The emphasis on continuous learning is captured in Bernstein's idea of a 'total pedagogy' which means a 'continuous disposition of the subject to be trained for the requirements of his/her entire life' in a process that is 'permanently open' (Bonal and Rambla, 2003: 174).

Such prospective pedagogic identities of future-facing, flexible, lifelong learners are now the subject of attempts to influence the future of education from outside of the usual organs of the state, including non-educationalists and other new kinds of specialists from different political and sectoral positions (Young 2008). Early in the twenty-first century, education is increasingly being shaped and enacted through the participation of private sector organizations and other cross-sectoral actors such as think-tanks, consultancies, philanthropies, nonprofits and all manner of other hybrid, intermediary agents and agencies that increasingly act globally as well as locally (Ball 2007; 2012). Many of the new actors in education deploy cybernetic styles of thinking and metaphors which function by erasing the boundaries between formal schooling and the everyday participatory media cultures within which powerful informal pedagogies are now presumed to operate (e.g. Bentley 1998; Hargreaves 2004; Leadbeater 2010). Within the future imaginaries of education deployed by these new actors and organizations working within education, learner identities are increasingly understood in terms of being networked, flexible, de-centred, hybrid, and self-fashioning. This is, by now, a familiar litany. Thus, the preferred prospective pedagogic identity emerging today is to be 'made up' in the official, institutional pedagogies of school but also in the informal pedagogies of everyday life.

Portfolio-based pedagogic identities

What we are trying to characterize, then, is a pedagogic identity which is shaped by the socio-technical processes and resources of new technologies and digital media and by pedagogic resources in a changing landscape of schooling. As the domains of schooling and new technologies have increasingly been synthesized a new prospective pedagogic identity has been constructed, that of a digital learner, and promoted in the hope that young people will identify with it, and aspire to their own futures in its image. Such a new identity is perhaps best captured in James Gee's (2004) ideal of 'shape-shifting portfolio people.' Shape-shifters are learners who think and act in terms of their 'résumé,' who view themselves in 'entrepreneurial' terms as 'free agents in charge of their own selves as if those selves were projects or businesses':

> Their set of skills, experiences, and achievements, at any one time, constitutes their portfolio. However, they must also stand ready and able to rearrange these skills, experiences and achievements creatively (that is, to shape-shift into different identities) in order to define themselves anew.
>
> (Gee 2004: 105)

Rather than viewing young people as possessing a core identity, shape-shifting expresses identity as a collection of experiences to be constantly updated and rearranged according to situated context. The 'portfolio,' for Gee, is a collection of transferable skills and achievements that people need to be able to self-manage. It is the portfolio or the résumé which for Gee embodies the ideal learning identity in 'fast capitalism'.

For Gee, a shape-shifter identity is best exemplified by the identity projects involved in playing videogames. According to Gee (2008), videogames stimulate a very high order of learning through pedagogies that are far more challenging, complex, yet more engaging and motivating than the traditional pedagogies of school. Similar arguments have been made in terms of complexity theory, systems thinking and business management theory (Barham 2004; Johnson 2006; Veen and Vrakking 2004). Drawing on constructivist and interactive sociocultural accounts of learning, Gee (2008: 31–3) argues that game-based learning involves model-building and knowledge construction; 'microcontrol over objects in virtual space'; 'embodied empathy for complex systems', whereby players learn to 'enter imaginatively into a system'; distributed intelligence between players and artificially intelligent virtual characters; and 'cross-functional' team-working. These affective and organizational dimensions of gaming practice work together to structure player identities. The conditions for deep learning from experience 'go beyond the individual to include the individual's participation in social groups that supply meaning and purpose to goals, interpretations, practice, explanations, debriefing, and feedback', and games do this by:

> ... recruiting distributed intelligence, collaboration, and cross-functional teams for problem-solving; offering players 'empathy for a system'; marrying emotion to cognition; being challenging while still keeping frustration below the level of the affective filter; giving players a sense of production and ownership; and situating the meanings of words and symbols in terms of actions, images, experiences, and dialogue, not just 'definitions' and texts read outside of contexts of use.
>
> (Gee 2008: 37)

Gee (2004: 111–12) describes three identities that coexist during the playing of videogames:

1. *Virtual identity*: one's fictional identity as a character in a game
2. *Realworld identity*: a non-virtual person playing a computer game, though this reflects the variety of real-world identities of the player
3. *Projective identity*: (a) the identity which results from realworld players projecting their realworld values and desires onto their virtual characters; (b) working on a virtual identity as a personal project in the making.

The projective identity becomes the source for reflection not only on one's virtual character but on one's real-world identity, values, and desires. The projective identity is the effect of constantly juggling multiple realworld and virtual identities, shape-shifting, and working upon one's self as a personal portfolio.

As Shaffer (2006) has elaborated, this understanding of gamer identities makes games highly appealing as pedagogic technologies to induct learners into the epistemic communities, practices and social identities of other professions. Shaffer (2006: 181) has created a series of 'epistemic games' that model the professional practices, ways of thinking, skills, knowledges, values and social identities of scientists, bio-mechanical engineers, urban planners and environmentalists, to 'show what effective learning might look like in a high-tech, global, digital, post-industrial world.'

The projective identities and the shape-shifting portfolio people they embody, with their personal projects in the making, are thoroughly hybrid identities, understood to be produced actively and reflexively as players negotiate worlds that are simultaneously near to hand and virtually at a distance. In the age of the internet individuals work on 'project' or 'portfolio' identities that expand their identifications well beyond their specific real contexts, projecting their identities into diverse affiliations, communities and networks which are defined by socially and economically distinctive forms of knowledge, information, skills, experiences and lifestyles. Salen (2008:2) argues that 'today's kids are crafting identities for themselves – hybrid identities – that seemingly reject previously distinct modes of being.' Defining these identities simply as 'kids', characterized by their 'digital kidness', Salen suggests they hybridize identities such as 'writer, designer, reader, producer, teacher, student, gamer' and bind them together all equally. This definition of 'kids' and 'digital kidness' inscribes identity in the vocabulary of videogames. It manufactures the subject position of the videogames player, the shape-shifting masters of their own projects of virtual identity, as ideal–typical figures of the digital age. It is important to reiterate that shape-shifting projective identity associated with videogames is itself a historical invention which addresses and represents videogames players as if they possess identities of a certain kind. Projective gamer identities are subjects that are made up, made visible and intelligible as people with certain features, modes of conduct, and forms of relation with themselves and others.

But who is doing this 'making up'? The recent surge in advocacy for the educational potential of videogames is not confined to the videogames industry itself, which is ultimately ambiguous about education as a market. Instead, videogames are being reframed as an educational medium by a cross-sectoral mix of experts from think-tanks, nonprofits, university research departments, and management consultancies. Their claims to expertise draw on emerging research findings carried out in academic research departments that cut across social and computer science disciplines. Key videogames advocates like the nonprofits The Institute of Play in the US and Futurelab in the UK, as well as the think-tank Demos and the government spin-off the Innovation Unit, sit alongside hip management gurus and funky culture theorists, all of whom draw intellectual force from research in areas like cognitive science, the learning sciences, and other interdisciplinary blends of psychological and computer science discourses. Together, these new experts have seemingly been invested with authority to redefine the future of learning, as a future modelled on the ostensible pedagogic effectiveness of videogames. Along the way, they have been responsible for reshaping ideals about pedagogic identities as self-hybridizing subjects who can shape their own futures.

The politics of second life itself

Are videogames 'political'? To the extent that, among myriad other things, they act to shape individual and collective conduct according to particular norms and values generated and disseminated by diverse experts from a variety of cross-sectoral and disciplinary positions, then videogames should now be considered political technologies. For the videogames theorist Bogost (2007) videogames are a 'persuasive' medium with the potential to support existing ideological hegemony, distribute corporate advertising, and promote capitalist interests. For example, in contrast to the utopian interpretation of videogames as ideal learning machines, an alternative reading is that playing videogames sculpts and promotes identities that are appropriate for participation in the affective work regimes of post-industrial global capitalism.

It is now suggested, for instance, by many management theorists and consultants, that children are developing from computer gaming the skills of multitasking, 'zapping' between different information flows, non-linear behaviours, learning through enquiry, and collaboration, all skills which will be important for entry into knowledge-based work and for the corporate governance of high-tech labour (Dyer-Witheford and de Peuter 2009). Videogames are 'ideal-type commodity forms' for a digital era characterized by perpetual innovation, style and fashion, fluid electronic consumer experiences, digitally enabled enterprise, and the reorganisation of work and business, and function as 'a sort of low-level domestic socialization for high-tech work practices' (Kline, Dyer-Witheford and de Peuter 2003: 76). As such, games are 'perfect training for life' at a time when 'daily existence demands the ability to parse sixteen kinds of information being fired at you simultaneously'; 'kids weaned on videogames are not attention-deficit, morally stunted, illiterate little zombies,' but 'simply acclimated to a world that increasingly resembles some kind of arcade experience' (Herz 1997 cited in Kline, Dyer-Witheford and de Peuter 2003: 76).

For critics, instead of shape-shifting portfolio people, videogames players are fabricated as immaterial labour in the new 'play factories' of the cultural industries and creative media (Scholz 2010b), or, as Kucklich (2005) has brilliantly neologized them, 'playbour'. Researchers at the British think-tank Demos have argued, as if to illustrate the point, that the successful 'leading-edge "techy" organisations' of the creative and cultural sector are already 'tapping into the skills developed by a generation that has grown up with Nintendos, Xboxes and more recently online multiplayer games' (Green and Hannon, 2007: 23). The exemplary post-industrial organizations of this type of analysis, such as the main videogames corporations, have successfully exploited the idea that work can now be more like play, that the 'work ethic' of efficiency, routine, restraint, stratification and deferred gratification can be replaced by a 'play ethic' of affective passions, enthusiasms and feelings (Kane 2004). The pleasure of gaming is not innocent, neutral or decontextualized but instead deploys 'an array of metaphors, narratives and codes for the interpretation of life … . Minds, bodies, and social interactions are thus increasingly "occupied"' by videogames, which become a dominant source of identification (Kline, Dyer-Witheford and de Peuter 2003: 126).

Such readings draw more attention to how gamers' playful identities are shaped in ways which bind them into practices of control, surveillance and discipline. A socio-technical analysis of videogames by Dyer-Witheford and de Peuter (2009) takes these observations further. Drawing on the theories of Deleuze and Guattari, they argue that videogames are 'social machines' constituted as a 'functionally connected assemblage of human subjects and technical machines, people and tools' (Dyer-Witheford and de Peuter 2009: 70). Within these social machines, new subjectivities are created. These 'subjectivities are not natural or given but assembled from biological, societal, and technical components' and 'fabricated, machined, made up from elements that include, among others, technical machines' (2009: 70). Technologies and human subjects are co-constitutive; the historical development of devices is paralleled by genealogies of persons (Osborne and Rose 1999b).

For Dyer-Witheford and de Peuter (2009: 84), therefore, videogames generate 'machinic subjects', configuring their players by inviting and amplifying 'major gaming subjectivities' while 'ignoring or actively repelling possible minority participants.' These major gaming subjectivities include the hyper-masculinized militarism associated with the violent military action genre, as well as the flexible immaterial labour of networked communication required by twenty-first century global hypercapitalism. Videogames are thus understood to simulate identities, to train flexible labour for flexible jobs, to domesticate consumer identities, and to shape militarized subjects.

Ultimately, these machinic subjects and gaming subjectivities are configured as post-human 'cyborgs', where subjects are understood not just as users of machines but where machines are increasingly integrated prosthetically into the minds and bodies of subjects themselves (Haraway 1991; Hayles 1999). Thus bound into technical machines, 'this machine subjectivity will be a component part to a larger social machine':

> To become an Xbox or PS3 or Wii player is to plug oneself into a network of techno-human relations, which even as it offers cognitive skills and affective thrills also inserts subjects into a commodity web … and a whole branded identity built around … a grid of machinic coordinates engineered to the tolerances of corporate profit.
>
> (Dyer-Witheford and de Peuter 2009: 93)

It is in this sense of human–machine integration that the idea of the cyborg, or 'cybernetic organism', a 'hybrid assembled of body parts and mechanical artefacts', has made all too clear how 'humans are intrinsically technologically fabricated and "machinated" ' (Rose 1996: 5). The cyborg is the ideal figure for an era in which biological and corporeal life has been integrated into the technological and the political, and life looks increasingly like a 'semi-artificial' system in which humanity and software are both being assembled together (Thrift 2005: 178).

Understood in this way as an extension of our biological selves, software such as videogames must therefore be understood in terms of a new politics of the body, or 'biopolitics'. Biopolitics denotes new ways of exercising power based on practices of correction and optimization at the level of 'life itself' (Foucault 1990: 143; Lemke 2011). Rose (2007) talks of 'the politics of life itself' in a context where biotechnology and bioscience increasingly seem to allow human beings to be re-engineered and 'optimized.' In the context of videogames, then, we are witnessing the emergence of a 'politics of second life itself' where players' machinic subjectivities are being configured through assemblages of the technical capacities of virtual worlds and the larger social machines of which they are components.

The biopolitics of second life itself, then, refers to the correction and optimization of virtual kinds of living, which are now components of 'real' kinds of living in a world where virtuality is increasingly constitutive of reality. In this biopolitics of second life itself, persons are made up as machinic subjects endowed with the technical prosthetics of networked technologies as well as the social prosthetics of networked communication. Such observations demonstrate why caution is required about techno-utopian claims which make up 'kids' in terms of their own personal projects of self-determination and shape-shifting identities. Indeed, such expert claims and their intellectual basis are themselves part of the assemblage of biological, technical and societal components which are composited together in the new cybernetics of identity in the digital age.

Conclusion: Cybernetic pedagogic identities

In this chapter we have seen how emerging social theories of identity in the digital age have been assembled together as a new prospective pedagogic identity of the digital learner. The projective gamer identity of shape-shifting portfolio people has been made up as the ideal figure of the digital age, largely through the expert advocacy of a loose network of globally mobile academics, management theorists, nonprofits, think-tanks, and the new ideas and innovations that they are able to generate and propel. The projective gamer identity is equipped with the digital skills, ways of thinking, and empathetic and imaginative connections with digital systems to thrive in changing technological futures. Such a socio-technical identity has been configured for the new cybernetic order of the digital age, and increasingly promoted in the cyberpedagogies of gaming and other networked forms of learning.

Embodied by this gamer subjectivity, the new prospective pedagogic identity is characterized as being a DIY project, a self-fashioning hybrid, assembled together as a subject integrated with technical systems and the larger social systems of which they are components. In trying to comprehend prospective pedagogic identity, we therefore need to be looking beyond traditional notions of stable private identities, or even beyond standard notions of hybrid identities. Instead, a prospective pedagogic identity is constituted as a functioning network of biological, technical and societal components.

In sum, the prospective pedagogic identity of the digital learner captured in the notion of the half-real/half-virtual projective identities of gamers, resonates with the idea of the cyborg as a semi-artificial, and thus optimizable, form of life itself. But the idea of the cyborg implies more than a prosthetic attachment between bodies and machines. It links people into assemblages of biological, social and technical components (Lee 2001; Prout 2005). Indeed, as Rose (1996: 171) phrases it:

> It is within these assemblages that subject effects are produced, effects of our being-assembled-together. Subjectification is thus the name one can give to the effects of the composition and recomposition of forces, practices and relations that strive or operate to render human being into diverse subject forms, capable of taking themselves as the subject of their own and others' practices upon them.

The composition of a projective gamer identity is a new effect of this process of subjectification. The cybernetic pedagogic identities implied by the shape-shifting character of the portfolio learner, the DIY learner, and the digitally networked learner, and so on, are therefore a heterogeneous assemblage made up out of the discourses of the digital era and 'mashed up' (Fenwick and Edwards 2010: 168) from prospective aspirations for the future, projective desires and projects of the self, and prosthetic attachments and extensions between bodies and technologies. Through the integration of new technologies into such assemblages, the identity of the learner as a digital learner is increasingly written in code, with modes of conduct, cognition and action all packaged up and configured in devices and software. Within such assemblages, the ideal prospective pedagogic identity has been made up as a DIY self-learner who, empowered by the networked connectivity of the web, is able to make his or her own life into an ongoing and ceaseless enterprise, a project of self-transformation, correction and optimization.

The digital lives of young people, acted out in the mundane everyday sites of their bedrooms and classrooms, are now linked up to a political apparatus with its own norms and objectives related to assumptions about the role of digital technologies in the economic and cultural dimensions of existence. Prospective identities and regimes of personal conduct are being sculpted, programmed, shaped, guided, channelled, directed and controlled from afar by forms of authority from 'beyond the state' that act at arm's length through the trivial features and everyday acts of living and 'by means of persuasion, education and seduction rather than by coercion' (Miller and Rose 2008: 209). The gamer subjectivities idealized as prospective pedagogic identities for high tech futures are not just creatures of pleasurable play summoned up out of their own self-determining efforts. Rather, they are made up as ideal-type citizens and actively responsible individuals who can maximize their own lifestyles and their corporeal lives, become experts of themselves, in a world in which politics is mediated by the intervention of new experts of everyday life and diffused throughout every individual's personal aspirations and pleasures, anxieties and problems. These are new active subjects and ideal citizens made up for the digital age.

5

ASSEMBLING CREATIVE LEARNING

Creativity thinking

How has creativity been made intelligible in the digital age? In recent years, creativity has been positioned at the centre of debates in areas as disparate as post-structuralist philosophy and literary theory; chaos and complexity science; cosmology; evolutionary biology and genetics; neuroscience, cognitive psychology and artificial intelligence; quantum mechanics and theoretical physics (Pope 2005). In the field of education, creativity has been linked to a series of debates going back half a century to the birth of progressive child-centred education and, in a different vein, to Raymond Williams' ratification of the everyday creativity of working class 'lived culture' in the 1960s (Jones 2009). It is now integral in research and debates on youth media cultures, where 'creative production' and 'creative expression' using social media have become part of a 'common parlance and consciousness' (Ito *et al.* 2009: 246), while 'creative learning' has itself gathered force and momentum within educational debates (Sefton-Green 2008). In the years that straddled the turn of the century, creativity became a central educational orthodoxy, with a kind of taken-for-granted privilege to access all areas of education. Creativity has been invoked by educational policymakers, by educational psychologists, developers and researchers of educational technologies, and deployed in relation to all manner of activities (Craft 2005).

For our own purposes we are mostly interested in creativity as a concept as it has been adapted and deployed in relation to education and technology, from the creative model-making associated with constructionist technologies to the do-it-yourself identity creation associated with the everyday uses of social media. Yet we argue that current meanings of the word 'creative,' even narrowed in relation to education and technology, are ambiguous and used for various purposes amongst different communities and contexts. Like the 'digital age' itself, 'creativity' has a complex genealogy.

Our approach in this chapter, then, is to interrupt the taken-for-granted definitions and assumptions about creativity that have been yoked to education and technology. Dean (2010: 31) argues that 'our taken-for-granted ways of doing things ... are not entirely self-evident or necessary'. Instead, an analysis of any taken-for-granted set of practices in education should seek to identify the emergence of those practices, examine the multiple sources of the elements and knowledges that constitute it, and follow the diverse processes and relations by which these elements are assembled into relatively stable forms of organisation and institutional practice. Taking up such a genealogical approach, we trace a number of different ways in which 'creativity' has been made thinkable and thought in the field of education and technology, identifying the emergence of three families of creativity, the elements that constitute them, and the ways in which they have been assembled into educational practices.

What we aim to show is how the creativity concept may be understood as part of the ensemble of terms, concepts, theories and techniques that constitute the distinctively cybernetic style of thinking that is characteristic of attempts to reform education and re-fashion young people's pedagogic identities for the digital age. In such a cybernetic style of thinking, the digital age has itself been made intelligible in terms of networks and cool culture, and identity has been thought in terms of hybridity and DIY self-enterprise, concepts which have in turn been translated and assembled into new ways of rethinking and acting upon education, curriculum, pedagogy and learning. Through such a cybernetic style of thinking, new prospective pedagogic identities are being put together and promoted to young people as sources of personal and collective identification. However, we need to recognize that many different kinds of creative identities have been sculpted and promoted to young people, whether in the formal institutional pedagogies of school or in the informal pedagogies of everyday relations, according to different definitions and presuppositions about creativity. There is no single fixed creative identity being assembled together but a range of possible identities associated with different fields. They can be recognised in various contexts and communities fulfilling different purposes, from Apple stores to artists' studios. These identities can be acknowledged and fostered within and on the margins of education systems, and they can co-exist whilst generating tensions, contradictions and dilemmas. Our understandings of these identities and the close relationship between them and the wider context of a digital age have implications for our thinking, action and policy. They will influence our adoption of learning theories; our design and making of curriculum; and our design of pedagogy.

We examine three deployments of creativity. First, we explore how creativity has been developed in cognitive terms within the psychological domain. Second, we explore how it has been translated into economic and educational policy objectives, particularly through being linked up to new technological ideas. And third, we explore how creativity has been 'encountered' in education through creative and entrepreneurial practitioners sharing their practice with young people. The ways in which creativity is thought shapes experiences and choices for young people as they develop their learning identities.

Cognitive creativity

The digital age would seem to require approaches to learning which respond to the need for fluidity, flexibility and uncertainty, as well as distributed networks, connection and representation. These characteristics of learning in the digital age have been noted by many researchers of creativity and cognition to be closely related to descriptions of the dispositions of creative people (Claxton and Lucas, 2004, Craft, 2011, Robinson, 2001). Such accounts seize on a variety of psychological concepts and ways of understanding creativity as a form of competence. These include qualities such as openness to experience; independence; self-confidence; willingness to take risk; sense of humour or playfulness; enjoyment of experimentation; sensitivity; lack of a feeling of being threatened; personal courage; unconventionality; flexibility; preference for complexity; goal orientation; internal control; originality; self-reliance; persistence are recognized in people's engagement in creative activity. (Shallcross cited in Craft, 2000: 13). A 'confluence model' of creativity offers an image of the convergence of six elements of personal qualities such as intellectual abilities; knowledge; styles of thinking; personality; motivation and environment (Sternberg and Lubart, 1999). Robinson (2001, 2010) draws attention from general processes back to the context and medium in which creative people have some control yet are confident enough to act playfully, take risks and exercise critical judgements.

Furthermore, it is argued that individual states of intuition, rumination, reverie, even boredom, can play a role in creativity and problem-solving (Claxton, 2000). Such day-dreaming is represented as more than drifting and hoping for lucky ideas, but acknowledges a less conscious way of knowing which draws upon existing resources of knowledge, skill and experience yet makes new combinations, explorations and transformations (Boden, 1992). 'Flow' is a familiar description of a common characteristic of creative people who are capable of a seemingly automatic and effortless, yet highly focused state of consciousness. This focus is observed when people are engaged in activities that involve an element of discovery, novelty or originality, yet can often be painful, risky or difficult. The state of being 'in flow' often weaves together clear goals, immediate feedback, balance between challenges and skills, merging of action and awareness, elimination of distractions, lack of fear of failure, lack of self-consciousness, distortion of sense of time, and autotelic activity, that is, enjoyment for its own sake. Flow enables the stretching of capability, skill, understanding and accomplishment in the task – from scrimshaw carving to jazz improvisation (Csikszentmihalyi, 1996, Nachmanovitch, 1990). Csikszentmihalyi (1996), for example, has articulated a kind of 'everyman' creativity which combines smartness with naïvety and playfulness with discipline.

In the terms established by these vocabularies, there are close similarities between the qualities of creative processes and engagement and the demands of learning in a digital age in which people need to cope with questions, problems, failure and disappointment, in order to learn from these experiences and demonstrate perseverance, resilience and a disposition to seek more inventive solutions. They also need to think about patterns and connections in their experiences, and reflect upon how new situations might relate to earlier problems solved, or require novel suggestions. They need to be capable of drawing upon a wide range of resources from tangible materials and personal memories to networks and nodes of information and other people. Above all, they need to be aware of, and engage in, meaningful and mutual relationships with other people and places (Loveless 2009). The assimilation of creativity into education has thus been achieved through a shift in thinking about creativity as an individual attribute to a much more social and cultural event (Craft 2005; Jones 2009).

It is important, however, to note that these cognitive, psychological and sociocultural understandings of creativity should not be taken for granted as some species of reality. Rather, these 'psy knowledges' generated through psychology have come to inform a whole host of fields, including but certainly not confined to pedagogy (Lawler 2008). The psy knowledge of creativity allows us to comprehend human competences through its new discourse of flow, problem-solving, risk-taking and so on. It is in this discourse that creativity is now being deployed in education. Indeed, as Lucas and Claxton (2009: 8) have shown, creativity is associated both with 'innovation skills (typically associated with international competitiveness)' and with 'personal skills associated with individual potential (more likely to be connected with achievement and well-being)'. Creativity is thus a mobile concept that links up personal well-being with innovation and international competitiveness. Indeed, as Foucault (2008: 231) showed, the contemporary 'problem of innovation' and the 'permanent stimulation of competition' is to be solved through investing in the 'economic-psychological' well-being and improvement of 'human capital'.

Creative policy

Understood in these economic–psychological terms, creativity is now vigorously promoted in global economic and educational policy developments, from early years' education to the promotion of creative industries, financial services and hi-tech engineering. In the last two decades, policymakers have offered creativity as an unproblematic 'good thing' to benefit economic competition and growth and thus the well-being of society (e.g. Bacon *et al.* 2010). The years have been fruitful for international agencies and national governments producing reviews, reports, research, recommendations and responses to the challenges of applying creative processes in education to economic and political spheres.

The 1990s saw the stirrings of interest and activity, from the UNESCO report *Our creative diversity* in 1995, to the UK National Advisory Committee on Creative and Cultural Education (NACCCE) producing *All Our Futures*, which explicitly linked creativity generated imaginatively in purposeful fashioning activity to outputs demonstrating originality and value (NACCCE, 1999). In the UK, the New Labour Government produced *Culture and Creativity: The Next Ten Years*, with a foreword from Prime Minister Tony Blair, which echoed the spirit of 'Cool Britannia':

> This Government knows that culture and creativity matter. They matter because they can enrich all our lives, and everyone deserves the opportunity to develop their own creative talents and to benefit from those of others. They matter because our rich and diverse culture helps bring us together – it's part of our great success as a nation. They also matter because creative talent will be crucial to our individual and national economic success in the economy of the future. Above all, at their best, the arts and creativity set us free.
>
> (Department of Culture, 2001: 3)

These assertions were supported in the UK by a wave of initiatives to promote creativity in the school curriculum (QCA, 2004); nurture creativity in young people (Roberts, 2006); consolidate creative partnerships between practitioners and schools (Creative-Partnerships, 2002); and establish relationships between creative industries, research and education through organizations such as National Endowment for Science, Technology and the Arts (NESTA) and the think-tank Demos (Mulgan 2007; Bentley and Gillinson 2008).

National governments have included imperatives for creativity in education reform, notably in Singapore, New Zealand, the UK and the Scandinavian countries (Birch 2008). Philanthropic foundations, such as the MacArthur Foundation in the US, have focused on 'creative people and effective institutions committed to building a more just, verdant, and peaceful world'. The World Creativity Summit was held in Taipai in 2008, and 2009 was declared the European Year of Creativity and Innovation, supported by a series of conferences, workshops and reports which brought together diverse groups interested in the implications of creativity for economic development and education systems (Cachia *et al.*, 2010). Viewed through the policy prism, there is an unproblematic close fit between a competitive knowledge economy, social coherence and cultural production and exchange. However, despite such a positive vision, there is some irony in the publication of a joint report from three departments in the British government, entitled *Creative Britain: New talents for the creative economy* was published in 2008 – the year of the Lehman Brothers' crash (Department of Culture *et al.*, 2008).

An illustrative example of how ideas about creativity have been imported into education policy debates is supplied in *The Creative Age: Knowledge and skills for the new economy*, published by the New Labour think-tank Demos (Seltzer and Bentley 1999). The so-called 'creative age' of the title is presented as an increasingly 'weightless' era dominated by intangible resources including information, organizational networks and human capital, horizontal relationships and 'thinking skills' and 'intellectual capital', or brainpower rather than musclepower. In a weightless world creativity has taken on enhanced importance:

> Creativity is the application of knowledge and skills in new ways to achieve a valued goal. To achieve this, creative learners must have four key qualities:
> - the ability to identify new problems, rather than depending on others to define them
> - the ability to transfer knowledge gained in one context to another in order to solve a problem
> - a belief in learning as an incremental process, in which repeated attempts will eventually lead to success
> - the capacity to focus attention in the pursuit of a goal, or set of goals
>
> (Seltzer and Bentley 1999: viii)

In a follow-up pamphlet focused on learning for a 'creative nation', Jupp, Fairly and Bentley (2001: 7) explain that 'Unlike some skills, creativity cannot exist in isolation and be performed "on demand". Rather it is a form of interaction between a learner and their environment', which depends on trusting relationships, freedom of action and personal responsibility, contextual variation and the extension of networks, and the interactive exchange of knowledge and ideas across the boundaries of existing institutions. In setting out these qualities and organizational environments as a series of new objectives for the education system, the Demos reports are involved in the task of engineering new creative learning identities. The new learning identities are characterized by adaptability, anticipation and commitment:

> First of all, it means that creative people view learning as an ongoing, incremental process. They are adaptable in that they don't see skills or knowledge as something you either have or you don't – they view them as learning 'realms' with more limitless and contiguous boundaries. Secondly, it means that creative individuals can engage in progressive learning, the ability to uncover new problems and redefine old ones. They anticipate the problems that will lead to tomorrow's solutions and find novel ways to apply what they have learned in the past. Thirdly, it means that they have goals which drive their ongoing learning, and the discipline to focus their attention and energy in positive and original ways. They are committed to doing what it takes, however long it takes, to solve the problems that will help them to reach their goals.
>
> (Seltzer and Bentley 1999: 22)

Pope (2005: 50) views the Demos vision of the 'creative age' as a 'radically hi-tech corporatist democracy' which is 'shadowed by techno-fascism and planned obsolescence'. It represents a blend of 'social engineering and skills-based education in the service of a model combining democratic citizenship and competitive commercialism. This is frankly a corporatist model of creativity' or 'creativity with attitude' (Pope 2005: 26–7). Such 'creativity with attitude' can be seen to be concerned with both the surface detail of lifestyle and consumerism, and the deeper construction of identities of workers who are required to be continually innovative and productive, playful, social, competitive and entrepreneurial. These creative pedagogic identities are homologous with the image of 'smart people' who are able to foster the powers of creativity in order to drive innovations who are now the 'fast subjects' of the new economy or the knowledge economy (Thrift 2005: 135). The characteristics of technologies are often inscribed on to such fast pedagogic subjects (as, eg, 'networked' learners and constructionist learners), while, moreover, schools are being reimagined as spaces in which creativity can physically take place, such as through flexible classroom design, more emphasis on interactive collaboration space, and so on (Rudd *et al.* 2006).

The translation of creativity into part of the discourse of the new economy has been underpinned by an explosion in the management and production of creativity in a wide range of communities and groupings, and Osborne (2003: 510) notes:

> ... as a combination of doctrine and morality, the creativity explosion is unquestionably variegated and double-edged; it can be captured by business gurus and management writers, Californian lifestyle sects, new age groups, post-identitarian philosophers, literary critics turned cultural theorists, intellectuals, postmodern geographers, anti-globalization protestors, whoever.

Although there are some who are placed in positions of cultural advantage and economic advancement, not everyone benefits from a universal sprinkling of creative fairy dust. Creativity can be viewed in terms of its marketable value, as creative capital. In a policy research working paper produced for the World Bank, Yusuf (2007) claims that a 'competitive economy' must be supported by 'large numbers of creative individuals', and suggests that a key component of building creative capacity is 'wikicapital', arising from networks:

> ... as knowledge deepens and becomes more variegated, human capital can be more creative when it is pooled into 'wikicapital' through the formation of local and global teams, partnerships, associations and learned societies which facilitate the deepening and sharing of knowledge and bring together diverse talents with different perspectives, viewpoints and spheres of knowledge. Creative solutions to complex problems are becoming more feasible because wikicapital can harness a vast array of expertise and to attack a problem from many directions by exploiting the potential of heterogeneity. The accumulation of wikicapital is growing because ... the opportunities for collaborative work have been enormously facilitated by ICT. ... The creativity of wikicapital – of teams that combine diverse skills – has been reinforced by advances in techniques of measuring physical as well as social

phenomena and the sophistication of measuring devices, in the techniques for assembling and storing vast quantities of data, and by the automation of discovery in certain areas.

(Yusuf 2007: 6)

Darras (2011:91) draws attention to the convergence of interests between international agencies appropriating creativity for cultural and economic purposes, and 'the lifestyle of a new privileged stratum of the population whose creativity drives both their professional activity and their free time'. The idea that capital can be more creative has found its iconic figurehead in Richard Florida (2003), whose 'creative class' and 'creative cities' thesis has been adopted by businesses and regional governments worldwide. Florida describes members of the 'creative class' in five groups: artists, designers and workers in the entertainment, sport and media industries; health workers; computer science and engineering professionals; workers in the education, training and libraries sector; and creative professionals within these groups such as senior managers, lawyers and accountants. He observes that they tend to gravitate to groups, locations and networks that are characterized by '3 Ts' of technology, talent and tolerance, often in urban centres.

Although now critiqued and developed, Florida's descriptions have stimulated discussion and a refiguring of the debates. Peck (2007, 2010) describes the new 'creative type' of human actor animated by Florida's creative class thesis as '*homo creativus*', an atomized subject with a preference for intense but shallow experiences, not commitments, who seeks free-market self-actualization through self-indulgent over-work, expressive play and conspicuous consumption habits. *Homo creativus* is economic man but with a better social life or economic man 'dressed in black', and the creative class to which he belongs yearn to 'validate their identities' in 'plug and play' communities that maintain experientially intensive work–life balance and which are characterized by 'creative comingling', heterogeneity and loose social ties (Peck, 2007: 5).

Indeed, public investment is made in services and facilities that are seen to attract creative talent and creative communities to cities and neighbourhoods. As Peck (2010: 221) states, creative individuals have seemingly become 'the pre-eminent carriers of economic-development potential, so the pursuit of economic growth becomes neatly synonymous with the publicly-funded seduction of the Creative Class'. The preoccupation with 'wikicapital', 'creative cities' and the 'creative class' is an outgrowth of a more extended network of discourses, practices and material realities that Liu (2004) describes as 'cool' post-industrial 'knowledge work' and which McGuigan (2009) understands as 'cool capitalism'. Developing on Boltanski and Chiapello's (2007) analysis of the 'new spirit of capitalism', cool capitalism describes the capacity to incorporate critique and turn it to the advantage of capitalism itself, in particular by deploying discourses of countercultural rebellion and resistance:

'Cool' is actually the dominant tone of capitalism today. Corporations have incorporated countercultural traditions and deployed signs of 'resistance' in order to market their wares. Where the original 'spirit of capitalism', often associated with puritanical Protestantism, emphasised deferred gratification and hard work, the 'new spirit of capitalism' is much more hedonistic and, indeed, 'cool'. Immediate gratification is sought and sold in the sphere of consumption. Consumers are, in effect, seduced by the delights of high-tech and 'cool' commodities, promising to satisfy their every desire, especially if they are 'different' and vaguely rebellious in tone. Great stress is placed on individual autonomy and the more complex notion of 'individualisation'. The individual perpetually on the move, accompanied by a personal soundtrack and in constant touch, is the ideal figure of such a culture.

(McGuigan, 2009: 124)

Following Rose's (1996) characterization of an 'enterprising self', McGuigan (2009) argues that the seductive discourse of 'enterprise' is a key element of cool capitalism that is the dominant cultural and political expression of capitalism in a market-based context. The 'enterprising self' or the 'entrepreneurial individual' which seeks self-actualization, 'enterprises' its own life, and works upon itself, is the ideal figure of the learner within the cool capitalist vision of contemporary economic globalisation.

This kind of post-modern version of enterprise culture is epitomized by the 'creative industries' which seek to maximize value from the commodification and commercialization of 'expressive value', but even more particularly by the ostensibly 'transformative function of information and communication technologies (ICTs) in the "new economy" ' (McGuigan, 2009: 156). The style of creativity of cool capitalism is not without power and effect for those who work and live in it. In the world of 'furious networking' and the 'meritocracy of "creativity"' promoted by New Labour in the 'relentlessly upbeat business' of the creative industries, 'workers are required to work upon themselves, to fashion a useful self and to project their selves through strenuous self-activity'(McGuigan, 2009: 187–8). Creative capital exercises influence in the organization and culture of places and patterns of work, educational institutions, community facilities and their associated lifestyles. Darras (2011: 95–6) draws attention to how a 'creativity-based society' produces:

> ... new ways of living, thinking, acting, organizing, sharing, which require more and more adaptability, flexibility, mobility, fluidity, diversity, and entrepreneurship, leadership and competitiveness, and thus invention and innovation in all fields of science and technology, and imagination and creation in all sectors of culture and media. Everyone is creative, everyone is a leader and an entrepreneur, so everyone is in competition with everyone else. The members of the creative class and their institutions therefore make sure the contents, values, manners and tastes that characterize their lifestyle are reproduced.

Similarly, Fougere and Solitander (2007) argue that the creative class consists of workaholic, consumerist and apolitical 'bohemians' who value individuality, meritocracy, diversity and openness, but are also positioned as flexible immaterial labour, working in increasingly precarious conditions. Further, those on the margins or beyond the boundaries of such a 'creative class' might experience these changes not as enabling and contributing to growth, but as provoking loss of tradition, security and expertise.

It is in this context that Osborne (2003) has written scathingly of 'compulsory creativity'. It is important to note that for Osborne the 'creativity explosion' is primarily the result of a combination of psychology and new practices and discourses of business management (also see Thrift 2005). Popular and management psychology has increasingly emphasized the creative powers of people who can change the domains and conditions of their own work and, moreover, act to change their own lives. That this psychological perspective has affinities with the view of identity as a self-creative enterprising process requiring a commitment to lifelong learning should be clear. Hence too, for Osborne (2003: 509) 'the importance of the field of education for the creativity explosion, for, in a "knowledge society" such as ours, education comes to be recognized as more a way of life than a stage that is preparatory to maturity'.

Further, the value of creativity has been turned by popular psychology and creative management discourse into 'fashion', or the endless repetition of permanent imitation, which is tied to economic performance and efficiency or, as Osborne (2003: 523) puts it, 'the capitalisation of creativity':

> ... creativity is a value which, though we may believe we choose it ourselves, may in fact make us complicit with what today might be seen as the most conservative of norms; compulsory individualism, compulsory innovation, compulsory performativity and productiveness, the compulsory validation of the putatively new.
>
> (Osborne, 2003: 507)

Precisely because of its compulsory character in the fashionable sense, creativity has conservative effects. It has been transformed from something like experimentation into something more like machinery–creativity. Creativity, then, has been translated from a set of concepts and theories that have been validated as 'psy knowledges' into a series of prescriptions for a meritocratic new economy, and from there projected into every nook and cranny of contemporary society. Indeed, the compulsorization of creativity makes everyone into a creator, with the result that we are beginning to see ourselves as very different kinds of 'creatures' with the ability to constantly create ourselves anew, characteristics which are compatible with the principles of liberalism and democracy (Rose 1999a).

How have these ways of making creativity intelligible been adopted in the educational environment? Hartley (2006) charts how creativity has been translated into government education policy as part of an attempt to 're-enchant' schooling.

In the re-enchantment of schooling the 'expressive dimensions of education' have been revived at exactly the same time as the 'high-tech' practices associated with technology have taken on enhanced significance. Schools have therefore been subjected to pressure to ensure students possess the flexible 'human capital' required by the 'high tech' economy as well as the 'emotional capital' to participate in delivering 'high-touch' services (Hartley 2006: 65).

In this new affective ethos, the production of new knowledge, created through innovative and entrepreneurial methods, original and creative combinations, often by using the most state-of-the-art technology, has become the central dynamic of a globally networked society. As such, there is a shift from viewing school knowledge as a legitimated and authoritative body of content for transmission to a more fluid, creative and constructivist understanding of knowledge which supposes that students themselves can be responsible for creating or making knowledge within communication networks. This involves new arrangements and selections of knowledge, the basis of which is creativity. As possessing disciplinary knowledge diminishes in importance, it becomes more important to be able to seek out relevant information and make sense of it through creative application in practice. The task, in other words, is to develop a curriculum, pedagogies and assessment procedures that position students as 'knowledge creators'.

Furthermore, within the high-tech/high-touch economy, creativity is required to produce innovation and new products that are appealing and desirable to consumers, that may be advertised, marketed and retailed as lifestyle products or identity accessories that can be bought at a price. The new mode of production, with its regimes of design, innovation and the production of desire requires new modes of consciousness. Whereas routinized labour required an emotionless, instrumental and 'mechanical' orientation, the high tech innovations economy requires 'maximally creative' workers who put their emotions to work alongside their creativity and their high tech acumen (Hartley 2006). The creative knowledge economy requires, above all else, self-regulating individuals with the capacity to be flexible to meet the changing demands of the economy through engaging in continual self-improvement and lifelong learning. Hay and Kapitzke (2009: 151) describe how:

> ... international anxieties coalescing around the need to ensure the competitiveness of national and regional economies in the context of globalisation have prompted authorities to focus on strategies to secure economic advantage by enhancing human capital resources. Thus, policy documents in recent years have sought to improve productivity by urging people to be more innovative, enterprising and entrepreneurial.

A key aspect of this adjustment is what Hay and Kapitzke (2009: 159) refer to as 'the emergence of creativity as a way of understanding, managing and transforming the self-governing capacities of modern social subjects,' and they show 'how the creative self is fabricated out of particular truths told about the present and the obligations of the citizen worker that flow from this'.

According to these accounts, creativity is an educational concept that has been reassembled from a genealogical hybrid of corporate and public sector management disciplines by governments attempting to manage the demands of a global creative economy. Education systems are therefore repositioned as a futures-oriented investment in creativity and committed to perpetual innovation in order to ensure competitive advantage. Governments around the world are now seeking 'smart' strategies to ensure a steady stream of creative subjects who can permanently add value to the economy, regardless of the stability or uncertainty of its future trajectories. Consequently, policy discourses seek to reconstitute and domesticate creativity as a mainstream attitude that can be promoted rather than viewing it as the privileged psychological preserve of a gifted élite. The appeal to an emotional, self-centred or affective dimension in education is part of the re-enchantment of the technocratic orthodoxy of productive technical efficiency by the new cultural ethic of personal identity creation and self-expression. It represents 'education for (re)creativity and reflexivity' where creativity has been attached to the understanding that a successful knowledge economy 'cannot be constructed and sustained unless more of the creative and emotional self can be appropriated for instrumental purposes' (Hartley 2006: 67–9).

In sum, this is a 'new creativity' but at the same time it is imitative and conservative creativity. As Jones and Thomson (2008: 720) put it, 'the attempts to re-enchant the school through art and creative practice have clear progressive antecedents in the educational movements of the three decades that followed 1945', but these are antecedents which policymakers strategically choose to forget. It is not, however, the final word. It co-exists with other approaches, experiences and embodiments of imagination, practice and creative intent. As Darras urges, 'if there is no room at the top for everyone, let's be really creative: let's imagine other geographies' (Darras, 2011: 97).

Encountering creativity

In the midst of all the activity of policy practice and evaluation in the field of creativity and learning, it may be that 'other' creative people in all domains have been getting on with their practice, often without even mentioning or bothering about the word 'creativity' itself. Many of the people involved in policy, research and practice are not necessarily fully committed cool capitalists, but have found ways to work with the grain of activity in the field in order to generate and explore new openings for creative experiences for young people, whilst engaging in a variety of contradictory 'rhetorics' of creativity. Nevertheless, many recent initiatives to promote and foster creativity in learning and teaching have enabled and provoked encounters between young learners and creative practitioners that have afforded different perspectives on ways of knowing, doing and being.

Although the economic imperative and the psychological well-being of the identities of *homo creativus* in the weightless knowledge economy might seem to predominate in debates and policy development, there have been other 'rhetorics of creativity'(Banaji *et al.*, 2007) emerging from academia, research, policy and practice. These rhetorics flow in the interaction between the communities of education, psychology, social policy and the creative industries. They are constructed, contradictory and raise interesting questions about the development of creative activity in education contexts because:

> ... public discourse about creativity is characterised by a lack of clarity that allows participants to gain the benefits of aligning themselves with conflicting or mutually incompatible ideas and views without being seen to do so.
>
> (Banaji, 2011: 42)

In their study of different rhetorics of creativity, Banaji *et al.* (2007) contrast how '*creative genius*', '*democratic and political creativity*' and '*ubiquitous creativity*' offer three different expressions of creativity. Understandings of creativity as an innate characteristic of exceptional individuals with the notion of 'divine anointing' is contrasted with a more inclusive, democratic view of creativity being found in the symbolic expressions of culture and identity in everyday life, where the balances between identities, consumption, production, canons and censorship are negotiated. Ubiquitous, 'little c' creativity for all, supporting 'possibility thinking' in problem-solving in new situations, opens up approaches to creativity as enabling and empowering in daily life. It does, however, exist in tension with constructions of creativity as a special quality, or expressions of thinking and activity that are disruptive or uncomfortable. '*Creativity as a social good*' and '*Creativity as an economic imperative*' are linked in the appropriation of creativity in the discourse of development and growth in fluidity in the economic conditions and demands of the twenty-first century. '*Play and creativity*' and '*Creativity and Cognition*' draw together different psychological frameworks of intelligence and development of individuals also situated in social and cultural contexts. '*The creative affordances of technology*' and '*The creative classroom*' present questions about the use of digital tools for creative purposes, and the demands of pedagogy for both creative teaching and creative learning in school environments (Banaji *et al.*, 2007).

These rhetorics circulated amongst all those actors engaged in the revival of interest in creativity in the 1990s and 2000s. In England, examples of initiatives to model creative processes and partnerships between schools and active creative practitioners were supported by the Arts Council of England (ACE). Teacher Development Posts, for example, were established in the 1990s, establishing project collaborations between practising artists, university researchers and schools to explore approaches to planning, preparation and modes of working together in creative projects (Loveless, 1997, 1999, 2003; Sefton-Green and Sinker, 1999). The most significant recent initiative was Creative Partnerships, set up in 2002 and closed in 2011 in the wake of cuts to arts and education by the UK Coalition Government. Creative Partnerships (later renamed 'Creativity, Culture and Education') brought together creative practitioners with the creative industries, educators and policymakers. The aims of Creative Partnerships were to 'develop the skills of children and young people across England, raising their aspirations and achievements, and opening up more opportunities for their futures', thus encompassing the imperatives to raise standards of achievement across the curriculum, as well as provide access to cultural and artistic experiences in order to 'unlock' creativity in learners and teachers. In bringing together different communities, networks and enterprises, Creative Partnerships enabled children and young people to engage in creative activities and goals themselves, but also to encounter the people who embody creative work.

The reach of Creative Partnerships was wide, including Change Schools which worked with creative agents and practitioners for a sustained period of three years, focusing on whole school curriculum planning development; and Enquiry Schools which addressed a specific topic or issue over one year; and Creativity Schools which supported wider networks. Creative Partnerships was well documented, evaluated and researched over the nine years of its activity, exploring not only the impact on achievement, motivation, engagement and vernacular change in schools, but also reviews of areas of literature in the field, and the influence on and implications for the creative practitioners themselves contributing to a wider context of creative industries (see for example Parker and Ruthra-Rajan, 2011, Kendall *et al.*, 2008a, Kendall *et al.*, 2008b, Ofsted, 2006, Sharp *et al.*, 2006, Thomson *et al.*, 2009a, Thomson *et al.*, 2009b, BOP-Consulting, 2006). At a farewell gathering of a regional Creative Partnerships organization, representatives of the local schools regretted their demise and thanked the group for 'showing us that there is another way of doing things, although the ambition for creative and cultural transformation in curriculum and pedagogy was not fully realized and cultural critique was often marginalized in favour of enjoyment and inclusion (Hall and Thomson, 2007, Selwyn, 2011a).

The workshops, projects, expert groups, national and local initiatives, conferences, publications, networks, partnerships, pressure groups and motivational speaking circuits associated with this programme meshed together a wide range of motivations and intentions. In noticing and describing the rhetorics of creativity circulating in this particular policy moment, Banaji and her colleagues drew attention to the complex nature, complications and contradictions contained in the phenomenon of creativity in education policy at this time (Banji *et al.*, 2007). They demonstrate its potential not only to address particular goals and targets in the appropriation of creativity for standards and economic growth, but also to model the contradictions and ambiguities that can emerge in creative processes and communities themselves.

The research projects and evaluations emerging from the Creative Partnerships programme have sought to show how learners' encounters with creative practitioners – from musicians to mathematicians – reveal two distinct aspects of creative processes: a focus on the substance of the work itself; and the dispositions or habits of mind that support ways of working. Such studies are informed by the latest thinking on creativity as a form of action and practice. Robinson (2010), for example, emphasises the need to recognize that creativity and innovation involve 'doing something', often by people who are passionately immersed 'in their element' – in different subject areas, with different media and materials. 'Whatever the task, creativity is not just an internal mental process: it involves action. In a sense, it is applied imagination' (Robinson, 2001: 115).

Other thinkers on creativity stress how practitioners rarely discuss the concept of creativity unless questioned by psychologists and education researchers interested in articulating and analysing creative processes (Csikszentmihalyi, 1996, Gardner, 1988, Claxton and Lucas, 2004). Others have found that creative people rarely work in isolation. Their ideas and outcomes are likely to have been generated through interaction with other people's ideas and responses. Many exceptionally creative people tell tales of their supportive families, or engaging network of friends, or group of like-minded people in studios or laboratories. John-Steiner's (2000) observations and commentaries about creative people, for example, explore the nature of their collaborations, in which they challenge, discuss and try out their ideas for their work. Creative activity is not easy or straightforward, indeed, is not always desirable in every situation. There are dangers of creativity being perceived as just the elements of 'having good ideas' or 'making pretty things'; rather than the challenging, and often painful, disruptive or frustrating, experience that characterizes the practices of creative people – the 'hard fun' and the 'flow' (Papert, 1993, Csikszentmihalyi, 1996).

The skills, inclinations and alertness to opportunities that generate such creative work have been described by Hetland (Hetland *et al.* 2007, Hetland 2008) in a framework for Studio Thinking in the arts that outlines eight allegedly key dispositions that underpin wider creative work in relationship to education. According to Hetland's framework, '*Developing Craft: technique and studio practice*' is fundamental in mastering the tools and media of the domain. '*Engage and persist*' requires an understanding of the conceptual depth and problems in the field, and a capability for perseverance, resilience, an acceptance of slow growth and a desire to focus and perform the process as well as possible. '*Envision*' relates to the imagining of possibilities not yet realised, whilst '*Express*' enables the communication of ideas and meanings in the different domains and media. '*Observe*' demands the paying of attention to the surface and depth, micro and macro dimensions of detail and meaning; '*Reflect*' involves the openness to explain, question and converse with others about the work, leading to evaluation of the work in a wider context in the field. '*Stretch and explore*' allows movement towards boundaries and margins, playful conjecture of possibilities, and openness to mistakes and serendipity. Finally, '*Understand Art World*' links explicitly to an awareness of the place of the creative work within a wider domain, field and community which might recognize, ignore or reject the contribution and value of the endeavour.

It is not only creative practitioners who model these characteristics and qualities whilst focusing on a broader vision and purpose. For example, it has been claimed that when young people encounter social entrepreneurs who engage in activity to effect change for a wider social good, they also witness the hard work of imagination, commitment, conjectural thinking, negotiation, persuasion, dealing with disappointment, learning from mistakes, collaboration, co-operation, perseverance and the identification of responsive partnerships and alliances (Facer, 2011). Such enterprises not only reflect the changes in creative ways of working in a digital age, they also adopt and appropriate the affordances of digital tools to support their goals, from communication to crowd-sourcing, collaboration and show-casing. Activities to promote social entrepreneurship and creativity in learning have often emerged more from the informal creative, cultural and social sectors of youth work, more than formal education.

There are many examples. Weekend Arts College (WAC) in London, has worked for 30 years providing training in the arts as well as career and personal development projects for children and young people (www.wac.co.uk). Livity (http://livity.co.uk) is a youth engagement agency committed to working with young people in the combination of business and social responsibility, through co-design and co-creation of campaigns, content and communities. Their clients include Google, Coke, PlayStation, BBC, Home Office, O2 and Channel 4. The Nominet Trust (www.nominettrust.org.uk), established by Nominet, a large UK internet registry, supports internet-based projects that make a positive difference to the lives of disadvantaged and vulnerable people. In the US the MacArthur Foundation (www.macfound.org) has a strand of substantial grant support to understand how digital media is changing the way young people learn, play, socialize, and participate in civic life, and one of the initiatives, the Mozilla Open Badges (http://openbadges.org), focuses specifically on the recognition of people's accomplishments, skills, achievements and capabilities in online spaces and contexts which are outwith formal education. Educurious (http://.educurious.org) is a non-profit organization which develops curriculum and pedagogy by connecting young people at risk of dropping out of school with experts in a wide range of fields and professions, from epidemiologists to a film producers, to engage in a series of authentic, problem-based challenges, using digital media.

These creative, entrepreneurial activities offer encounters with role models and mentors who expect participation and focus, and they are often marginal to mainstream education institutions and systems. Role models and mentors have a pedagogic role in sharing experience, expertise and advice on substance and on ways of working, and their approach might contrast or contradict that of the teachers in school, college or university classrooms. Hall, Thomson and Russell (2007), for example, observed and analysed the pedagogical approach of artists working in a primary school project for Creative Partnerships. Using Bernstein's framework of 'competence' and 'performance' pedagogies, they noted the differences between the predominantly 'performance pedagogy' of the classroom teachers and the 'competence pedagogy' of the artist: where 'performance pedagogy' focuses on the outputs produced by individual learners and evaluated and assessed by teachers who regulate the space, time and discourse in the classroom:

> Bernstein argues that the 'social logic' of competence theories is a view of the subject as active, creative and self-regulating. Because an inherent

competence is assumed, there is 'an in-built procedural democracy' ... a sceptical view of hierarchical relations, a focus on the present tense and what is presented (rather than on what is missing). Competence pedagogies therefore tend to focus on the learner and what the learner has achieved. Control is implicit or 'invisible'; that is, it tends to inhere in personalised forms of communication and an assumption of self-regulation. Learners are likely to have a greater degree of control over what they learn, the pace and sequencing of lessons and the spaces in which they occur.

(Hall et al., 2007 p. 607)

According to the researchers, when young learners encounter such creative role models and mentors, they experience alternative ways of developing processes and achieving goals. Their potential and capability to participate and contribute is understood and taken as a starting point. They are encouraged to engage in their tasks in order to perform to their best abilities, to persevere in developing skill and technique, and to subject the quality of their outcomes to critical review and suggestions for improvement. They are introduced to practitioners who know the tools of their trade, who are familiar with the concepts and substance of their field, who know why their work matters to themselves and to others in that moment and beyond, and who are able to point the way to a wider variety of prospective learning identities.

Conclusion: Beyond compulsory creativity

In this chapter we have seen how creativity is deployed as a polyvalent concept across psychological, management, policy and practitioner discourses. We first saw how psychological accounts have positioned creativity as a high form of competence, then how policy and management discourse has translated it into images of the worker–citizen of the new economy; and finally how a more practitioner-based discourse has been mobilized in education which focuses on the values and dispositions of creative work.

Perhaps, roughly following the actor–network theory approach of Fenwick and Edwards (2010) what we can say about creativity in education is that it is constituted of a heterogeneous array of elements. Amongst these elements are some that are conceptual–psychological theories, policy imaginaries and new management ideas. Some are organizational and institutional – schools, government departments, businesses, creative industries and practices, and other 'intermediary' organizations. Other elements are practical – arts practices, creative 'partnerships', pedagogies. Some of the elements are material – tools, technologies, environments and spaces, as well as bodies and books. And, related to the materiality of books, many elements that constitute creativity are textual – textbooks, curriculum documents, competency lists, software, exam papers, websites and so on. Within all this, subjectivities are made up and promoted – creative teachers and creative learners with identities characterized through the definition of certain kinds of capacities and competences. In order to capture what might be meant by creativity in the educational field, it is necessary to trace the ways in which various bits and pieces of all these kinds of elements are joined up together and assembled into programmes that can be enacted in practice.

Our brief discussion of the Creative Partnerships programme has indicated how 'creative learning' has been enacted in UK schools as an effect of government priorities in a knowledge economy, creative industries' rhetoric, psychological and socio-cultural theories of creative practice, the development of relationships in the form of partnerships and collaborations between schools and artists, the production of texts, the equipping of classrooms to afford possibilities for certain kinds of pedagogy, the generation of research evaluations, literature reviews and the publication of research findings—all of it generating creative identities for both teachers and students. All of these elements and more make up the 'assemblage' currently known as creativity in UK schools, although the stability and durability of such an assemblage is constantly being threatened by alternative creativities.

In the following chapters, we now wish to turn our attention to the 'master discourses' of learning, curriculum and pedagogy as they relate to the rethinking of education, technology and creativity that we have been trying to articulate.

PART II

Thinking, curriculum and pedagogy

6

THINKING WITH DIGITAL TOOLS

Agency, tools, context and improvisation

If as educators we are seeking to foster learners' prospective identities in a digital age, then we need to understand how to approach four aspects of being a learner:

1. *agency*: active participation in the social and cultural contexts in which we are learners;
2. *tools*: our relationship with technologies and the role they might play in our engagement in intelligent action;
3. *context*: creating and shaping learning environments which are appropriate for the demands of our lives and futures;
4. *improvisation*: imagining and constructing new contexts and communities to meet the challenges of our learning lives.

Our theories of learning can influence not only how our learning lives and worlds might be constructed, but also the questions we might ask about *how* we might improve them to benefit the learner. It is the distributed nature of intelligence in context, with the potential for creative and improvised action that is the focus of this chapter, which was prompted by conversations with a student teacher, and by witnessing a change in his understanding of the complexity of the 'toolbox' he would need for his developing practice in the context of a 'digital age'. After engaging with the concept of learning with tools for the first time, he changed his views of being a teacher away from a model of delivery of information to assembled individuals. He understood his role instead as designing learning experiences to enable his pupils to use the tools, resources and other people's expertise purposefully in order to learn. He realized how his expertise in his own subject area was not a discrete body of knowledge to be transmitted, but a key part of a complex system of purpose and activity that he was learning to design and orchestrate. He imagined how the intelligence in the room might be distributed, and thought about how he might prepare lessons that enabled his pupils to build up a useful toolbox for learning in his subject and beyond the classroom. His view of the modes of schooling was expanded from a model of reception and reproduction, to one of design and performance. He understood some of the complexities and contradictions of his task as a new teacher, yet recognized that the characteristics of digital technologies that had caught his own interest and enthusiasm were those of tools for learning as well as the content of a curriculum. It was this engagement that motivated him to teach his pupils; to shape their thinking; to connect with others; to construct knowledge in their environment; and to understand the spaces and places of their learning something well.

The ways in which we understand being a learner in a digital age will make a difference to the experiences and environments that we recognize, design and make available for young people now, and in the future. If we believe that learning is fostered entirely through reward and reinforcement, or transmission and information-processing, then the appearance, activities and expectations of the work of classrooms will have a particular look and feel for learners. But if we believe instead that learning is fostered through experience, participation and purposeful activity, we might well not have classrooms at all. Clearly, the rationales for the ways in which we educate our young are not choices between the extremes of one model of schooling or the other. Human beings learning across the millennia have devised many different solutions to the problem of passing on, sustaining and developing our societies and cultures.

A characteristic of human learning and creativity is that we can't help ourselves using and making tools to extend and enhance our abilities. Digital technologies are tools, amongst many, that are integral in shaping the potential and constraints in our learning, our knowledge and our culture. Yet, educators in a digital age must not presume that we will learn with digital technologies just because they are there. Prolific use does not mean sophisticated use, and many digital technologies are used by learners as consumers rather than as constructors and creators of knowledge and identity. Evidence of direct causal links between using digital technologies and improvements in measures of learning is notoriously difficult to demonstrate, particularly to those advising policymakers who need to make an immediate case for the spending of public money on new technologies in schools (Selwyn 2011a). Indeed, a study of Web 2.0 technologies for learning in groups of 11- to 16-year-olds in the UK, for example, highlighted only a few embryonic signs of criticality, self-management and meta-cognitive reflection (Crook et al. 2008). We suggest that seeking such a causal link is asking the wrong questions about the phenomenon. Rather than attempt to establish direct links between the use of Digital Technology X to offer higher test scores than Traditional Technology Y within Timescale Z, it would be more useful to consider a more complex view of qualities of learning for different purposes in different contexts. We need not only understand agency, tools, context here and now, but also be able to improvise and pre-figure our future as creative, innovative learners across generations.

All of these considerations should be underpinned by finely tuned and well-informed skepticism in approaching claims for transformation in human learning and progress that underpin the appropriation of digital tools. Digital technologies don't bring about transformation in learning and teaching; change is brought about or constrained by people enacting their theories of learning and engaging in their politics of purpose in education. Digital technologies are, however, tools embedded in our wider culture and as such have an effect on metaphors for creativity and learning in our times. The tools and artefacts that we use to mediate our learning experiences are many and various, from language shared with other people, to knots in our handkerchief to help us to remember things. Digital technologies are certainly not the only tools for learners in a digital age, yet they are increasingly ubiquitous in local and global contexts. We engage our imaginations in designing and using them with their potential and their constraints in the activities they afford. They shape the nature of these activities – in opening up new possibilities for retrieval, representation and communication, whilst restricting or closing down other modes of connection and communication. Saljo argues that:

> ... one of the main consequences of why these technologies are so significant is that they affect the manners in which society builds up and provides access to social memory, that is, the pool of insights and experiences that people are expected to know about and to make use of ... the technology does not facilitate or improve learning in a linear sense, rather it is currently changing our interpretations of what learning is and changing our expectations about what it means to know something
>
> (Saljo 2010: 56)

Learning with agency

Over the years the focus of our thinking about how we learn has shifted from the behaviours of solitary individuals to the interactions of people in social and cultural relationships. Our active learning identities emerge through intention, activity and participation. Our theories are useful in helping us to explore questions about learning in particular circumstances, from learning our multiplication tables to learning to build and operate a space station and participate in a just society. They are also useful in making explicit our understanding of learning in our society and culture, from models of training and transmission to networks of collaborative knowledge-building.

In the early 1970s established courses on the Psychology of Learning presented theories of behaviourism and reinforcement; information processing; sensory perception; motivation and emotion; the impact of Piaget's work on construction of knowledge and the stages of child development; and recent developments in social psychology in the laboratory and in the field. It was the era of programmed learning machines, early models of Artificial Intelligence, and Stanley Milgram's laboratory experiments in obedience to authority. New courses in cognition, language and mental processes were being introduced; and at least one institution offered an optional course on the Psychology of Art, which considered more recent questions of creativity and introduced early ideas of ecological approaches to visual perception and a theory of affordances (Ehrenzweig 1973, Gibson 1972). Learning theories at that time focused predominantly on learners as individuals who developed their behaviours by response to stimuli, and constructed knowledge through active adaptation to the external environment.

Forty years later, socio-cultural theories of learning reflect understandings of knowledge as emerging in social interactions, contexts and networks. Vygotsky's theories of learning in social and cultural environments opened up wide horizons for thinking differently about learning with other people, using mediating tools, through activity, and in meaningful contexts. Socio-cultural theories, and the development of ideas of subsequent schools of thought in different countries and cultures bring into focus the characteristics of theories of learning which include understandings of human agency. Concepts such as mediation, activity, intention, context, culture, identity, connection, participation, scaffolding, authenticity, community, ecology and narrative offer insights into the complexity of human learning (Wertsch 1998, Engeström 1999, Nardi and O'Day 1999, Luckin 2008, Bruner 1996, Pea 1993, Castells 2009, Wenger 1998, Goodson *et al.* 2010). These offer radically different landscapes of learning which have profound implications for our understanding of knowledge, learning, mastery, pedagogy and the structures and systems of education. (Daniels 2001, Somekh 2001, 2007). Learning is active and dynamic, not only in approaching and solving problems of new experiences, but also in creating new ones to be solved. Pachler and Daly explain their understanding of learning as:

> ... the twin processes of 'coming to know' and 'being able to operate' successfully in and across new and ever-changing contexts and learning spaces, as a process of meaning-making through communication and as an augmentation of inner, conceptual and outer, semiotic resources ... .
>
> (Pachler and Daly 2011: 17)

Learning to be a participant in a digital age, and not just a consumer or commodity, demands an engagement with the potential of people, tools and contexts to foster knowledge, capability and agency for intelligent action. Identity and agency are closely linked, and we develop our identities as learners through participation with others in our communities. We engage with purposeful activities which have meaning in our wider culture, from reading, writing and arithmetic, to gardening, playing the saxophone, devising health care policy, and designing an electric car. Inden defines agency as:

> ... the realized capacity of people to act upon their world and not only to know about or give personal and intersubjective significance to it. That capacity is the power of people to act purposefully and reflectively, in more

or less complex interrelationships with one another, to reiterate and remake
the world in which they live, in circumstances where they may consider
different courses of action possible and desirable, though not necessarily from
the same view … .

(Inden 1990: 32 in Holland et al. 1998: 42)

Learning with tools

Traditional views of intelligence, such as IQ for example, considered it to be fixed,
and influencing how well, or how much a person could learn. Contemporary
understandings of intelligence are more dynamic, recognizing that intelligence can
be learned and practised. Research evidence over many decades indicates that
intelligence is composite, expandable, practical, intuitive, social, strategic, ethical
and distributed.

> … we should strive toward a reflectively and intentionally distributed
> intelligence in education, where learners are inventors of distributed-
> intelligence-as-tool, rather than receivers of intelligence-as-substance. In the
> court of worldly experience, such learners may be far more ready not only
> to adapt to change but to contribute substantially to it.
>
> (Lucas and Claxton 2010: 82)

Digital technologies have been described as 'just a tool' in education for many
years, yet our understanding of the implications of such tools in our education
systems has not been particularly well-developed in changing practice. Some claim
that digital technologies have transformed learning. Such a view focuses on the
technologies and not on the complex and mutually shaping interactions between
people, the tools and artefacts that they use to pursue a goal or solve a problem, and
the context in which they are making decisions and acting. Earlier chapters of this
book have considered how we are using digital technologies to participate in a
variety of contexts, from global to local, which themselves have been shaped and
changed by the presence and meaning of those technologies. The tools that are
available to us in our socio-cultural settings are 'in place, already "there", deeply
entrenched in culture and language' (Bruner 1990: 11). In a 'digital age', such as
we have argued earlier in this book, digital technologies can therefore be considered
as mediating tools, not just to be efficient in the storage and presentation of
information, but also to shape the meaning of activities themselves and help learners
to understand and represent their worlds.

Our identities as learners are formed and shaped through active engagement
with the matters of what, how, when, where and why of learning. We can pull
back from seeing and using digital technologies as instructional aids that mimic
more traditional tools in learning activities, and consider how they might afford
opportunities for changing our relationship with knowledge and knowing. We can
think differently about educational 'tools of the trade' in designing contexts and

cultures for learning and pedagogies for intelligent action. Our designs can reflect an understanding of the implications of both cyber utopianism and cyber skepticism in shaping and being shaped by tools for learning and identity.

Many of the learning experiences and opportunities for creativity for many young people in schools can be described as 'Person-Solo', relying on 'bare brains', rather than 'Person-Plus', drawing upon the potential of tools, from language to laptop computers, to help us to be intelligent learners (Salomon and Perkins 2005). The view that intelligence is accomplished in collective, social and cultural contexts, rather than being an essential mechanism in individuals, opens up interesting questions about the role of technologies in what it means to be 'smart'. Salomon and Perkins argue that intelligence is cognitive performance in solving problems, making decisions and drawing upon a range of technologies in complex environments. They also argue that dispositions to be attentive, persistent and alert to possibilities are as important in the potential and performance of intelligence. They describe the learning effects of, with and through technologies. Learning effects 'of' technologies are recognized in the changes in behaviours and capabilities prompted by their use. Learning 'with' technologies enhances and extends our capabilities to perform tasks from retrieving information to representing what we know. Learning 'through' technologies offers a more profound change in the nature of the task itself.

The learning effects of digital technologies are recognized in the lasting effects which persist after using the technology. Digital resources might be designed as instructional aids, offer opportunities for people to practise motor responses and skills, or reward users for accurate responses in numeracy and literacy tasks. An example of this is the effect of playing videogames on improvements in visual processing tasks (Green and Bavelier 2003). Such direct effects of the use of digital technologies in causing clear, focused impact have been sought, but not clearly found, in other areas such as the use of computer programming languages as a 'mental gymnasium' for more general and complex cognitive developments, or the general access to computers in classrooms leading to improvements in attainment in subject-based tests (Selwyn 2011a).

Learning with digital technologies is more of an intellectual partnership in which cognition is distributed between the tools and the learner. Wertsch describes the 'irreducible tension' between humans as active agents and mediating cultural tools such as computers. He illustrates the concept of 'distributed memory', using the example of trying to remember the name of a book to recommend to a colleague. Unable to recall the title, he used Amazon.com to remind him, and then asked 'Who did the remembering?'. He understood how to use the technology of Amazon.com, and both he and the technology were involved in a system of distributed remembering (Wertsch 2002). We use tools and artefacts in our environment or 'surround' to assist and enhance our activity of becoming knowledgeable and capable.

> Complex human cognition is typically distributed cognition - distributed over social and physical support systems. Person-Plus is the norm for the

human condition, and human beings as intellectual agents are best considered not stripped of, but suitably equipped with, tools … .

(Salomon and Perkins 2005: 76)

A fruitful surround for learning will offer particular access characteristics in the system. The first characteristic is the knowledge that is available both as content and as the higher-order problem-solving strategies and modes of enquiry within a discipline, from particle physics to plumbing. The second is the range of representations of this conceptual knowledge, captured in devices such as documentation, visual models, tables, formulas, simulations, and the like. Third is the capability for effective and meaningful retrieval of the knowledge, from straightforward searches to problem-based approaches in understanding a subject in context - from using Google to search using keywords, to working in apprenticeship alongside others with expertise. The final access characteristic is construction which enables people to assemble the knowledge represented and retrieved into new knowledge structures. Such access characteristics might be recognized in a variety of environments with digital tools. A school student doing their Physics homework with a computer in their room might have access to the content and conceptual areas of the subject through a variety of representations in books, broadcasts, simulations, websites and multimedia activities. She will be able to retrieve knowledge and representations by having access to search engines, the school virtual learning environment, online communities, social media and networks, writing, presentation and media production tools, and communication with friends, peers, teachers and experts in the wider community of interest and practice. Informal, distributed learning communities draw upon all these characteristics, whether it be supporting each other in learning how to fix a particular model of vintage motorcyle, to study for a doctorate at university, or develop networks for sustained political activism. Construction and sharing of new knowledge might be with a wide range of tools, from using a scratchpad or workbench, to writing up a text, making a movie, or mixing and mashing a variety of media.

Access to tools, physical and virtual, is not sufficient, however. The 'fingertip effect' describes our being surrounded by potentially useful tools without the capability of using them purposefully as '[w]hat technologies afford they do not typically demand' (Salomon and Perkins 2005: 82). At the time of writing this chapter, the Centre for Learning Performance Technologies conducted an online survey of 'Top 100 Tools for Learning' (http://c4lpt.co.uk/top-tools/top-100-tools-for-learning-2011; accessed 20 August 2011). Of course, such a survey would reach those engaged with digital technologies who listed the top ten tools as:

- Twitter (microsharing)
- YouTube (videosharing)
- GoogleDocs (collaboration suite)
- Skype (instant messaging and voice communications)

- Wikipedia (collaborative encyclopedia)
- Prezi (presentation software)
- Facebook (social network)
- EduGlogster (interactive poster)
- WordPress (blogging tool)
- Moodle (course management system).

By the time this chapter is being read, the list and pattern of digital tools being used for learning will have changed, yet the need for the capability to make purposeful choices of tools in a personal learning environment will remain. Agency, capability and expertise in the use of tools can take time to develop, needing the involvement of others to design and scaffold meaningful experiences, resources and feedback on progress, an approach not always reflected in conventional instruction.

The executive function also needs to be distributed in a Person–Plus surround. This is the means by which we make choices, ponder the consequences of decision points and select action paths. A good learning support system will offer instruction, organization, step-by-step guidance, and will break down concepts for novices. This function can be expressed in resources and materials, as well as in the other people and teachers in the situation. The aim is to enable learners to take on this executive function themselves in the knowledge, representation, retrieval, and construction of higher-order knowledge in new situations. In the meantime, the design and choreography of the process of giving access to tools for intellectual partnership is an important role of a teacher.

Learning with technologies enables us to extend and augment the learning experience. Learning through technologies takes us further in understanding how our thinking is shaped and transformed more substantially in our use of tools. There is an intimate relationship between human intelligence and technological tools which act across mental, material, cognitive, non-cognitive, biological and cultural aspects of the evolution of human nature itself. The human brain has developed in social and public environments modified by technology and culture, and interaction with tools plays a role in both amplifying action and transforming human thinking.

> Thinking consists not of 'happenings in the head' (though happenings there and elsewhere are necessary for it to occur) but of trafficking in significant symbols – words for the most part but also gestures, drawings, musical sounds, mechanical devices like clocks.
>
> (Geertz 1973: 45 in Salomon and Perkins 2005: 220)

Such understanding takes time and practice with new technologies. The early products of photography, for example, resembled more traditional modes of painting before the distinctive features of capturing light on the medium of film were explored technically and aesthetically. Similarly, word processors could be used for straightforward copy typing and spell-checking, or could afford opportunities to change understandings of literacy and authorship through format, hyperlinks and multimedia. Graphics software, for example, could be used to mimic physical painting techniques, or to manipulate visual images to make meaning which couldn't be expressed with other media (Loveless 1997).

Learning through digital technologies in a virtual culture challenges us to re-examine thinking itself in a digital age. Learning with, and learning through the use of technologies are on a continuum, rather than being polar, but there is a shift in the relationship between the learners and the tools as the partnership in thinking becomes more interactive, reorganized and the location of the cognitive work is shared more evenly. Some tools such as spreadsheets, calculators, dynamic geometry tools, simulations and serious games, not only support the storing, retrieval and presentation of knowledge, but also offer the potential for modelling and conjecture. They afford opportunities to ask the question 'What would happen if I tried this …?'; devise algorithms and procedures to explore these questions; and then play a dynamic role in the working out of the problem and representing possible solutions to the questions. Using digital tools to encourage playful exploration through the manipulation and testing of ideas can enable learners to set up their own models and test hypotheses. Learners are in control of the activity, considering the consequences of decisions that produce predicted or unexpected outcomes. Using programming languages such as Logo or Scratch, or following a series of questions in interrogating a database to test hypotheses are examples of learners constructing their own models and trying them out. Such resources have been described as 'cognitive toolkits' and 'mindtools' to help describe the qualitative difference between applications for instruction, automation, speed and storage, and applications for computation, conjecture and exploration (Underwood and Underwood 1990, Jonassen 2000).

Shaffer and Clinton (2006) go further in coining the term 'toolforthoughts' to represent the concept of mind being distributed between human actors and tools, each contributing symmetrically to the location of thinking together. Thoughts and tools are shaped by each other. New tools are designed and made when the old tools aren't fit for a new purpose, thus shaping and being shaped by an activity. Modelling and computational tools in mathematics might enable learners to solve problems without the need for traditional tools such as logarithm tables or abstractions of algebra. Similarly, new forms of reading and writing texts are required in the use of simulations, games, multimedia and hypermedia. These tools 'push back' in interactions with humans, shaping the nature of the learning activities (Shaffer and Clinton 2006, Shaffer 2006, Gee 2004). Such a strong approach to toolforthoughts raises questions again about the location of the thinking in an activity, particularly in the assessment of the thinking and learning with tools in a virtual culture. They contend that the use of such tools is not cheating, but enabling learners to demonstrate what they know and have come to understand. The final outcome of the activity is the significant benefit from the process of interaction and purposeful use of the tools, from calculators to immersive virtual environments.

A vivid way of approaching learning through technologies can be seen in the design and playing of serious games which present an epistemic frame of the toolkit of knowledge, skills and values in an activity. This supports the learner in coming to understand the goals, rules, roles, strategies and content of the game . These games can be focused on simulations of specific competences, such as flying an aircraft; on a more open exploration of particular scenarios, such as IBM's City One business game to solve realworld business problems; or adopting a wider range of roles in virtual worlds, such as SimCity or World of Warcraft. Shaffer and Clinton argue that current schooling in the developed world does not usually engage with such learning through technologies, as its current focus is on thinking in the head of the learner which is then assessed in abstract forms. There are multiple pathways to knowledge, and achievement is 'what students will be able to accomplish in collaboration with toolforthoughts - what matters are the actions we value - and the new possibilities for action that new toolforthoughts make possible' (Shaffer and Clinton 2006: 287).

The mutual relationship between tools for learning and the meaning and purpose of the learning activities is vividly illustrated by Saljo (2010), who describes the role of technologies in transforming the metaphors of learning which are embodied in many practices of schooling. He offers an argument for the potential of digital tools to radically change metaphors of learning in a digital age, and places his discussion in a wider context of historical changes in the purposes of schools and their relationship to technological developments. He argues that our tools and artefacts for learning have shaped and influenced the purposes and contexts for learning, but not directed them. Institutions and teachers have adopted and adapted different technologies to meet their purposes appropriately. Supposed low 'take-up' of digital technologies in schools and universities might be not so much to do with teachers' resistance to or lack of competence with the technologies. It might well because they are making good decisions about what is needed to meet the purposes of learning within a particular curriculum and assessment system.

Over 5000 years ago, the Sumerian edduba (tablet house) were schools where early cuneiform writing on clay was taught as a skill to underpin knowledge in matters of trade and law. The role of the teacher in the ancient world was to lecture, and the role of the docile pupil was to listen, copy and practise reading and writing, not only to document but to build up social memory. The metaphor for schooling of knowledge and skills was one of reproduction and preservation of content and form. Later, Western school practices developed to reflect the changing purposes of schooling. In the Middle Ages, the focus was on hearing and reading proscribed religious texts to instruct others and preserve religious authority. The mediaeval technologies for reading and writing required intensive, skilled labour. In later centuries, the technologies of print promoted literacy as a capability to read and synthesize a wide range of texts, such as fiction and non-fiction books, newspapers, posters, pamphlets, and manuals. At the end of the twentieth century, learners were expected to make sense of information, incorporate it into what they already knew and apply and express their new knowledge within their life and activity in a variety of settings.

Digital technologies, however, have the potential to take us further than metaphors of learning as reproduction, synthesis and expression, to a metaphor of learning as production, performance and 'remix'. Learners can have access to tools for capturing multimedia data, composing, editing, mixing, mashup, and dynamic representation. Digital literacy has developed, not just from page to screen, but to synthesis, composition, participation and response through personal and mobile media (Saljo 2010, Carrington and Robinson 2009, Cook *et al.* 2011). Multi-modal texts represent meaning through the juxtaposition of written text, sound, still and moving visual images, and hyperlinks, thus making the reading of them no longer linear, but more related to design. Thus Saljo asserts that learners have personal perspectives and interests that guide the selection of and attention to information in multi-modal forms:

> The 'reading as design' metaphor emphasizes the creative element in the interpretive activities of readers/learners; reading and interpretation go beyond giving back what is already there. What is expected is cognitive work aimed at producing a version of what is seen that is significant for some purpose.
>
> (Saljo 2010: 60)

Access to knowledge and other people is no longer restricted and controlled by institutions, and learners can make choices about how they engage with a range of media, networks, communities and places. Learners need to make decisions about how to access, filter and harvest relevant information in order to question, interpret, make meaning and represent their understanding using a range of literacies of reading and writing in different modes. They can be inspired and engaged by many pathways and modes of connection, and use multiple tools to construct, represent and communicate their new knowledge and ways of knowing.

Learning in contexts

Learners and tools interact with each other in contexts that can be complex and located, yet not necessarily bounded by physical space and episodes in time. Learning in context is situated, adapted, localized and connected through a dialogue between learners and their environment. Our theories of learning in a digital age need to be able to hold understandings of not only the mutual shaping of people, tools and purposes, but also of the interactions within wider learning environments. Person-Plus in a digital age should not evoke an image of individuals placed passively in the centre of a rich environment of tools and connections, hoping for the best by serendipity. Intention, motivation and interaction between people help learners to make sense of their situation and understand what they might need in order to move on in action. Understanding our learning as 'Person-Plus' can change the way in which we perceive the world around us which we perceive as a variety of contexts in which we use tools to learn. Context is connected to people and their surround and can extend over space and time and also be mobile as we move through place.

Context matters to learning; it is complex and local to a learner. It defines a person's subjective and objective experience of the world in a spatially and historically contingent manner. Context is dynamic and associated with connections between people, things, locations and events in a narrative that is driven by people's intentionality and motivations. Technology can help to make these connections in an operational sense. People can help to make these connections have meaning for a learner.

(Luckin 2010: 18)

'Context' can be described as the circumstances that surround our behaviour, represented in concentric circles around a person's activity, rather like nested Russian dolls. Such an image of concentric circles can, however, be limiting in evoking context as a container for activity, rather than being part of the activity itself. Michael Cole suggests a metaphor of weaving together the many elements of context as they influence the nature, construction and pathway of the activity.

In short, because what we call mind works through artifacts, it cannot be unconditionally bounded by the head or even by the body, but must be seen as distributed in the artifacts which are woven together and which weave together individual human actions in concert with and as part of the permeable, changing events of life.

(Cole 1996: 136 in Luckin 2010: 10)

The idea of a context which is rooted in physical space that can be mapped can be a limiting, Western view. Dillon *et al.* (2008) argue that nomads, such as the Daur pastoralists in Mongolia, have a concept of context which moves with them on a journey through a changing landscape. Life for the Daur is being in a landscape, not following directions to positional goals. Learning contexts are therefore more complex, interactive and idiosyncratic than conventional descriptions of the location of learning in classrooms and institutions. They can be more usefully considered as the weaving of elements in trajectories, as learners move between different contexts, orchestrating their use of digital media, tools and networks of people appropriately for their needs and interests. The challenge to educators is to understand the kinds of contexts which might be generated particularly in a digital age, and how learners' imagination engages with agency to recognize the affordances of digital tools.

Ecological views of learning draw attention to the mutual relationships between people and all the potential resources within their environment (Dillon 2008, Nardi and O'Day 1999, Loi and Dillon 2006, Luckin *et al.* 2008). Perspectives on learners and their environments as ecologies have been influenced by understandings of ecosystems in natural environments, in which all elements and organisms shape and adapt to each other. Significant change is called a disturbance, and the response to this is a perturbation. Transient perturbations are managed to maintain the environment and resist major change, whilst permanent perturbations bring about a different state of relationships within the environment. The elements of education systems at all levels – from classroom groups to university league tables – respond to disturbances and innovations on a day-to-day basis, either maintaining equilibrium or effecting change in the purposes and conduct of activities. Loi and Dillon (2006) note how an education system such as a school which has specific objectives for examination success might align its strategies for teaching, management and general conduct to these external demands for success in league tables, and resist changes which might disrupt these objectives in the short-term. Schools which engage with objectives with different purposes, such as fostering equality or co-operation, might introduce interventions and initiatives which disturb the curriculum being taught, the pedagogical approaches and the nature of recognition of achievement and success, thus changing the learning environment and culture. In the experience of most schools, these objectives are not mutually exclusive, and there is an understanding of the contradictions and tensions that exist in the range of purposes of schooling activities within the community. Jeffrey and Woods' ten year study of a school noted many examples of how the staff and parents negotiated the numerous demands on their identity as a creative school, from designing the outdoor learning spaces to participating in national assessment tests, sustaining the balances and perturbations, both to maintain stability in some activities and to allow change and development in others (Jeffrey and Woods 2003).

The concept of Person-Plus with digital tools can be seen as an ecological approach to learners engaging with the technologies for access, retrieval, representation and construction in their surround. These digital tools can 'push back' in shaping the nature of the activity itself, causing disruption and perturbations with different consequences. In school classrooms, for example, they might maintain familiar activities such as using interactive whiteboards to mimic teacher-centred instructional approaches, or the interactive whiteboards might be used as a tool to open up innovative spaces for dialogue through talk and reflection with pupils (Warwick *et al.* 2011). The presence of multimedia tools for composing presentations with text, image, sound and hyperlinks might disrupt traditional understandings of school curriculum subjects. In English and Art, for example, they might perpetuate the discrete disciplines in their traditional forms, or they might provoke learners and teachers to experiment with multidisciplinary approaches to making and communicating meaning with multimedia texts that cross boundaries between visual and textual representations (Ellis 2004, Long 2001).

The ecological concept of niche construction can help us to understand how humans shape and are shaped by their world at macro and micro levels. The niches which we make, and in which we might thrive or fail, emerge from the interaction between the features of the individuals and the factors of the environment. Such niches might be at the levels of classrooms, museums, and Brownie packs; or in virtual groupings using social media to support doctoral students or international steam rail enthusiasts. The micro levels of these niches of human activity are very local and 'niches are wisely created when generalizations are adapted to local conditions rather than being imposed on them' (Dillon 2008: 115). Most noticeably in recent years, digital tools can provoke a change in niches which can be constructed by the relationships between teachers, students, and content, and by the time and place of networks for learning. Mobile technologies have shaped not only social and cultural contexts, but also approaches to, and environments for learning. Mobile learning focuses not just on the technologies and devices themselves, but on the changes in how we engage with information. Learning experiences in wide and varied environments can be more fluid, interactive and multi-modal. The learner can be placed centrally, having access to information and opportunities to capture, store, manipulate, make meanings and share in a variety of linked environments (Mahari 2011, Pachler 2007, Cook et al. 2011).

Personalisation in learning with digital technologies can therefore be approached, not as a series of differentiation activities designed for pupils to 'catch up' or be 'stretched', but as the recognition and design of learning contexts which offer choices in the people and resources that are available to support skills, knowledge and feedback in learning as 'Person-Plus' (Green et al. 2006). Personal learning environments can be designed as 'off the shelf' digital tools, such as e-portfolios for managing, collecting, curating and planning learning activities. They can also emerge from active learners' more diffuse and haphazard construction of networks, repositories, projects and links. Some argue that digital technologies are both providing access to and changing the relationship with information which is ubiquitous and dynamic. The technologies afford connection with networks of information and people as 'nodes' who are engaged in sharing and constructing links and ideas. This moves beyond retrieval, as learners therefore demonstrate their capacity to know more through making connections through search engines and social media. Personal learning environments and networks underpin the establishment of distributed activities such as Massive Open Online Courses (MOOC) in which people with experience and expertise provide support to others learning particular topics. They contribute to fluid 'digital stores' of knowledge, making choices and decisions rather than accumulating and reproducing what it already known (Siemens 2005).

An example of such a context of a Personal Learning Environment in action is offered by McCrea, presenting his work using the tools and virtual spaces that were themselves the focus of his research enquiry into student teachers' use of online learning space for learning to teach mathematics:

- I have chosen to approach both the doing of the research and the reporting of the research using the following digital, networked and open practices
- I have been using Twitter to connect to networks of expertise, providing access to highly current and relevant content, and as a way to share my thinking with others
- I have been blogging about my research, which has encouraged me to reflect on and articulate my thinking, and to create a space for discussion and feedback on my ideas

- I have analysed data using tools that allow them to be represented digitally and shared openly (after they have been anonymised) for reuse and scrutiny in meta-analyses and parallel studies
- I am publishing this report openly on the internet with a Creative Commons license so anyone (with access to the internet) can freely access and build upon my work
- I have built this report as a hyperlinked document to offer readers a 'connected' experience, where they can be transported directly to source material
- I have designed this report so that readers can comment on it if they wish
- I have linked this report to my digital identity so readers can easily evaluate my credibility as a researcher, and connect with me if they wish.

> As you can see from this list, digital scholarship is more than just using technologies for effective collaboration and research – it is as much about embracing open values and exploiting the potential of technology for the benefit of the academy and society. This includes: championing the importance of sharing and being generous; recognising the need to practice inclusion on a larger scale; developing new systems for licensing content; and exploring alternative models for resourcing learning.
>
> (McCrea 2012)

Improvisation: 'Making worlds' in a learning life

Our theories of learning are expressed in the pedagogic decisions that we make in designing learning environments that face the future. We wish to equip learners to be purposeful, imaginative, resourceful and wise as they develop the capability to pay critical attention, be rigorous, analytical and evaluative as they create new knowledge communities and networks.

There is a paradox of human improvisation in remaking the world in social and cultural contexts which might be experienced as constraining. Socio-cultural perspectives of learning are optimistic, making room for creativity and improvisation, contingency and surprise, as well as recognition of complex relationships between people, meanings, goals and systems. Holland *et al.* (1998) argue that identity is situated in activities which are formed collectively. Drawing upon anthropological understandings of the work of Vygotksy, Bahktin, and Bourdieu, their concept of identity in practice pulls together four threads: figured worlds, positional identities, authoring selves and making worlds.

- 'Figured worlds' are contexts which are imagined and populated by communities of people who share 'webs of meaning' in which the interpretations of human actions are negotiated and shaped through activities, performances, rituals and artefacts.
- 'Positional identities' relate to activities which constitute understandings of degrees of power, status, hierarchy, rank, distance, privilege and affiliation.

The ways in which we take up social positions can cut across our figured worlds, being expressed and understood in our speech, dress, movements and manners of relating to others.

• Our identity in the 'space of authoring' acknowledges how we 'answer back' to the world, drawing upon our resources from our position in a social field and orchestrating them in order to respond in time and space. Our responses might be scripted or automatic in the situation, yet might also be unexpected, challenging and risk going against the grain of the social and cultural context.

• 'Making worlds' is therefore the way in which we imagine and construct new figured worlds of new communities and new social capabilities requiring resourcefulness and improvisation.

We hold on to our beliefs in our own worth and identity by trying to maintain a degree of competence, consistence, control and comfort (Claxton 1984). Yet significant learning occurs when individuals take risks in not being competent, consistent, in control and comfortable, and when they experiment with new situations and untried ways of doing things. Innovation and change do place people in positions of anxiety and lack of confidence, but provide the opportunities for new learning and new competences.

Such 'making of worlds' can be linked to the ways in which we 'story' our lives at particular moments to make sense of past, present and future, and to imagine and act in moving forward. Building on Bruner's description of the narrative construal of reality (Bruner 1996), Goodson and Sikes consider individual narratives within the wider meanings, projects and politics in which we act, highlighting the importance of 'stories of action in theories of context' (Goodson and Sikes 2001: 86). A theory of narrative learning draws attention to how learners' identity and agency are expressed in the quality and efficacy of their life narratives, which can act as sites for learning, 'through the ongoing internal conversation and external accounts that are undertaken as a genuinely lifelong process' (Goodson et al. 2010: 131). The quality of life narrative is recognized to have five dimensions: intensity of elaboration, levels of analysis, organizing principles of plot, chronological or thematic presentation, and degrees of theorization. The efficacy of our stories is related to the potential of the narrative for learning and action, for making a difference to learners' identity and agency. Our capabilities to make new worlds are fostered through our participation and position in communities; through our capabilities in recognizing and using tools for learning; through our 'answering back' and shaping our context; and through our narrative capital in constructing, maintaining and creating the unfolding stories of our lives.

Erstad calls for a new approach to research of young people as they develop their learning identities in a digital age. We need to understand how their 'learning lives' encompass longer trajectories than their involvement in formal education, and recognize how they are mobile between different settings, how they create a variety of niches, and how they create and express their identities in diverse contexts (Erstad et al. 2009). The Digital Media and Learning Strategy of the

McArthur Foundation has also focused on learning of young people in order to inform the design of new learning environments; the formation of networks for learning; and the creation of 'a new vision of connected learning that is interest-driven and more motivating, engaging, social, and supported by a constellation of mentors, educators, knowledgeable peers, and parents'.

Many children and young people arrive at school with an ease and familiarity with digital media and a confident and curious approach to new technology and the skills required to help them explore. They also have the potential to contribute their experiences of more informal and participatory learning in other contexts. Identity, tools and context are drawn together in the narratives of people's learning lives. Turvey offers a model of 'narrative ecology' to help describe the complexity of people's purposeful, intentional appropriation of digital tools in learning and teaching (Turvey 2010, 2013). People bring their narratives of their particular biographies and contexts to their use of digital tools. They are also part of an ecology of learning, participating in the adaptive and interactive relationships between the features of the individuals and the autobiographical and contextual factors in the environment. There are many aspects of the contemporary digital age which we would question, critique, resist and work to remake in order to address the challenges of the immediate and long-term future. Our theories of learning in a digital age should help us pay attention to the world as it is, as well as help us make a world which reflects our values and desires across the generations. Active learning in uncertain times calls for the development of learners' identity and agency characterized by confidence in criticality, contingency, adaptation, design, improvisation and creativity.

7

PROTOTYPING THE CURRICULUM OF THE FUTURE

Re-imagining the curriculum for the digital age

What is the future of the school curriculum in the digital age? This chapter traces a genealogy of recent curriculum developments and examines a series of contemporary proposals and prototypes for a 'curriculum of the future' (Young 1998). By adapting a family of 'how' questions from Rose (1999b) and Dean (2010), it asks how these prototypical models of possible future curricula have been assembled together, to address what problems, to achieve what objectives, in pursuit of what visions of the future, and in order to shape what kinds of pedagogic identities? This approach gives priority to how the curriculum has to be *thought*, and how certain forms of thought give rise to certain practices, techniques, and rationalities. In focusing on a genealogy of the curriculum of the future, we are seeking to emphasize how present thinking about the curriculum, and the potential educational futures it might pre-figure, has been shaped by prior histories of ideas and practices, contests, compromises and conflicts. Our emphasis is on the cybernetic styles of thinking that circulate as everyday ways of understanding and explaining contemporary society. How has such a cybernetic style of thinking, with its metaphors of connectedness, networks, flexibility, multiplicity, and interaction, been translated as a cybernetics of the curriculum?

The main sections of this chapter describe:

- a series of curriculum variations since the 1980s as the cultural conservatism of curriculum reforms in the 1980s was challenged by a post-Fordist emphasis on computers in the curriculum in the 1990s;
- a soft constructivist shift to 'soft skills' and competencies at the millennium;
- a form of networked interactive curriculum in the early 2000s;
- the recent emergence of 'open source' models of curriculum; and

- the potential rise of 'bio-pedagogies' as children's bodies and brains are made increasingly intelligible and amenable to pedagogic intervention.

Each of these sets of proposals for the curriculum embodies specific ideas and images about the future and about the production of 'appropriate' pedagogic identities. Bernstein (2000) has distinguished between 'retrospective' and 'prospective' pedagogic identities that may be projected and distributed through curriculum reforms. Retrospective identities are promoted through curricula intended to conserve aspects of the past and preserve them into the future. Prospective identities, however, are intended to contribute to the shaping of imagined futures. The curriculum is a pre-eminent site for the sculpting and promotion of pedagogic identities with which students can be encouraged to identify and experience themselves. By focusing on a genealogy of curriculum developments in the digital age, our argument is that curriculum reforms are paralleled by the generation of pedagogic identities, and we are concerned with the kind of prospective identities being made up through the contemporary re-thinking of the curriculum for the future.

Microcosmic futures

Researching curriculum change is important because the curriculum is a microcosm of the wider society outside of school. It is the 'intellectual centring' of schooling, communicating 'what we choose to remember about our past, what we believe about the present, what we hope for the future' (Pinar 2004: 20) and designating what society has decided as the worthwhile knowledge and culture to be passed on from one generation to the next (Apple 2000). Despite popular claims that the school curriculum is simply an inert body of content, decontextualized from the lives of students and the needs of society, the curriculum is in fact always historically contingent, contested, and its organization, content and form are constantly being (re)aligned with preferred visions of the future of society (Scott 2008).

Since the 1990s curriculum debates have been increasingly influenced by the same systemic narrative that rapidly changing digital technologies and networked communications, accompanied by 'long waves' of change in all social dimensions of economic, political and cultural existence, make curriculum reform essential (Goodson 2005; 2008). The pretext in this change narrative is that school curricula provide forms of highly insulated and self-enclosed bodies of academic subject content that are out of touch with a networked world in which interdisciplinarity, collaboration, and creativity have taken on more importance both for work and for social life. In this mode of thinking, the curriculum is increasingly being re-imagined as a 'post-standardized' (Hargreaves 2008) fusion of different technologies and configurations of knowledge, or hybridizations of technologies and epistemologies. We use the neologism 'epistechnical systems' to refer to this binding of technologies and epistemologies into hybrid curricular reconfigurations. Within the epistechnical systems of new curricula, particular ways of conceiving of technologies and devices, particular theories of learning, pedagogies and epistemological assumptions, and particular ways of imagining the future of society and subjectivities are all assembled together. Epistechnical systems, like all technical systems, are both *socially shaped* and *socially shaping*. As the products of design processes that take place in social contexts and real material circumstances, they are socially constructed and historically contingent, while as technical products or artefacts they function and act to influence and shape thought and action (Monahan 2005). Viewing curricula as epistechnical systems therefore asks us to consider the styles of thinking that galvanize them and the politics and values they embody and catalyze; to trace the authorities and the forms of expertise that have contributed to their shaping and deployment; and to understand the kinds of prospective behaviours, actions and pedagogic identities which are to be organized and shaped through such systems.

Furthermore, the notion of epistechnical systems serves as a reminder that curricula are not straightforward microcosms of a social reality that already exists beyond the school. Rather, they have a productive role as microcosms of *imagined* social futures – *microcosmic futures-in-the-making*. As Gough (2002) argues, curricula are not just 'out there' waiting to be discovered, but must be imagined and constructed. Any curriculum is the result of effect of myriad different ideas, concepts, theories, practices, material objects, and their historical and political networks of connections, being assembled together into new conceptual vocabularies and practical possibilities for thought and action (Fenwick & Edwards 2010; Harris-Hart 2009). Rose (1999b) refers to such 'functional networks' as 'technologies of schooling'. A technology of schooling consists of pedagogic knowledges, educational theories, classroom organization, timetables, techniques of instruction, supervisory regimes, behavioural and regulatory codes, curricular guidance, inscriptions, and digital devices, amongst other things, assembled and infused with the aim of managing students' capacities and habits. It is 'not implanted through the monotonous implementation of a hegemonic "will to govern" ' but is instead 'hybrid, heterogeneous, traversed by a variety of programmatic aspirations' (1999b: 54). In the term epistechnical systems, then, we are additionally trying to register this meaning of the 'technology' of the curriculum as a complex assemblage of human, material, discursive, and technical objects and actions that have as their main aim the generation of pedagogic identities for students inscribed in particular normative visions about the future of society.

Minor reformers

Curriculum reform in the digital age is now taking place in a more globalized policy context within which new educational ideas, trends and fashions are being borrowed, copied, interconnected, harmonized, and hybridized across distant and local sites, the public and private sectors (Rizvi and Lingard 2010; Spring 2009). Educational policy is increasingly being done through the techniques of 'governance', especially through the cross-sectoral 'policy networks' that span the boundaries between government and commercial interests, public and private sectors (Ball 2012). Theories of governance by policy networks, or 'network governance', propose that parts of the work of public education can now be done by actors from sectors beyond the traditional bureaucratic organs of the education system (Bache 2003; Parker 2007). In all of this, education is 'now being "thought", influenced and done, locally and nationally, in many different sites by an increasing number and diverse set of actors and organizations' (Ball and Junemann 2012: 9).

The curriculum proposals, prototypes and projects described below are the outcomes of a variety of new curriculum 'gatekeepers and licensers' (Bernstein 2000: 76) who have sought to translate images of the future into legitimate curricular prescriptions and pedagogic practices. These new gatekeepers and licensers increasingly come from outside the formal institutions of the state, from think-tanks, non-profit organizations, non-governmental and quasi-governmental organizations, charities and voluntary groups, and the philanthropic outgrowths of corporations (Williamson 2012), all of them proffering and seeking to propel their own new forms of expertise and authority (McLennan 2004; Osborne 2004). Their ideas and their solutions traverse and bisect political and ideological boundaries and they make it possible to think about the curriculum of the future in their terms. Rather than 'big-P' Policy reforms mandated by state power, the new expertise of the curriculum of the future works by assembling a technology of schooling at a 'minor level' of innovation and ad hoc improvisation, through delicate affiliations, distant attachments, and diverse associations between bit-part players, actors and agencies (Ball, 1994; Rose 1999b). These minor level *reforms-in-action* and the experts and authorities galvanizing them act as 'loose relays' (Jensen and Lauritson 2005) linking up 'questions of government, authority and politics' with 'questions of identity, self and person' (Dean 2010: 20). According to Ball (2012) through network governance, educational institutions are treated in exactly the same way as the person – as autonomous organizations and self-managing individuals. In making up a new curriculum of the future, new cross-sectoral authorities and experts are now being permitted to make up new pedagogic identities and to promote new ways for young people to see, think, feel and act in school.

Learnifying the curriculum

Network governance therefore permits a wider array of sources of authority and expertise into curriculum innovation. Perhaps the dominant sources of intellectual expertise shaping the curriculum of the digital age, as we will see, are increasingly derived from psychological ways of comprehending and understanding 'learning'. As Young (2012: 141) has argued, in the context of the knowledge economy and the increased interest in new technologies and media in education, terms like curriculum, with their assumed elitism, have been replaced with the popular 'slogans' of 'personalized learning', 'learning styles', 'learner choice' and 'learning centres', with the result that policy has increasingly been 'emptying out content' from the curriculum. Likewise referring to the 'learnification' of education, Biesta

(2006: 16–17) describes the emergence of a 'new language of learning' from a composite of constructivist and sociocultural theories of active learning, generic learning outcomes and a narrowly individualistic and psychological view of the learner. This shift in the language of curriculum is evidence of new ways in which the curriculum is thought and acted upon.

The 'learnification' of the curriculum is perhaps best exemplified by the rising profile of 'learning science' as an interdisciplinary approach to educational modernization. Learning science amalgamates psychological, cognitive, sociocultural, and, increasingly, neuro-scientific subdisciplines, along with computer science and engineering. Selwyn (2010: 67) notes that 'a "learning science" perspective on educational technology now pays close attention to the technical and the social processes of learning with digital technology', and to 'the perceived technological and psychological strengths and shortcomings of individual learners, their tutors, and educational institutions', but it is far less concerned with 'the wider social contexts that make up education and society'. Moreover, Popkewitz (2012) has shown how the school curriculum is increasingly being organized through 'psychological eyes' and psychological concepts. Through curriculum reforms based on the new language of learning, and on the interdisciplinary expertise of learning science, schools are now being exhorted to evaluate, know and act upon the 'psyche of the learner' through the 'gaze of the psychologist' (Rose 1999a) in the classroom.

We have already begun to argue that the shape and structure of the curriculum of the future is being influenced by the shift to network governance, the entry of diverse new cross-sectoral authorities, and the concomitant rise of new intellectual sources of 'learning' expertise in public education. In the conjuncture of the digital narrative and its imagined trajectory into the future, with the political decentralization of network governance, and with the new science of learning, a shared conceptual vocabulary and a consensual style of thinking about the curriculum of the future is being fabricated, a new cybernetic technology of schooling with the management and optimization of particular kinds of prospective pedagogic identities as its objective.

Post-Fordism

In the US and the UK during the 1980s curriculum was dominated by 'New Right' or 'neoconservative' policymaking, which imprinted it with a culturally restorative agenda which sought to protect and reproduce the historic 'virtues' of Western culture, and restore particular forms of social authority (Apple 2006; Ball 1990; Berliner and Biddle 1995; Jones 1989; Pinar *et al.* 1995). It was a 'curriculum of the dead', 'made up of echoes of past voices, the voices of a cultural and political élite' (Ball 1994, 45–6). These culturally restorationist impulses were, though, accompanied by more industrial and economic arguments favouring educational modernization and curricula appropriate to equip students with the habits, attitudes and self-discipline for the technical demands of the workplace. The recent history of curriculum reform can be seen as a series of ongoing attempts to accommodate both the restorationist and post–industrial modernizing impulses in educational politics (Young 2008).

In the 1990s, as Hartley (1997) noted, the curriculum was increasingly being 're-worked, re-tuned, made flexible', and 'framed by the imperatives of global capitalism' (1997: 45). The modernizing imagination produced a raft of proposals for a 'new vocationalism' of entrepreneurship and enterprise to be taught in 'high-tech' or 'post-Fordist schools' (Ball 1990). Such schools were to be transformed through the implantations of technological infrastructure, systems, devices and instructional programmes. In this post-Fordist context Goodson and Mangan (1996) argued that programmes of 'computer literacy' popularized in North American schools in the 1990s were based on a modernizing ideology, one embraced and embodied in the practices and beliefs of teachers and students, which assumed the future economy would depend on equipping students for jobs based on technology. By the end of the 1990s, as Selwyn and Brown (2007) showed, the establishment of 'education superhighways' and the boosting of 'human capital' had become a global education policy narrative.

As a consequence of this modernizing post-Fordist imagination, new technology and global cultural, economic and political trends have begun to exert more and more powerful influences on the curriculum (Rizvi and Lingard 2010). The conservative restoration of the 'curriculum of the past', with its specialist modes and hierarchies of knowledge, has come under siege from a 'curriculum of the future' characterized by connective integration and modularization, and by the promotion of generic skills and 'flexible learning' to meet the perceived demands of the job market for more 'flexible workers' (Young 1998). New technology and the internet specifically have been positioned as a 'policy device' to align schooling with 'global economic concerns of national competitiveness, the up-skilling of workforces, performative logic of the labour market, the dynamics of global capitalism and the intensification of the economic function of knowledge' (Selwyn 2011a: 66). According to Monahan (2005: 60), however, these technologies are 'ideally suited for the production of workers who can meet the needs of global capital without challenging the political status quo'. They are part of the 'nightmare of the present' and the 'politics of public mis-education' in the curriculum, 'the latest technological fantasy of educational utopia, a fantasy of "teacher-proof" curriculum' (Pinar 2004: 8). Too often, technology has been assumed to be a politically neutral, values-free and efficient means for presenting material to the learner, when in fact it embodies powerful value statements regarding the nature of education that are derived from the models of thinking of computer programmers (Pinar et al. 1995). Permitting the 'geeks of Silicon Valley' to make decisions about the 'future of education in the digital age' suggests that the curriculum will 'be determined by our judgement of which aspects of the information we pass between generations can be represented in computers at all' (Lanier 2010b, np).

It is important to put these arguments in the context of the shaping of pedagogic identities. Bernstein (2004) derived an important distinction between 'autonomous' and 'dependent' curricula. The autonomous form is justified according to the apparently intrinsic 'worthwhileness and value of the knowledge it relays', whereas the dependent form is justified by its market relevance; it promotes 'relevant skills, attitudes, and technology' and 'allows for an almost perfect reproduction of the hierarchy of the economy within the school or between schools' (Bernstein 2004: 212–13). These different forms of curriculum have major implications for the production of pedagogic identities. For Bernstein (2000: 60) in the post-Fordist restructuring of school curricula learners were encouraged to respond flexibly to whatever the economy required. This 'flexibilization of the self' was a complete reversal of the understanding that identity is derived from the dedicated specialization of subjects in strongly knowledge-centred curricula. Thus, while an autonomous and 'insular' curriculum of the past dominated the 1980s and 1990s it has been challenged by advocates of a more dependent and 'hybrid' post-Fordist curriculum of the future which is consistent with the boundaryless and flexible character of modern economies (Young 1998). As a result, contemporary education simultaneously faces towards 'an imaginary past' of 'heritage, traditional values and social order and authority' and towards an 'imaginary future of a knowledge economy, high skills and innovation and creativity' (Ball 2008: 205).

Soft constructivism

In the early twenty-first century, the 'imaginary' of the 'knowledge economy' has become the dominant political style of thought worldwide in education reform today, shaping shared thinking and common understandings in society (Kenway *et al.* 2006; Lauder *et al.* 2012; Rizvi and Lingard 2010). In the knowledge economy imaginary, knowledge is assumed to be at the heart of economic competitiveness. Better educated nations therefore have an advantage in the global economy, while well-educated students can aspire to high status, high skills knowledge jobs which can in turn assure them of rapid upward social mobility. Boundaryless portfolio careers replace lifelong employment. Muscle power is replaced by brainpower, and value is derived from integrating behavioural competencies with modular task components (Brown, Lauder and Ashton 2011).

The knowledge economy is a seductive and persuasive concept. Where critics of post-Fordist developments have pointed out its basic ideologies and economic reductionism, which appear to lock students and teachers into oppressive pedagogic routines and surveillance regimes, the knowledge economy is based on a 're-enchanting' policy discourse which appeals to the emotions, feelings, and other expressive dimensions of learning, and owes as much discursively to marketing theory as to economic policy (Hartley 2006). Through its distinctively 'soft' discourse, the knowledge economy has been accepted as an imaginary to which, despite the global economic recession, there appears to be 'no viable political alternative on the horizon' (Lauder *et al.* 2012: 5). The knowledge economy, then, should not be seen as functionally pre-determined by economic interests and needs, nor even as a reflection of an already existing reality or pre-given world, but as an imaginary construction being made up as a new social reality in which people are offered new ways of thinking, acting, and feeling. In this sense, the knowledge economy is part of the new discourse of 'soft capitalism' which speaks in metaphors of flows, complex networks, plasticity, and other 'looser organizational forms which are more able to "go with the flow"', rather than in post-industrial metaphors of hard structures and systems (Thrift 2005: 33).

Within this softening of the discourse, the curricular emphasis has been put on soft skills, competence, thinking, and other categories of 'know-how,' rather than 'know-what,' since most knowledge contained in the curriculum is presumed to become outdated very quickly in a globally fluid and fast-changing era. Many such arguments have been encouraged by researchers from the interdisciplinary field of the 'learning sciences' which prioritizes the design and application of new instructional programmes and ICT applications based on constructivist, constructionist, socio-cognitive and socio-cultural theories of learning. Learning scientists focus on such things as enhancing intelligence and thinking, boosting brainpower, building learning power, transforming learners' behavioural competences, enhancing cognition and metacognition or 'learning how to learn', and so on – a constructivist science of brainpower (Lucas and Claxton 2009). The hybridization of the learning sciences with the cyber-utopia of a knowledge economy suggests that it is possible to make calculations and predictions about the future by investing in brainpower and 'human capital.' As Foucault (2008: 229) argued, the formation of 'human capital' required for 'technical innovations' depends on making 'educational investments' not just in 'simple schooling or professional training' but in all kinds of cultural, health, psychological and behavioural enhancements. The soft skills and competences promoted by the knowledge economy narrative are, then, an amalgam of technical and psychological skills, capacities and abilities, or a unification of the inner-focus of 'mind and character' with economic purpose (Lauder *et al.* 2012: 11).

In sum, the knowledge economy imaginary has been assembled together through a particular interpretation of economic modernization with a re-enchanting discourse within which soft capacities have been aligned with constructivist theories of learning in order to 'create future learning environments and cultures in which the promises of constructivist, social, situated, and informal learning are realized' (Weigel, James and Gardner 2009: 8). Such soft constructivist pedagogies are intended to shape an 'independent, constructivistically oriented learner who can identify, locate, process, and synthesize' the resources of the internet and other new digital media (2009: 10). In soft constructivist pedagogy, less emphasis is placed on the control and dissemination of knowledge by educators and there is more investment on the part of the learner in hands-on, active problem-solving and knowledge construction.

A number of interesting curriculum developments have been galvanized by this soft constructivist unification of mind and character, technical and soft skills. Opening Minds, launched as a pilot project in the UK in 1999 by the Royal Society of Arts, Manufactures and Commerce (RSA), offers a 'competence' curriculum. Its competencies approach:

... refers to a complex combination of knowledge, skills, understanding, values, attitudes and desire which lead to effective, embodied human action ... at work, in personal relationships or in civil society.... Competence implies a sense of agency, action and value ... [T]he spotlight is on the accomplishment of 'real world tasks' and on a multiplicity of ways of knowing – for example, knowing how to do something; knowing oneself and one's desires, or knowing why something is important, as well as knowing about something.

(Candy 2011: 286)

Flexibility in the Opening Minds curriculum allows learners to concentrate on interconnected contemporary topics, community sources and real cultural contexts. In practice, Opening Minds is usually arranged as thematic and cross-curricular projects, with learners given greater apparent control over the selection, sequence and pace of their learning. It emphasizes the active, creative, meaning-making potential of the individual, and combines an entrepreneurial vocabulary of initiative, risk, team work, and brainpower with a softer discourse of community values, empowerment and cultural diversity.

Learning Futures is another UK programme that aims to support students to 'work and thrive as the world grows more interconnected, the environment becomes less stable, and technology continues to alter relationships to information' (Price 2011). It was developed by the philanthropic Paul Hamlyn Foundation in collaboration with the Innovation Unit, a non-profit spin-off from the former government education department under New Labour. Learning Futures re-imagines the future of school as a 'learning commons', a 'base camp' and a 'hub that creates connections' amongst a web of 'extended learning relationships' (Learning Futures 2010). In 2012 Learning Futures collaborated with High Tech High, a network of San Diego charter schools assembled to meet the challenges of preparing individuals for the high-tech workforce, to produce guidance on 'project-based learning'. The booklet speaks of project-based learning being 'passion-led', 'fun', 'exciting', 'inspiring' – it should have 'real world' relevance, stretch students' 'intellectual muscles' as 'expert learners', and 'ignite students' imaginations'. Its project-based pedagogy involves designing, planning and carrying out an extended project' using 'digital technology' to 'conduct serious research, produce high-quality work', and to 'foster a wide range of skills (such as time management, collaboration and problem-solving)' (Patton 2012).

Moreover, 'Learning Futures schools are seeking to develop pedagogies which transform the identity of the learner from "recipient of information" to thinking (and being) like a scientist, geographer, artist, entrepreneur' (Learning Futures 2010) and which also shape 'how students think, feel and act in school' (Price 2010). Here there is both an appeal to the technical skills associated with particular professions and professional identities, and a more affective appeal to students' cognitive, emotional and behavioural capacities. Clearly the project pedagogies of Learning Futures and High Tech High, like the competences curriculum of

Opening Minds, all lay emphasis on the production of the independent, constructivistically oriented learner who is able to mobilize the resources of new media and the internet, using his or her soft skills of interpersonal collaboration, problem-solving, and self-management. These are successful examples of a soft constructivist form of curriculum that is both 'linked to the reconstitution of education as a central arm of national economic policy, as well as being central to the imagined community the nation wishes to construct through schooling' (Rizvi and Lingard 2010: 96).

An additional dimension of these programmes, however, is the emphasis they put on the self. In focusing on competences, Opening Minds proffers a vision of the future of schooling which emphasizes the invisible, internal learning of the child. As Bernstein (2000) showed, the concept of 'competence' refers to the intentions, dispositions, relations and reflexivity, open narratives and personal projects of the individual, and the cognitive, affective and motivational dimensions of learning, rather than to the grand collective narratives of the disciplines that make up the subject-based curriculum. The student subject announced by 'competence' is active, creative, constructivist, and self-regulating (Hall, Thomson and Russell 2007). The image of the 'competent' child is largely derived from the psychological sciences, and linked to theories from the science of child development that flourished in the 1960s, particularly in the rise of radical and progressivist pedagogies which sought to emancipate the child from social disadvantage and repressive forms of authority through more 'child-centred' forms of education. Competence would thus be taken from the field of developmental psychology, translated into pedagogic norms of cognitive development, and realized in the 'pedagogic machinery' of 'new techniques for the cognitive maximization of the child' (Rose 1999a: 203). As Hartley (1997: 66–7) has found 'the "new" learner-centred subjects of the self' introduced as a result of progressive psychological intervention in the curriculum are intended to '*educate* us into the skills of personal effectiveness and emancipation. This is self-regulation of a very high order'. It is these self-centred subjects that have now been reworked in terms of competences and soft skills for the knowledge economy – a new image of the learner as a self-supervising, constructivist self. The psychopedagogies of soft constructivism teach students how to conduct and regulate themselves.

In competencies-based approaches, the curriculum is therefore being reformed as a set of psycho-techniques for intervening in the competences and capacities of learners in order to release future economic potential. As noted earlier, in the recent proliferation of dynamic social psychological subdisciplines in education – such as those embedded in learning science approaches – the subjectivities of students are being ordered through 'psychological "eyes"' (Popkewitz 2012: 177) which generate psychological concepts of motivation, problem-solving, learning to learn, and so on, in the curriculum. These 'curricular competences are not merely about what the child knows' but translate normative 'cultural theses' about 'who the child is and should be', which in turn embody 'learning how to see, think, act, and feel' (2012: 176–7).

A review of 'competencies curricula' and other 'wider skills' frameworks in Britain conducted in 2009 shows how such psychological concepts, and the perceptions, thoughts and actions they shape, have been reworked in terms of the human capital required for innovation in the knowledge economy. The report surveys the range of 'new smarts', 'creativity', 'orientations', 'capabilities' and 'capacities', 'dispositions' to learning', 'multiple intelligences', and the 'mental and emotional habits of mind' which are required 'if innovation is to be effectively developed in young people' (Lucas and Claxton 2009: 4). An accompanying report on the emergence of new theories of intelligence details all the 'smart elements' of contemporary psychological thinking required to transform pedagogy in a fast-changing world (Lucas 2007). These reports emphasize psychological discourses of cognitive competence, emotional resilience, resourcefulness, reciprocity and self-reflection, in line with recent claims that contemporary education is increasingly 'feelings'-centred and preoccupied with 'therapeutic orthodoxies' (Ecclestone and Hayes 2009) .

To sum up this section, soft constructivist curriculum programmes like Opening Minds and Learning Futures in the UK, and High Tech High in the US, hybridize inner-directed psychological discourse with economic entrepreneurialism to produce a blueprint for a psychotechnological curriculum of the future that has as its objective the production of new kinds of pedagogic identities made up to be constructivistically oriented and actively self-supervising. This curriculum of the future is to be built by amalgamating theories of competence, originating in the emancipation of individuals' active creativity in the 1960s and 1970s, with emerging twenty-first century theories of creative intelligence, the constructivist discourse and techniques of learning science, and the entrepreneurial 'new smarts' associated with innovation in a knowledge society. These initiatives and the models for the curriculum of the future they embody have all emerged from outside of the formal governmental and state institutions within which educational policy and reform is conventionally understood to be produced. Instead, they are the result of educational thinking in places like think-tanks, philanthropies, learned societies, commercial groups, and other organizations and agencies which are only loosely allied to the formal organs of public education. They represent how the reform of the curriculum in the digital age is increasingly being done by a heterogeneous range of actors from across the public and private sectors, especially by networks of cross-sectoral or 'third sector' actors and agencies which are stretching, dispersing and reconfiguring public education both globally and more locally.

Networked neo-progressivism

Some of the factors discussed above have been intensified even further in an emerging curriculum model we call 'networked neo-progressivism', which combines concerns about the relevance of the curriculum in a dynamic networked era with a more progressive and 'radical' emphasis on learning through active, authentic and situated inquiry. In the UK, Enquiring Minds was intended as a curriculum approach which would recognize that 'the relationship between pedagogy and curriculum and between 'school' knowledge and students' 'informal' knowledge is central to the search for more effective and powerful educational strategies for the 21st century' (Morgan *et al.* 2007: 15). Enquiring Minds (EM) stressed the need for students working with cultural knowledge – understandings and meanings related to specific events and objects – and with critical knowledge that would allow them to understand and critique the forces that shaped the world. Instead of fixed school knowledge, it advocated 'dynamic knowledge' to be the subject of a reinvigorated future curriculum. Dynamic knowledge is open to change; it is recognized as constantly in production, often contested, socially contextual, and transformed in reality. The EM guide stresses that 'the development of the curriculum starts with students' interests, ideas and experiences', and that the task for teachers is to help them 'explain, expand and explore further from that starting point ... to illuminate or decode aspects of their experience' (2007: 29). Moreover, EM acknowledged that young people's uses of digital media and technology offered a challenge to the curriculum:

> ... media corporations have figured out their own 'pedagogies' and become modern society's best teachers. The corporate curriculum of consumer culture has, in turn, become a yardstick against which the school curriculum and its associated pedagogies are assessed. ... However, consumer-media culture teaches particular sorts of knowledge, and these are based on affective pleasures rather than the more reflexive pleasures of knowing about and being able to interpret the world.
>
> (Morgan et al. 2007: 24)

In Enquiring Minds, critical pedagogic approaches are juxtaposed with the progressive concern to recognize and value the informal learning that occurs outside of school, including the learning that occurs in highly seductive, networked and mediated environments.

The New Basics programme developed and trialled in Queensland, Australia also blended a progressive agenda with the problematics of twenty-first century globalization. It promoted 'futures-oriented categories for organizing curriculum' and a way of 'managing the enormous increase in information that is now available as a result of globalization and the rapid change in the economic, social and cultural dimensions of our existence' (Queensland Education 2000). Its architects draw from Dewey and Freire, alongside the socio-cultural psychology of Vygotsky, to craft an approach which requires the solution of 'substantive, real problems' in learners' worlds, 'integrated, community-based tasks', and involves teachers as mentors, 'scaffolding the activities of 'novice' students (Queensland Education 2000). But as Rizvi and Lingard (2010: 107) have put it, the title 'New Basics' appealed to a cross-section of the educational community, from progressives who liked the notion of the 'new', to conservatives who liked its 'basics.' Family, locality, history, civic institutions and scientific understanding are established as the basics or the foundations to which the new demands of diversity, global communities, global forces, and new technologies must now be added. The New Basics project documentation speaks of 'new student identities,' 'new workplaces', 'new technologies', 'new times', 'new citizenship', 'new knowledges', and 'new epistemologies' in order to construct its futures-oriented curriculum. Rejecting the curriculum as a 'central authority' based on 'economies of scale for publishing, distribution and implementation of texts using print media', the project advocates 'using online, interactive technology for local, regional and global curriculum development and renewal' and the 'rapid prototyping, development and revision' of more specialised materials based on 'economies of scope'. Like Enquiring Minds, New Basics adopts a child-centred progressive vocabulary and conceptual repertoire which emphasizes the participatory democratization of the curriculum and increased freedom of choice for students, and interlaces this with the seemingly emancipatory potential of new technology and media.

The third example of the networked neo-progressive model is Quest to Learn (Q2L), a 'high school for digital kids' in New York City. The school's curriculum emphasizes 'systems thinking' and learning about the globally networked world' as a 'set of interconnected systems' (Salen *et al.* 2011: 2). Q2L students are described as 'socio-technical engineers' enabled to 'think analytically, and holistically, to experiment and test out theories, and to consider other people as part of the systems they create and inhabit' (2011: 46). It re-imagines school as a 'node' within a network that spans in-school, out-of-school, local and global, physical and digital, teacher-led and peer-driven, individual and collaborative learning spaces. The curriculum is organized as integrated interdisciplinary knowledge domains instead of separate subjects, each focused on 'researching, theorizing about, demonstrating, and revising new knowledge about the world and the systems of which it is composed' (19).

The theories underpinning Q2L's curriculum and pedagogies are explicitly based on constructivist and socio-cultural psychology, particularly insights generated by the learning sciences and the design of 'effective learning interventions' (33). Q2L 'posits learning as context-based processes mediated by social experiences and technological tools', a 'highly social endeavour' which takes place through 'situated practices' within 'communities of practice':

> In this way, a situated-learning view stipulates that learning cannot be computed solely in the head but rather is realized as a result of the interactivity of a dynamic system. These systems construct paradigms in which meaning is produced as a result of humans' social nature and their relationships with the material world of symbols, culture, and historical elements. The structures, then, that define situated learning and inquiry are concerned with the interactivity of these elements, not with systems in the individual mind.
>
> (Salen et al. 2011: 32-3)

Q2L mobilizes highly interactive pedagogies, modelled on dynamic social psychological understandings of tool-mediated learning and the interactivity of a dynamic system. Again, Q2L draws on the progressivist legacy of John Dewey, emphasizing pedagogies of 'inquiry', 'experience' and 'learning community', which it remixes through its technical discourse of open systems, networks, self-organization, non-linearity, connectivity, complexity, dynamism and interactivity. Q2L's 'evidence-based inquiry curriculum' is modelled to drop learners into 'inquiry-based, complex problem spaces that are scaffolded to deliver just-in-time learning' (Salen *et al.* 2011: xi). The pedagogies of the Q2L curriculum stress complex networked interactions and dynamically webbed learning, with students as knowledge producers, organizing and constructing knowledge as they interact with one another and with technologies and media.

In these three examples of networked neo-progressivism, with their emphasis on inquiry pedagogies and interactive technologies, an 'interactionist' model of curriculum is announced. 'Interactive pedagogy' centres on the importance of social interaction between teacher and learner, and it draws its conceptual force from twinning sociocultural psychology with aspects of human–computer interaction (Fendler 2001). Interactive pedagogy requires teachers to respond flexibly to the thoughts, feelings, questions and actions of the learner. The pedagogies of situated inquiry-based learning of programmes like Enquiring Minds, New Basics and Quest to Learn are the ideal flexible interactive pedagogic formats of such a curriculum. They elicit and promote an interactive pedagogic identity based on a new image of the school student as continually involved in a reflexive project of self-improvement and self-realization, perpetually developing competence through responsive forms of interaction and change. Or, as Hartley (2010: 788) terms it, an 'interactive social identity' which is 'at ease with interdependence' and 'making a contribution'.

However, in curriculum programmes like Q2L, interaction is no longer confined to interpersonal relations between teachers and students. Instead, Q2L also stresses dynamic interactive systems of networked technologies, complex systems, and human–computer interactions. These concerns are taken from the computer science aspects of the learning sciences that underpin the Q2L curriculum design. In particular, Q2L links its situated learning approach to insights from human–computer interaction. As Thrift (2005: 165) has pointed out, the recent study of human–computer interaction, along with more general developments in the social sciences, have stressed 'the situatedness of action, the importance of interaction and adaptation, and emergent properties'. This identifies the importance of situated learning, human–computer interaction, and complex emergent systems which form the basis of the Q2L curriculum.

In the kind of networked neo-progressivism of the learning sciences embodied by programmes like Quest to Learn, we are witnessing the birth of a new hybrid of cybernetic computer science (CompSci) and psy discourses, a new 'CompPsy ' complex. The characteristic style of thinking of CompPsy – its explanations, its ideas, its theories, its concepts, its key terms, its references and its relations – are derived both from psychological ways of understanding and representing human beings, and CompSci ways of thinking about technologies as connected, networked, interactive, and so on. But as a style of thinking, CompPsy does not merely explain; it also shapes and intervenes in the objects of its explanations – it shapes the conduct, thoughts, actions, and feelings of human subjects at the same time as it shapes computer code, software programmes and technical systems. Indeed, as Edwards and Carmichael (2012) suggest, the code in which educational technologies are programmed acts as a new kind of 'hidden curriculum in electronically-mediated learning' that encodes specific assumptions about students. Likewise, the design of educational technologies by learning scientists has been described by Popkewitz (2008: 155-6) as a method for 'designing people', or a 'technology of making people', through 're-engineering' particular forms of learning, actions and dispositions. CompPsy assembles and encodes a particular representation of learner subjectivity and pedagogic identity, and it promotes particular kinds of interactive technologies which elicit, promote, facilitate and foster the capacities, capabilities and qualities of such a pedagogic subject. The gaze of the psychologist in the classroom has been augmented with the code of the computer scientist. The result is the invention of a new kind of student subjectivity, an interactive pedagogic identity, that is both psychologically competent and inner-focused, and cybernetically coded to be interdependent, outwardly extended and networked.

The growth of CompPsy in the curriculum is no mere accident. Enquiring Minds and Quest to Learn are both curriculum interventions which originate in nonprofit organizations with particular stated objectives to explore the role of new technologies in the improvement of the future of education and learning. Enquiring Minds was developed by Futurelab, an educational R&D 'lab,' with funding from Microsoft's global philanthropic Partners in Learning programme. Futurelab acts as a cross-sectoral relay between commercial organizations and public sector institutions, bringing new discourses of technological change, new technological practices, and new kinds of subject positions for teachers and students into education.

Likewise, the Institute of Play, the nonprofit originator of Q2L, states that: 'Many social institutions are challenged to fulfil their missions in the complex new global reality arising as a result of advancements in digital technology' and it promotes educational technologies and institutions in which technological activities of 'creating, sharing, mixing, modifying, searching out, curating, critiquing and commenting' are seen as the foundations for building 'new kinds of communities and ecosystems of engagement' (www.instituteofplay.org/context). The Institute of Play's ideal model of learning is a persistent ecosystem of real and virtual learning, where pedagogic activities are networked and connected, spanning sites of public education and spaces of informal learning, and blurring the traditional differentiation of domains like work–play, politics–entertainment, school–home, and global–local. These organizations, and the initiatives they promote, are precedents for a new and emerging imaginary of education that is distributed, networked and convergent across a variety of media, across formal and informal spaces, and across public and private sectors and hybrid cross-sectoral, and which increasingly takes place through human–computer interaction.

Curriculum 2.0

In this section we examine the recent proliferation of a 'futures' discourse in thinking about education and new technology, particularly the educational futures thinking of British think-tank Demos and nonprofit Futurelab, although also in the connectionist style of thinking deployed by US nonprofit the Institute of Play and in the 'connected learning' programme in which it plays a significant role. These organizations all operate cross-sectorally, spanning boundaries between private and public sector approaches to education reform, bringing new discourses into the curriculum, and they advocate for educational futures in which activities hitherto carried out by public sector institutions are to be thoroughly distributed into networked ecosystems of learning.

In one of several collaborations, Futurelab and Demos authors have written about a 'post-school era' in which 'schools wither away as young people increasingly learn through networks, drawing on personal and domestic digital technologies as sources of learning and ways of connecting with others', within which the 'Curriculum 2.0' prizes 'experiences such as collaborative learning, personal development, self-monitoring, creativity and thinking skills' (Facer and Green 2007: 52). A provocative series of hypothetical 'educational visions' for 'future schools' is provided in another Demos/Futurelab collaboration by Green, Facer and Rudd (2005), who explore scenarios such as: the complete dismantling of formal educational institutions to be replaced by home-based digital online learning; the 'dissolving' of schools into the businesses and cultural resources of individual cities, towns and communities; and the 'extension' of school into community life itself. The scenarios are constituted particularly by a discourse of flexibility. All boundaries between informal and formal education are imagined as increasingly flexible; formal learning is imagined to be optional or flexible in terms of attendance; learners are imagined as taking more control over the selection of learning resources and sources, with learning content more customized, malleable and adaptable; new spatialities and temporalities of learning are opened up by the flexing of timetables, the compression of space by realtime digital communication; and schools are reconceived as 'learning spaces' designed to afford different ways of working (team working, personal reflection, information access) rather than being organized rigidly around faculties and subject disciplines. The curriculum in such future schools is replaced by learning, and is imagined to be taking place in the connections and links that young people are empowered themselves to make between different learning satellites and hubs. Young people are encouraged to become network experts who are able to locate resources and people to support their learning. They are to become, in effect, the creators of their very own self-curriculum empowered by a radically democratic, informal pedagogy of self-learning via the internet, and fully active participants in the shaping of their own learning futures.

The notion that learners can be involved in shaping their own educational services has been a main plank in the educational futures thinking at both Demos and Futurelab. Demos advocates educational services which have been 'co-produced' through 'open source methods' such as 'stakeholder engagement', 'flexible experimentation', 'participatory consultation', 'open innovation', and a culture of 'pro-innovation governance', and 'open public learning collaboratives' (Mulgan and Steinberg 2005: 39–40). This is in line with other think-tank ideals of 'open source' public services and education (Owen *et al.* 2006; Parker and Parker 2007), including those modelled on 'open innovation' methods in the private sector, especially in high-tech design and science parks (Horne 2008; Bentley and Gillinson 2007). Similarly, building upon an educational futures programme carried out by Futurelab, Facer (2011: 9) proposes conceiving of formal education as 'a primary motor for *shaping* social values, ideas, beliefs and capabilities rather than as a servant of society.' Rejecting the idea that schools should act normatively to 'future-proof' young people for the challenges they might confront in adulthood, Facer (2011: 10) calls for schools to be understood as 'future-building' institutions, with the 'right' to 'act as resources for their communities to imagine and build the futures that they want rather than simply training them for the futures they have been given'.

The post-schooling scenario reanimates the counter-cultural 'de-schooling' agenda of the 1970s for the era of eBay and MySpace, reaffirming its assault on institutionalized schooling, its attack on assembly-line learning, and its commitment to self-determined learning through informal networks and community bonds. The radical idea of learning webs imagined by de-schoolers is now, it seems, more realistic as learning networks are made possible through the internet to society as a whole (Jarvis 2004). A much more convivial new hidden curriculum, like the de-schooled society of progressivist imagining, facilitates communication, co-operation, caring and sharing between free agents and distributes learning into a nomadic network of authentic practices, cultural locations, and online spaces (Suoranta and Vadén 2010). Whether the desire for a 'technical fix' expressed in the post-school utopia will, however, as Hartley (1997: 155) anticipated, lead to the high-tech de-schooling of society, 'leaving us all enmeshed in Illichian webs and nets' – is debatable, and it seems more likely that education will continue to be 'framed within the competing claims and complexities of democracy and capitalism'.

Moreover, the kinds of pedagogies imagined by the post-schooling scenario need to be understood in the context of the 'productive' effects of conducting interactions and transactions with non-human smart technologies, databases, and all manner of devices and software in 'code-textured worlds' (Mackenzie 2006: 48). As Thrift (2005: 156) argues, software operates like a 'pocket dictator' generating 'mass-produced series of instructions' for conduct in everyday life.

Indeed, in the post-schooling scenario of connected, networked learning, we are witnessing the emergence of a new mode of transactional pedagogy in which pedagogy may be understood to reside in the transactions between humans and non-human devices, in the instructions provided by computer code, software, and smart data. The power of database-driven technologies such as search engines and social networking sites shape and configure users in subtle ways, not least by collecting, sorting and aggregating personal data and using the results to build up rich personal and aggregate user profiles. By turning these database-driven technologies to pedagogic purposes, tools like Google search and Facebook have become some of society's most powerful teachers, experts in personalization, gradually building up personal data profiles of their 'students' and in turn offering them experiences and information that have been selected, sifted and sorted according to each one's personalized needs.

But what of pedagogic identity in this post-school imaginary? Instead of the 'schooled' identities associated with mass schooling and the centralization and standardization of the curriculum (Austin, Dwyer and Freebody 2003), the pedagogic identity promoted by post-schoolers is a smart, self-fashioning identity augmented with digital extensions. Indeed, the curriculum in the post-schooling era is no mass-produced product, but reconceived as a self-curriculum, a personal 'project of the self' (Bernstein 2000; Rose 1999b) to be pursued in a borderless eco-system of online and real pedagogic spaces, formal and informal sites, schools and homes, through public and private sector providers and increasingly through cross-sectoral agencies and actors taking on the job of public education (Ball 2012). Within this new ecosystem, interactivity becomes a key capacity, as learners are encouraged to construct pedagogic experiences for themselves through constant ongoing interactions with informal pedagogues sourced at a distance through the internet, as well as through transactions with non-human devices, software and databases.

Biopolitical pedagogy

A further development that is beginning to show signs of potential future impact on curriculum is the optimization of life processes through medical, neurological and pharmaceutical technologies. Life itself has increasingly become available to experimentation (Lemke 2011; Rose 2007). Neuroscience and 'smart drugs' designed to enhance cognitive function are visible examples of new techniques of life enhancement and optimization that have the potential to impact significantly on the purposes and organization of the curriculum in the future. Facer (2011: 54) has documented some of the more spectacular implications of bio-technology for the design of the school of the future, arguing that 'we need to recognize that the people in the school will be mobilizing, in their lives outside it, a range of digital, biological and pharmacological resources.'

Perhaps more subtly, research has also begun to explore biopolitical issues of the management and control of children's bodies for political and economic purposes. New concepts of 'biopedagogies' and 'body pedagogies' (Evans and Rich 2011) refer to how students are increasingly expected to work on their selves and their bodies. Evans, Davies and Rich (2009: 401–02), for example, suggest that the body will become a 'credential' for future employment as employers look for 'aesthetic labour skills' such as appearance, size and body shape, 'making the bodies of young people "legitimate" sites for intervention and control and raising the question of whether schools should have a role in developing such presentational awareness in them in preparation for the labour market.' The preparation and optimization of bodies as aesthetic credentials for the economy is a powerful dimension of biopolitical pedagogy, with young people positioned as a biopolitical resource to colonize the future economic order (Lee 2008).

A rather different example of a biopolitical intervention into curriculum has been provided by the Learning Futures programme in the UK. Learning Futures promotes a pedagogy of 'spaced learning' based on neuroscientific theories concerning the repeated stimulation of neural pathways connected to recalcitrant memory (Learning Futures 2012). According to the theory, credited to R. Douglas Fields of the National Institute for Child Health and Development in the US, the formation of memory does not just depend on the stimulation of neural pathways, but on the gaps or spaces between stimulations. These insights have been translated into the pedagogy of spaced learning, a highly structured form of transmissive pedagogy where lessons are organized as a series of three fast 'inputs' separated by breaks or pedagogic spaces for 'distractor' activities. The first input focuses on presenting information, the second focuses on recalling information, and the third focuses on understanding information. The distractor breaks inserted between these three inputs must be designed so that they do not stimulate the same neural pathways as those of the inputs but allow those parts of the brain to 'rest.' The implications of spaced learning for curriculum organization are significant, not least because its advocates claim that it is possible to condense and accelerate a normal school year of curriculum material into just a few hours of pedagogic activity. In the Learning Futures approach, spaced learning methods are juxtaposed with enquiry-based project methods, with spaced learning viewed as the ideal transmissive approach for efficient and fast acquisition of relevant subject content and student-led project-based learning promoting the application of skills and knowledge in context.

In the spaced learning approach, the constructivist and interactionist pedagogies of inquiry and projects, with their roots in progressivist education and development psychology, have been combined with neuroscientific theory to produce a more biopolitically significant form of pedagogy. Learning Futures, as stated in other documents, promotes pedagogies based on extended learning relationships, with the school as a 'base camp' in a network of formal and informal learning opportunities, including the use of mobile devices and social media to provide open connectivity to the curriculum and peer learners. Learning Futures seeks to activate a pedagogic identity which is extended and connected to networks of people, technologies and knowledge, yet also neurologically optimized through a pedagogy of neural stimulation and neurocognitive dynamics.

This may seem to be fairly banal form of biopedagogical intervention, but it is significant insofar as it represents a concrete pedagogical intervention into the neural pathways of the brain itself. It is a biopolitical pedagogy 'centred on the body as a machine' and on its 'disciplining, the optimization of its capabilities' (Foucault 1990: 139). This is not to suggest that other pedagogies do not already do the same thing, only less overtly in relation to the neuroscientific evidence. Rather, it is to claim that in Learning Futures we can see the expertise of neuroscience being translated into a new way of understanding and acting upon children in schools – a new way in which the curriculum is being *thought*. Spaced learning is a new 'neuropedagogy' using neuroscientific theories and findings to shape teaching and learning (Patten 2004).

It is important to state here that neuroscience is first and foremost a technological discipline which depends on a complex apparatus of devices, instruments, techniques of measurement and visualization, such as MRI and PET scans. Any pedagogy derived from neuroscience, therefore, must be understood as being shaped by technology rather than a response to the 'nature' of learning in the human brain. As with biopedagogies of body work which seek to optimize aesthetic labour skills, or with psychopedagogies which seek to maximize children's psychological well-being, spaced learning, as a nascent form of neuropedagogy, anticipates a possible future in which children's brains will be subject to repeated interventions with the aim of cognitive enhancement and optimization. This presages the construction of a new prospective pedagogic identity, a source of identification shaped and promoted to deal with social and technological change through pedagogies of repeated neural stimulation and relaxation. This prospective neuropedagogic identity is a biopolitical construct, encouraging students to understand, relate to and manage themselves in terms of their neural optimization, and encouraging a culture of education in which educational achievement is measured in terms of the efficiency and effectiveness of neuropedagogy.

Social realism

In contrast to the cybernetic imaginaries associated with many recent curriculum innovations, an alternative emerging trend in curriculum theory focuses on the importance of the 'powerful knowledge' contained in school subjects. In social realist accounts, there is broad agreement that students need access to socially powerful knowledge so that they can navigate the differences between theoretical and everyday knowledge and the differences between school and non-school knowledge (Allais 2010; Moore 2004; Wheelahan 2012; Whitty 2012; Young 2008; Young and Muller 2010). The concept of 'powerful knowledge' refers to the epistemological status of knowledge itself, its conceptual basis, its structure, what it can do and how it is organized. According to social realist perspectives, socially powerful knowledge provides reliable and 'testable' explanations or ways of thinking; is always open to challenge; is conceptual as well as based on evidence and experience; enables those who acquire it to see beyond their everyday experience; is acquired in specialist educational institutions, staffed by specialists; is organised into domains associated with specialist communities such as subject and professional associations; and it is often but not always discipline-based.

However, again, according to social realists, in increasingly globalized debates about education and the knowledge economy, the concept of knowledge is increasingly being emptied out as the boundaries between theoretical knowledge acquired in school and everyday common-sense knowledge acquired through experience outside of school are collapsed. Young (2012: 141) argues that this collapsing of the boundaries between socially powerful knowledge and experiential knowledge is reflected in the replacement of institutional terms such as education, curriculum and school with concepts such as 'learning styles' and 'personalized learning', and by 'the idea of 'user-generated knowledge' that is associated with YouTube and Facebook.'

In contrast to both the content-based curriculum and the competence-based curriculum, a social realist model of the curriculum of the future recognizes that knowledge is socially constructed, but that it is the very fact of its social constructedness within highly specialized communities of enquiry that gives it its legitimacy. Specialist conceptual content and knowledge provides students with access to the ways of thinking that they will need in order to make sense of the world and to build their identities as learners. This means that it is not enough for a curriculum to focus only inwardly on the self and on the experiences of the learner, nor to focus only on the acquisition of esoteric powerful knowledge. A social realist curriculum of the future represents, as Young (2008: 34) states, 'the historically located collective achievement of human creativity'.

The social realist position and its translation into new scenarios for a curriculum of the future challenges many of the assumptions in which learning takes place through a learning web of loosely connected nodes of knowledge. It also challenges the idea that learning ought to be associated with generic competences acquired independently from specialist knowledge *or* the conservative idea that knowledge is fixed, static, and universal. Instead, it proposes that a curriculum of the future should recognize the dynamism of how specialist knowledge is produced and acquired, particularly in the context of network-based globalization.

Conclusion: Smart schooling

The prospective pedagogic identities promoted by many recent curriculum initiatives are all derived from a smart, cybernetic style of thinking about the future of education. Such thinking proposes that students' learning will be increasingly network-based, spanning boundaries between school and out-of-school sites, formal and informal spaces, public, private and cross-sector provision, and will consist increasingly of human–computer interactions as well as enhanced interactivity between teachers and learners.

These programmes represent a futuristic vision of education for the next century which challenges the acquisition of pre-packaged 'schooled identities' as embodied in formal curricula and instead extends the schooled identities of young people into an ongoing process of self-fulfilment and personal lifestyle creation that has now become the characteristic feature of lifelong learning in a modern consumer-media society. However, the social realist perspective questions the extent to which such approaches can take students beyond the common-sense knowledge acquired through everyday experience and introduce them to the socially powerful theoretical and conceptual knowledge associated with specialist communities.

The proposed reconfiguration of formally schooled identities as fluid, self-fashioning digital learning identities embodied in many recent curriculum programmes also links young people more forcefully to changing working circumstances where the emphasis is on workers who can continually improve themselves, upskilling and retraining as changing job descriptions require. These enterprising selves, permanently unfinished projects, and interactive social identities are represented as the necessary human capital required by the globally networked knowledge economy. In the smart, post-school imaginary of the future of learning where the curriculum is more an individual project of the self, a self-curriculum focused on the interactive development of the individual, students' pedagogic identities are refashioned through a variety of technological extensions, informational reticulations, and communicational connections.

Moreover, through advances in neuroscience and biotechnology, life itself may now be technologically manipulated, enhanced and optimized, and the potential for educational optimization is now a real possibility, as indicated by new 'smart drugs', 'biopedagogy' and the emergence of new 'neuropedagogies'. In such futures, it seems, human functions are to be extended and distributed through new material syntheses with technical systems, instructed by software code, and reticulated into networks of increasingly post-human hybrids. The challenge for educators is to rethink the future of the curriculum as it is emerging in the present. This chapter has aimed to make different curricular futures intelligible, to show how the curriculum is being made thinkable, and thus to make it amenable to being thought and made another way.

8

BEING A TEACHER IN A DIGITAL AGE

Ready, willing and able to teach in a digital age

Our understanding of how we might learn with and through the use of digital tools is growing, and we are aware of the changes in the roles of teachers in the learning of others. Digital technologies afford opportunities for thinking differently about how, when and where we engage with networks of knowledge, expertise, experience, practice, feedback and challenge. Their use can challenge many of the familiar ways in which we design learning environments, both formal and informal. Yet there are core questions of our pedagogy – 'What do we teach?', 'How do we teach?' and 'Why do we teach this in this way, here and now?' – which ground us in our cultural purposes for education and the relationships between teachers and learners in our societies. Digital tools for learning have a presence in the wider context of a digital age which has economic, social and cultural implications for education settings and arenas. We argue, however, that although these tools might create a disturbance in our more familiar learning environments, there are characteristics of good pedagogy that endure and manifest their strength in the ways in which they are flexible and adaptable, not brittle and unchanging. Our focus is not just on teachers in schools, since the places and contexts for learning in a digital age extend beyond these boundaries. The role of teacher is conceptualized as pedagogical – that is, a role that relates to the design of and engagement in learning experiences which are grounded in values and purpose within society and culture.

A 'teacher' in a digital age is not a technical deliverer of an instrumental curriculum, but a curriculum-maker who draws upon knowledge and experience, and is able to improvise in pedagogic moments and relationships. The pedagogic identities of teachers weave together micro and macro elements of 'making worlds' for learning. We would expect that teachers would be as purposeful, imaginative, resourceful and wise as they would wish their students to be. On a day-to-day basis, they would demonstrate ways of paying critical attention, being rigorous, analytical and evaluative, creating and participating in knowledge communities and networks. These moments and relationships are played out in the macro structures of policy, politics and the state's purposes of education. We argue that the learning identities of teachers in these times are developed in the interaction between the depth, scope and reach of their individual knowledge, and the wider context of their values, culture and practice.

Becoming ready, willing and able to teach in these times is a complex puzzle, a reticulation of interconnected elements and dimensions. Teachers' 'stories of action in theories of context' (Goodson and Sikes 2001: 86) reveal a breathtaking choreography of the relationships between people, knowledge, pedagogy, tools and a complex interaction of contexts. A teacher is engaged with the learning of others, either formally, with a professional identity associated with an educational institution and a process of accreditation; or informally as a person from whom others learn through interaction, mutual interest and support. Spiritual teachers have been described as those who walk with learners in the 'borderlands' between the sacred and profane, supporting them in the discipline and mastery of coming to understanding (Countryman 1999: 96). Teaching is not just a performance of trained competences to a recognized standard, but a profound expression of ourselves, our ways of knowing, our cultures and our contexts. Not everyone can teach (even among those accredited to do so), but there are many from whom others learn.

Teaching demands imagination, value, purpose, knowledge, ability, practice, reflection and perseverance. Teachers are often recognized in their communities, formally and informally, as engaging meaningfully with other people – peers and novice learners – and with their field of expertise and knowledge. They are often seen as being in their 'element', with an engagement in and passion for their area of endeavour. They are reflective about their practice, have a desire to improve and do better in both their teaching and in their field in order to do things well. They engage in dialogue with learners to create a space for conversation, consideration and knowledge-building. They are also in dialogue with their subject domain. They embody a pedagogical presence – physically and virtually – offering scaffolding, feedback and mentorship for learners. They bring experience and knowing to a situation to help make vivid the concepts, connections and values in a subject area. Their deep understanding of a field enables them to open up learning experiences for contingency and improvisation; and to ask challenging questions that reveal wider horizons and complex possibilities.

We argue that being a teacher, as a professional or as a member of a learning community, requires conceptual depth, contextual scope and pedagogic reach. We also consider the concept of 'didactic analysis' which offers a useful framework for thinking about pedagogy that is grounded in a critical approach to the purposes of teaching, and presents a series of questions which help to link pedagogy with the wider context of the digital age. We conceptualize teaching in the 'digital age' as a creative endeavour of depth, scope and reach rooted in imagination and value, whilst recognizing the tensions and contradictions in the formal purposes and contexts of education.

Conceptual depth

What might it mean to 'know your subject'? This discussion takes place against a backdrop of debate about the nature of subjects and curriculum in our education systems – from curriculum for nursery schools, to subject departments in universities. Do 'subjects' represent the core truths of ways of knowing in human intellectual endeavour or exist solely as social practices of people in contexts of power and dominance? In chapter seven we presented an overview of seven prototypes of curriculum knowledge: cultural restorationism, post-Fordism, soft constructivism, networked progressivism, Curriculum 2.0, biopolitical pedagogy and social realism. We suggested that social realism and disciplinary specialisation offer a useful way to describe and explain 'powerful knowledge' which is conceptual as well as experiential, organized into domains with boundaries associated with specialist communities, yet open to challenge and social construction. Teachers and learners can develop their identities in relation to these subject boundaries and communities, as well as in relation to the social, cultural and political context of education and schooling adopting network progressivism and Curriculum 2.0 approaches.

The conceptual depth of educators' understanding relates to questions of knowledge in subject domains in which disciplinary structures, conceptual organizations and principles of enquiry are identified and debated. We use the term 'domains' to encompass an identifiable core and network of knowledge, skills, dispositions and modes of enquiry that underpin curriculum in all phases of formal and informal education, from early years to adult education. A domain might be characterized by thematic and/or epistemological coherence and integrity; capacity to contribute to educational aims; developmental, cultural and instrumental relevance; and continuity across age phases (Alexander 2010). Such a view of domains would include constructions of traditional and cross–disciplinary subjects such as mathematics, geography and citizenship, as much as dance, environmental science and jazz. Teachers demonstrate their depth of engagement in, and commitment to their chosen domains whilst recognizing some of the interdisciplin-ary connections. Such a view of teacher knowledge relates to the 'What?' questions of curriculum and culture. It is informed by understandings of social realism, discussed in Chapter 7 in which 'powerful knowledge' is seen as arising from specialized human, social activities within communities over time (Young 2008).

Underlying this discussion is an understanding of 'knowing a subject' as being intimately related to 'doing' within a community and culture. Subject domains are socially constructed by thinkers and actors asking questions and solving problems – the concepts, principles, procedures that make up a subject at any one time. Science, history, philosophy, for example are shared and passed on to others, but also shaped, contested, debated and developed. Subjects can't be captured and preserved in amber, because our quest to describe, explain and understand is dynamic, and is itself acted out within a culture and amongst other people. The debates about the meaning, canon and relevance of our 'subjects' have raged in craftsmen's guilds and university departments since mediaeval times. School knowledge of subjects is reflected in curriculum guidelines and textbooks that change frequently within generations and within regions. The placing of creationism in the subjects of science or religion in certain states in the US, for example, or the presentation of history as exceptional achievements of the powerful of a nation in the UK, are but tips of the icebergs of the debates about knowledge and knowing a subject.

An educator's depth of knowledge focuses on knowing with dimensions of skill, commitment and judgement grounded in understanding of conceptual organization and principles of enquiry in a domain. Robinson describes people as being in their 'element', drawing attention not to their celebrity, but to their motivation and talent in persevering in order to do it well (Robinson 2010). Gladwell's discussion of the 'outliers' – the extraordinarily successful in our contemporary society - also notes their 'success' is rooted in 10,000 hours of committed practice and 'flow' (Gladwell 2009). Knowing something well, and indepth, does not come easily or quickly – for some, it is a lifetime's work. Teachers who are knowledgeable in their field can model this skill, commitment and judgement with their learners. They are aware of how they are part of a dynamic construction of knowledge, rooted in the traditions and experience, yet always being updated and renewed. 'Depth' is recognized not in comprehensive coverage of content nor necessarily accreditation – each of which are problematic to define – but in a capability to demonstrate understanding of the 'subject imagination' of the field, to be able to draw upon traditions, concepts, themes, and expertise, and to honour those who have contributed to thinking and practice over time (Egan 2008).

Knowledge of 'subject' – its products, disciplinary questions, procedures, methods – is developed collectively and in a context. It is warranted, accessed and constructed with peer review and challenge contributing to communities of authority. Such an approach to 'powerful knowledge' raises interesting challenges in formal teacher education, from initial training to ongoing continuing professional development. Ellis argues that subject knowledge is as complex, dynamic, situated, active and participatory as other categories of knowledge (Ellis 2007, Ellis *et al.* 2010). Although this is the wider experience of informal educators' knowing in subject domains, he draws attention to three common 'problems' with the ways in which 'subject knowledge' is discussed and conceptualised in formal professional training and accreditation of teachers, namely – dualism, objectivism and individualism.

The first problem is one of 'dualism' in which subject knowledge is presented as content that is fixed, stable, principled, universally agreed and context-free, and such 'theoretical knowledge' is considered to be different from situated 'practical and professional knowledge'. Yet subject disciplines are characterised by discovery, change, disagreements, paradigm shifts and debates. He argues that:

> It is these dynamic, social processes that make subjects worthy of study and allow us to *work* in the subject. The word "discipline" captures the power that is distributed among those who work in the subject; learning in a subject is also a process of being disciplined into the ways of thinking and feeling about subject concepts, a process of both regulation and innovation that is intrinsically a collective activity ... .
>
> (Ellis 2007: 450)

The second problem of 'objectivism' is detected in the views of subject knowledge as a 'thing' or commodity, as reflected in much educational policy for curriculum and teacher education in England over three decades (Ellis *et al.* 2010). The subject-as-thing can therefore be measured, audited and 'topped up' on training courses if found wanting. Such knowledge can therefore be accumulated bit by bit in a linear fashion which does not reflect participation in a dynamic field. The third problem of 'individualism' conceptualizes knowledge as cognitive and personal, rather than in relation to other people and environments, and any deficits or cracks in a body of knowledge need to be repaired by the individual. Ellis argues that 'subject knowledge' is therefore interactive and emergent, and 'exists as much *among* participants in the field as it does *within* them' (2007: 458). Such a cultural and historical view of knowing a subject has profound implications for the design of teacher education in mutual partnership between different knowledge communities and networks.

In a digital age, our knowing something well, having skill, commitment and judgement in a field will include, not only developing expertise in a Person-Plus environment and context, as discussed in Chapter 6. We will understand the place of learning *with* technologies, but also recognise how digital technologies have played a role in shaping our ways of knowing in the subject domains themselves (Loveless and Ellis 2001). Digital technologies in music, for example, have not only enabled the storage, sharing, imitation, remix, transposition and transcription of music files, but also the creation of novel sound in composition and performance, changing the nature and qualities of sound with electronics, changing the nature of 'reading and writing' music (Landy 2012). In visual art, digital technologies act as tools working in the medium of pixels and vectors to make visual meanings. The tools offer affordances for mimicry of other tools and techniques, from paint to film. They also afford opportunities to manipulate visual images in new ways, incorporating novel combinations of filters, leaving traces of earlier versions and ownership, and introducing hypertextual dimensions and networks (Mitchell 1994, Loveless 1997). As the young children in a hypertext project noted, they were able to create 'fat pictures' that brought new combined purposes of illustration and connection to their place in more traditional text in their online topic books (Lachs 2000). The debates about literacy practices with digital technologies are longstanding and lively (Snyder 1997, Erstad *et al.* 2009, Gee 2003). Ellis argues that emerging multi-modal and mobile activities are not the end of literacy practices as we know them, but are texts in themselves and that we 'need to pay attention to technology as an intrinsic part of becoming literate' (Ellis 2001: 147). Selinger highlights the accessibility of mathematical ideas represented by digital tools in not only the cognitive support of tools such as calculators, but also the mathematical problems that could not be solved without computers, such as the four-colour theorem (Selinger 2001). Hawkey draws attention to how digital technologies have the potential to re-present 'the whole domain of the public understanding of science, rather than ... as a delivery mechanism representing a particular establishment view' (Hawkey 2001: 106).

Networked neo-progressivism draws attention to the wider context of the landscape of a digital age, yet social realism recognizes the knowledge of communities that contribute to those contexts and the identities shaped by knowledge relations and networks; understanding how the technology becomes part of the subject takes time for practitioners (Long 2001). The presence of digital technologies does not ensure depth of knowing, and the affordances for searching, storing and sharing can often facilitate a surface engagement with subject domains. Yet, if we engage with a subject imagination, we can recognise the affordances of the technologies for representing and extending concepts and principles within a domain. We can move from being a 'flaneur', strolling through an environment of information, to a 'connoisseur', recognising, appreciating and curating knowledge in action.

Contextual scope

An educator's 'contextual scope' is their awareness of their relationship to other people, ways of knowing, identity, culture, politics, networks and power within wider contexts. They know where they fit, or not, in the wider landscape, and how what they do as a teacher might matter and have value. Contextual scope is related to the 'why?' questions of the values underpinning learning and teaching. It is reflected in the relationship between knowing a domain and knowing why that might have significance in human endeavour and culture.

The German traditions of *Bildung* can provide a useful framework for thinking about contextual scope, although the brief description cannot do justice to the 'fuzziness' and complexity of meaning in translating these words. *Bildung* can be translated as 'erudition' – the qualities of learning which contribute to the overall aim of the growth of an educated personality that can participate in and contribute to the social and cultural context. It also contains understandings of Kant's ideas of a culture of freedom in which learners develop self-regulation of their cognitive, social and moral lives, through critical thinking, transformation of their worldviews and self-concepts (Hudson 2011). The roles of values and beliefs are explored by Alexander in his model of 'good primary practice' (Alexander 1996, Alexander 2010). He distinguishes mere practice, which draws upon *political* and *pragmatic* dimensions of teaching, from 'good practice' which draws upon three further dimensions. The *conceptual dimension* provides a map of the essential elements of teaching, learning and the curriculum; the *empirical dimension* provides evidence about the effectiveness of practice and particular teaching strategies; and the *values dimension* is related to the beliefs which shape views of childhood, children's needs, society's needs and a coherent view of what it means to be educated. He argues that the *values* and *empirical* dimensions are the key elements to good practice:

> Education is inherently about values; it reflects a vision of the kind of world we want our children to inherit; a vision of the kinds of people we hope they will become; a vision of what it is to be an educated person. Whatever the other ingredients of good practice may be, they should enable a coherent and sustainable value-position to be pursued. Values, then, are central.
>
> (Alexander 1996: 96)

The early chapters of this book explored the complexity of the contexts in which we develop our identities as learners in the digital age. The contextual scope of educators is reflected in their social, cultural and political relationships and connections with other people, communities and power, as well as in the values that shape wider understandings of what it means to be educated in a digital age. Our engagement with wider horizons and more complex connections is a reflection of Friere's call to read the world as well as to read the word, and intimately related to our own learning lives and biographies (Goodson and Gill 2011). Constructions of 'a digital age' – characterized by cybernetic thinking of communication networks and flows, mergers and emergence of identities, and the challenges to the place, time and communities for learning as valued by different communities – provide a dynamic social and cultural context in which teachers make pedagogical decisions. In parts of economically developed societies, technologies are becoming 'embedded in the fabric of every activity – they are part of the infrastructure that supports learning, communication and participation' (Livingstone 2008: 6). It can be argued that the contemporary world of childhood and youth in developed countries and socio-economic élites is permeated by digital media which shape not only communication and interaction, but also the material, cultural and political contexts and activities. These changes challenge our values of inclusion and participation at local levels. They also challenge our global ethical position on our 'connectedness', from understanding how digital media and networks might be used for 'social good', to acknowledging the implications of the means of production and distribution of digital technologies from PCs to mobile phones.

The 'digital divide' has both local and global implications, not just for the resources needed to provide infrastructure and devices for access to digital communities and networks, but also for the quality of experiences and agency that people have once they have gained access. The variety and relevance of digital content makes a difference to the engagement of groups of people of different ages, cultures, languages, interests and levels of literacy. Critical and inclusive digital participation demands knowledge, skills and understanding of the social, cultural, political and economic backdrops to everyday life (Carvin 2002, Selwyn and Facer 2007).

> To be a 'digital participant' in the context of such changes and the debates shaping them means making informed use of digital technology and media in one's own life. It means recognising how technology and media offer opportunities for people to participate in new kinds of social activities, civic life, learning and work, and it also means recognising that technology and media must be challenged and questioned rather than accepted passively.
>
> (Hague and Williamson 2009: 3)

As children and young people roam through unmediated sites and networks where they might encounter disturbing or inappropriate material, or experience bullying and unpredicted use of personal information, parents, teachers and policymakers express concerns about 'digital safety'. Guidelines, filters and policies have emerged, not only as codes of conduct for the protection and mediation of young people's experiences and privacy, but also as mirrors of the compelling debates in our wider society about control and surveillance as well as our wise and mindful participation through our digital media (Byron 2008, Craft 2011).

On the wider, global stage, we can see the potential of digital networks for information and activity to inform social and political challenge – from Wikileaks and the Arab Spring, to the Occupy movements and riots in England in 2011. The case of Kony 2012, a campaign video which went 'viral' in March 2012, attracted millions of viewers and a global social media campaign to capture Joseph Kony, leader of a group abducting children to be soldiers in Uganda. The global networks and communications through Facebook, YouTube and the mainstream media disseminated the campaign information. However, they also drew attention to a backlash of criticism of inaccuracies and simplifications in the story, and raised questions about the role of global activism through online discussion rather than engagement with structures of power to effect justice and change. Education networks and charities subsequently developed a range of teaching resources to help young people to engage with and understand the deeper issues of child soldiers and living in the midst of war (Drabble 2012).

In 1969 Postman gave a presentation, quoting Hemingway and declaring the purpose of education to be the nurturing a 'built-in, shock-proof, crap detector' (Postman 1969). The need for such detectors is as apparent in the early decades of the twenty-first century. Underlying the critical examination of the values that underpin the contextual scope of education in a digital age is the concept of 'cost'. We need to be aware of the commodification and individualization of education as a social good, and the gains and losses of the introduction of any new technologies in social processes (Postman 1993). We also need to acknowledge the actual human and environmental cost of our desire for ubiquitous and mobile learning identities. Hall (2011) argues for the development of three themes of critique and action:

against pedagogies of consumption; for social justice and ethical imperatives; and recognition of the place of energy availability and climate change. Pedagogies of consumption promote the desire for the latest upgrades and innovation and the commodification and privatization of content. Our involvement in social justice and ethical imperatives are highlighted in our position on the implications of the abuse of workers' rights in factories producing digital mobile devices; tax avoidance by mobile phone operators; and violence in areas, such as the Democratic Republic of Congo, where the mining of minerals for the manufacture of mobile technologies are drivers of conflict and wars. The sustainability of our consumption and renewal of personal digital technologies is questioned, from the resources in manufacture, to the carbon footprint of each server and search in 'the Cloud'.

Hall asks if it is morally acceptable to dissociate ourselves from the global impact of our development and use of digital tools. In discussing what is to be done to address these challenges, he suggests the following as starting points:

> ... educators might think about the following in their lives and practices.
>
> How do we lobby vendors, providers, re-sellers, commissioners, in order that they justify the extraction of the materials, and the production processes, that they use for their products? How do we do this in association with others and in our daily work? How do we work for technological decisions, like procurement, outsourcing etc., to be based on community need related to a critical analysis of socio-environmental impact and human rights, rather than on a discourse of cost-effectiveness, monetisation, economic value, and efficiency?
>
> How do we lobby for consensus in open systems architectures, focused upon open-sourced, community designed and implemented technologies?
>
> How do we work for a digital or technological literacy that is ethical? How do we work up an ethics of mobile learning?
>
> (Hall 2011)

The prospective identities of educators themselves are sculpted and promoted by 'styles of thinking' of a digital age. Contextual scope therefore touches upon our values, our capacity to pay attention to the world around us, and our critical and imaginative participation.

Pedagogic reach

'Pedagogic reach' describes the connection between educators and learners, where the purposeful designs of learning environments and experiences are successful in the transformation of understanding. Pedagogic reach is the joy of teaching – not in transmission of content or competence – but in those interactions and moments that Saljo describes as a 'shortcut to insights' (2004: 492). Hillocks argues that there *is* a recognition of a distinctive pedagogical knowledge which identifies 'good teachers' who have an understanding of how people learn and become knowledgeable. This distinguishes them from others with similar subject knowledge, but who lack the abilities to represent and 'transform the world' in order to support learners in the construction of their own knowledge:

> Like most other areas of teacher knowledge, pedagogical content knowledge appears not to be some body of pre-existing knowledge that teachers dip into, but knowledge constructed by the teacher in the light of the teacher's epistemological stance and conceptions of knowledge to be taught, learning theory and students. The most important of these appears to be the epistemological stance.
>
> (Hillocks 1999: 120)

It is the aspect of teaching where teachers do not assume a necessary shared understanding with learners and therefore take pains to represent, explain and provide opportunities for constructive learning processes, which Hillocks claims to underpin effective knowing and teaching. He quotes Aristotle: 'In general it is a sign of the man who knows and the man who does not know, that the former can teach and ... men of mere experience cannot' (Hillocks 1999: 244).

Knowing how to be a teacher is an active, social and authentic process, distributed between other people, tools and contexts (Putnam and Borko 2000). Our theoretical models of teacher knowledge have developed in response to the changes and challenges to the national and local contexts in which teachers practice. Here we argue that our ways of thinking about teacher knowledge have changed. We have adapted our understandings of the influence of digital tools on pedagogical knowledge, as well as placing such knowledge in a wider context of purpose and design in a digital age. Shulman's early descriptions of the integration of individual teacher knowledge which underpins pedagogical reasoning countered teacher education reform in the US in the 1980s which separated 'subject knowledge' that was taught in specialist university departments, from 'teaching methods' which were taught in education departments (Shulman 1987). His later work recognized the situated nature of teacher knowledge, and Shulman and Shulman (2004) analyzed and visualized the relationship between individuals, educators, their communities and the wider contexts of 'capitals' which influence the impact of policy and resources upon practice in these different levels. See **Fig. 8.1**.

More recent theoretical models of teacher knowledge and pedagogy acknowledge the cultural, historical contexts of activity and tools in building knowledge in practice (Ellis *et al.* 2010), the philosophical foundations of value and purpose in didactic analysis (Hudson 2011), and the influence and disruption of digital technologies in learning, as new subject, context and tool (Mayes and de Freitas 2007, Beetham and Sharpe 2007, Trifonas 2012, Webb 2011). Watkins and Mortimore offered a definition of pedagogy as 'any conscious activity by one person designed to enhance learning in another' (1999: 17), which draws attention to the role of design which affords opportunities for such moments. The term 'design for learning' encapsulates pedagogy as a 'systematic approach with rules

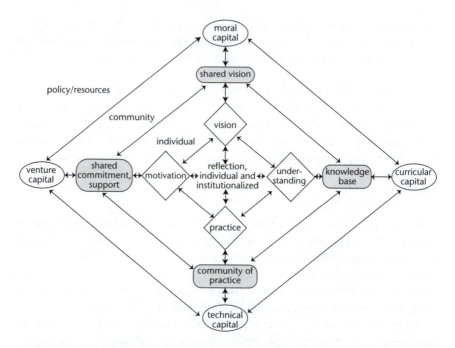

FIGURE 8.1 Levels of analysis of teacher knowledge; from Shulman, L. S. and Shulman, J. H. (2004) How and What Teachers Learn: A shifting perspective, *Journal of Curriculum Studies*, 36(2) March–April 2004: 257-71.

based on evidence, and a set of contextualised practices that are constantly adapting to circumstances' (Beetham and Sharpe 2007: 6). Pedagogical design expresses the congruence between the content, context, teaching strategies and underlying theories of learning and value (Mayes and de Freitas 2007, Kalantzis and Cope 2010, Hudson 2011). The concept of design encompasses preparation through planning, invention, drawing, pattern and intention. Hudson describes teaching as a design profession and elaborates on these activities:

> Planning is associated with intention and meaning, whilst invention is related to creativity, conceiving, originating and constructing. It is in the combination of these dimensions of planning and invention, or creative design that the professional judgement of the teacher is brought into focus
>
> (Hudson 2011: 224)

When digital tools are involved, there is an additional complexity in pedagogical reasoning, whether their role is as a resource, as a tutor, as an environment or as a tool (Webb and Cox 2004). Koehler *et al.* offer a model to describe the interactive, relational nature of teacher knowledge which encompasses content, pedagogy and technology. Building on Shulman's early framework, they conceptualise their model as 'Technological Pedagogical Content Knowledge' (TPCK) as the intersection of Content Knowledge, Pedagogical Knowledge and Technological Knowledge and 'argue that intelligent pedagogical uses of technology require the development of a complex, situated form of knowledge' (Koehler *et al*. 2007: 741).

Angeli and Valanides (2009) suggest that the model described by Koehler *et al*. does not discuss *how* the potential and constraints of ICT tools might 'push back' to shape both content and pedagogy. They argue that TPCK emerges from the interaction between pedagogy, content and technology and is new knowledge, which needs an explicit focus in order for teachers to make the connections between their knowledge and experiences. It is this 'new knowledge' that is a challenge to practising teachers, as well as to curriculum in initial teacher education and joint practice development. Research to date indicates that progress in this 'new knowledge' and pedagogical innovation is still slowly developing in formal education, both in the preparation and planning for purposeful learning with digital technologies, and in the understanding of TPACK in subject domains (Voogt *et al*. 2012, Valtonen *et al*. 2011).

The design role of a teacher in a 'Person-Plus' environment is to offer activities, spaces and tools for learning. Digital tools play a role in knowledge and identity construction through the mediation of human action, embedded in culture, and distributed through dialogue with others and the use of artefacts and tools (Wertsch 1998, Salomon 1993, Perkins 1993, Pea 1993, Salomon and Perkins 2005). Environments for learning can be designed to embody understandings of 'Person-Plus' showing the characteristics for access to knowledge, retrieval, representation and construction of new knowledge. Access to tools and artefacts alone does not necessarily lead to learning – indeed, Perkins refers to this as the 'finger-tip effect' (Perkins 1993). Teachers contribute a design purpose in context, synthesis of experiences, and guidance in making meaning, gradually ceding the role of 'executive function' as learners engage in higher order thinking and understanding. Indeed, involving learners in sharing the pedagogical reasoning underlying activities contributes to how they manage their own learning and support other students in the process (Webb 2011).

The pedagogic challenge to educators is far from trivial. There is the potential for significant change in the times and places for learning, as virtual and mobile environments for learning develop (Cook *et al*. 2011). The members of the networks and communities can also develop different approaches to pedagogical presence and role between themselves (Jared 2008). Digital tools cannot only support teaching by mimicking more familiar resources in the curriculum, but also change the conceptual frameworks within the subject too (Loveless and Ellis 2001). Laurillard calls for a focus on teaching as a 'design science', in which teachers have a professional responsibility to improve their practice by documenting and sharing their design patterns for learning. She places contemporary teaching practice clearly in a digital age in which digital technologies provide both the context and the tools for learning and teaching:

> The difference that marks out the early years of the twenty-first century from any previous period in education is that digital technologies not only enable a change to treating teaching as a design science, they also require it.
>
> (Laurillard 2012: 226)

Pedagogical reasoning and design in the context of a digital age, can be influenced by teachers' perceptions of the wider context and purpose of their practice. The social and cultural context frames the underlying purposes of the experiences that teachers design for learners. There is no one, shared and agreed rationale for the use of digital technologies to support learning and teaching, and teachers have expressed a range of different reasons why they think they incorporate them into their teaching. A study of the interaction between primary teachers' perceptions of ICT and their pedagogy, indicated that there were different reasons offered for the use of digital technologies in practice, reflecting the ambiguities in styles of thinking of educational technologies. First, teachers described the impact of the technologies in society and on their roles as teachers engaging with a curriculum which prepared learners for an 'Information Society'. Second, they discussed the role of ICT in the curriculum, as a discrete subject area to be taught which would have vocational benefit in the use of digital technologies in future work. Third, they described ICT as both a teaching resource to support content in other curriculum areas, and as a tool for learning in more autonomous and participatory ways. The future vocational potential of ICT was considered in more detail than the more immediate possibilities of using digital tools for learning in the present (Loveless 2003b).

A later study with primary and secondary teachers focused more closely on these more immediate possibilities for learning. Teachers were prompted to describe not only the surface level of the activity with different tools, such as word processors, spreadsheets, search engines, graphic packages and animation software, but also the deeper learning purposes that underpinned the planned activities. The analysis of the deeper learning intentions demonstrated 'clusters' of purpose within the curriculum subjects: distributed thinking, engagement, communication and collaboration and knowledge-building. The context in which the teachers were making their decisions in preparing, planning and assessing students' learning, demanded an interweaving of their knowledge of the content, the needs of their students, and their technological capability with a deeper understanding of purpose and value (Fisher *et al.* 2012). See **Table 8.1**.

We have argued that pedagogic reach is a characteristic of teacher knowledge which is expressed in designs for learning which are purposeful, complex and built on experience and expertise. It happens when there is a connection and understanding for a learner in relation to a teacher who has taken pains – explicitly or tacitly - to design an experience which has the potential for learning. Pedagogic reach is, however, not an instrumental model and soulless scheme for drawing up learning objectives and delivering lesson plans – it requires preparation which is rooted in moments of creativity, contingency and complexity rather than being predictable and easily planned. As such, it can be understood as improvisation

TABLE 8.1 Teachers' knowing how to use technology: Exploring a conceptual framework for purposeful learning activity

Conceptual categories	Purposeful learning activities
Distributed thinking and knowing	• accessing resources • finding things out • writing, composing and presenting with artefacts and tools which may structure activities in particular ways
Engagement	• exploring and playing • acknowledging risk, uncertainty and provisionality • working with different kinds and degrees of interactivity • responding to immediacy
Community and communication	• exchanging and sharing communication • extending the context of activity • extending the participating community at local and global levels
Knowledge-building	• adapting and developing ideas • representing understanding in multi-modal and dynamic ways • testing and exploring hypotheses. • evaluating ideas and understanding

(Loveless 2007). The playing of jazz has been used as a metaphor to describe teacher performance of professional knowledge, where 'the best teachers are not only well prepared, but also practised and skilful improvisers' (Humphreys and Hyland 2002: 11). Indeed, jazz improvisation between a group of musicians can be an expression of 'depth, scope and reach', indeed, Eagleton (2008) describes such moments as the 'meaning of life'! Improvisers are able to draw upon their established conceptual understanding of music and their practised techniques, and use them in flexible and novel ways. Jazz musicians can improvise together to high levels of skill and originality when grounded in elements of the history, philosophy, technique and practice of jazz, and aware of the possibilities of the moment for the music, fellow musicians and the audience (Nachmanovitch 1990, Purcell 2002).

> Improvisation is not just related to experience and skill, neither is it 'content-free', but it is expressed within and between subject domains. Creative individuals in different knowledge domains demonstrate understanding of the underpinning concepts and traditions, whilst knowing how to 'break the rules' to present original combinations of ideas and outcomes. Those with expertise in subjects are able to use their conceptual understanding in making decisions about tools and technologies to support and explore Didaktik analysis … .
>
> (Loveless 2007: 153)

Didactic analysis

Our discussion of educators' depth, scope and reach is framed by the concept of didactic analysis, prompted by questions which draw attention to the connections between the particular and focused designs for learning and underlying purposes of education in our societies (Klafki 2000). Didactic analysis offers a perspective on teacher knowledge that is rooted in human purpose, nurturing active and thoughtful design for learning, not instrumental transmission of information. We argue that it offers an approach to grounding our practice as teachers and educators in the wider context of a digital age. The model of technological pedagogical content knowledge (TPCK) is an attempt to draw together the complexities of content, pedagogy and tools. It does not, however, explicitly address the interactions with context and scope. A more substantial approach to the questions of pedagogic reach is offered by the concept of didactic analysis, which makes connections between designs for learning and the underlying purposes of education within contexts.

Understandings of the German word '*Didaktik*' are not familiar in the Anglo-American tradition, indeed the word 'didactic' is often used to describe a transmission approach to instruction from a teacher or lecturer to an assembled group of biddable pupils and students. The debates in the UK still lack the strong theoretical basis that can be found in continental Europe, where pedagogy is considered to be a subject domain taught within universities.

> ... a key characteristic of the different traditions was how the model for teaching in the United States came to be based on a business model. Under such a model teachers are perceived as a 'labour force' which is to be motivated and managed through narrowly conceived systems of control and accountability. It is further noted how such an atmosphere was not encouraging to independent and autonomous action.
>
> (Hudson et al. 1999: 8)

The concept of '*Didaktik*' in European traditions contains some powerful and useful approaches to planned support for learning and the relationships within the triad of student, teacher and subject–matter. The questions 'What shall we teach?', 'How shall we teach?' and 'Why are we teaching this?', bring together culture, knowledge and practice in teachers' intelligent action. There has been growth in recent publications and seminars to assist academics, policymakers and practitioners in developing new perspectives on the challenges to curriculum and pedagogy. Hudson and Meyer have edited an important collection of research papers from the European Didactics, Learning and Teaching community, which brings together debates in teaching and learning, teacher education, teacher research, didactical design and lesson planning, subject didactics and educational theory, and demonstrates how the concept of didactic in the European tradition might contribute to a more nuanced and complex understanding of teacher knowledge (Hudson and Meyer 2011).

We design for learning, selecting and interpreting what occurs in schools and educational settings, not because we are directed to do so by national curricula and strategies, but because it matters that learners move from being novices to experts within our society. Teachers and schools play a role in mediating between 'reality' – the natural and social worlds as shared within cultures and societies – and novices being initiated into those cultures and societies, developing their understanding of their potential to be human. Menck (1995) presents an image of learners and teachers in schools and classrooms engaged in activities of thought, practical action and performance – from embroidering a traycloth and painting a picture to singing Handel's *Messiah*. School children do not produce outcomes as accomplished as experienced practitioners, but these are accepted with pleasure and pride within a society because they indicate the learners' developing participation and contribution 'as if the future of the world depended on it' (Leach and Moon 1999: 120). This understanding of 'Didaktik' is useful in highlighting the role of mediation, symbolic representation and transformation of subject content knowledge for novice learners and children in a cultural context.

Preparing to teach is itself a 'draft' experience which requires an open mind in designing opportunities and possibilities for learning. Careful preparation for teaching and pedagogic reach requires substantially more than careful planning of particular teaching episodes. Wolfgang Klafki's approach to didactic analysis starts with the significance, meaning and value in preparing teaching activities grounded in relationship to learners as both individuals and as human beings with a cultural past and anticipated future (Klafki 2000):

1. What wider or general sense of reality do these contents exemplify and open up for the learner? What basic phenomenon or fundamental principle, what law, criterion, problem, method, technique or attitude can be grasped by dealing with this content as an 'example'?
2. What significance does the content in question or the experience, knowledge, ability or skill to be acquired through this topic already possess in the minds of the learners?
3. What constitutes the topic's significance for the learner's future?
4. What is the structure of the content which has been placed into a specifically pedagogical perspective by questions 1, 2 and 3?
5. What are the special cases, phenomena, situations, experiments, persons, elements of aesthetic experience, and so forth, in terms of which the structure of the content in question can become interesting, stimulating, approachable, conceivable, or vivid for learners?

The first three questions open up the analysis needed in the preparation for teaching, and the last two start the design process. Hudson argues that the design phase is extended explicitly to consider the relationships between teaching situations, pedagogical activities and learning environments which include digital tools (Hudson 2007, 2011). He then develops Klafki's five questions further:

In the *Design* phase, he includes:

6. What teaching situations, pedagogical activities and learning environments are to be designed?

In the *Development* phase:

7. What are the potential roles for ICT in terms of designing teaching situations, pedagogical activities and learning environments?
8. Which materials and resources are to be developed to support the creation of teaching situations, pedagogical activities and learning environments?
9. What is the role of the teacher?

In the *Interaction* phase:

10. How will students interact with the technology, with the teacher and with each other?
11. How will the students demonstrate their achievement of the intended learning outcomes?

And in the *Evaluation* stage, focusing on formal education:

12. How will students evaluate what they have learned in a formative way? How will this activity be recorded? How does this aspect relate to formal processes of summative assessment, examination and accreditation?
13. How will the quality of the teaching situations, pedagogical activities and learning environments be judged and evaluated?
14. How will the questions of the student learning through these experiences be judged and evaluated? (see Hudson 2011: 228-30).

These questions root understandings of pedagogy in the 'why?' questions, making critical connections with the wider landscapes of knowing in our society and time, embodying what is to be human through our teaching. *Didaktik* is therefore closely linked to universal, educational questions, placing the discussions of pedagogy clearly in wider social, cultural and political meanings for teachers and education systems as well as for educators who engage with learners in informal settings which are marginal to mainstream education. Hudson's work highlights how our growing familiarity with concepts of *Didaktik* has offered fresh perspectives on meaning and intentionality, attention to studying, tools for holding complexity, and the role of the teacher. Didactic analysis itself is creative: subject imagination in a meaningful context is able to make new connections between concepts, often novel, and metaphors, analogies, phenomena and examples. These are then fashioned purposefully in the design of teaching–studying–learning experiences and environments. Originality may lie in the moments of improvisation from the 'draft' character of careful preparation. Value is closely linked to the local and wider purposes of education, of *Bildung*, in which *Didaktik* is expressed (Loveless 2011).

Educators with depth, scope and reach can develop learning identities that reflect ways of thinking about the relationship between content, context, and the 'tools of the trade' for learning and teaching in our times. Fisher *et al.* describe the dangers of models of teacher professional development and identity which 're-tooled' individuals for new competences in a changing system, as components on a production line. They call instead for a 'renaissance' in understanding the complexity of teacher learning:

> We face a considerable challenge. The processes of teacher learning are complex, even messy, and teachers' current working circumstances contain inherent constraints. Yet the possibilities for real change in the system do exist. If we can bring the technologies into situations that resonate strongly with teachers' sense of professional and moral purposes, we may yet see what might truly prove to be a renaissance, in which teachers would employ digital technologies for 'understanding, reflection, ingenuity and creativity', and, through these, support their own learning in new ways.
>
> (Fisher et al. 2006: 41)

9

CONCLUSION

Final thoughts

In this book we have argued that education, creativity and technology should be understood as objects of thought, conceived and shaped by different types of questions, problems and forms of analysis. In writing the book we have tried to make sense of our own different ways of thinking, based on our different disciplinary perspectives and professional academic outlooks, and to account for how these differences have shaped our views and responses to education, creativity and technology. But we have also seen how, in the period named as the 'digital age', contemporary thought is increasingly saturated with cybernetic metaphors and vocabularies. Our own disciplinary perspectives are constitutive of this cybernetic infiltration of thought, as we have seen, for example, in the fascination of social theorists with ideas like the network society, mobility, flows, virtuality, and so on.

These terms have become something like an operative syntax for our times, inserted into a variety of social, cultural and organizational network theories and used to redefine contemporary understandings of everything from personal identity to cultural globalization to corporate restructuring. Terms such as network, then, do not just describe and explain things; they establish and shape the ways in which it is possible to think about them. Things and thinking are, in this sense, inseparable, indistinguishable from one another. The proliferation of network-based ideas in all sorts of places, including policy, economics, urban planning, the mass media, businesses, public sector reform, and a myriad of other places, though intensely contested by other researchers, is evidence of the circulation of a certain style of thought which seems increasingly taken for granted, common-sense – just everyday thought.

The future of education, too, is now increasingly thought and shaped in such terms, as they have been translated through a variety of educational theories derived from sociological, psychological, and computer science disciplines, and channelled through the objectives of an increasingly diverse array of authorities and experts.

Attempts to intervene in education are always, in a sense, utopian activities that presuppose a better way of doing things, a better type of person, a better society which is to be achieved (Dean 2010). The future of education is a translation of what various authorities, whether in government education departments, think-tanks, or the product development departments of technology companies, want to happen, according to what future visions of education, and in accordance with what dominant modes of thought. The term 'translation' is key here: it recognizes how formerly distinct ways of thinking, different vocabularies of thought, have been transformed and shaped into a shared language.

What this book has sought to trace is the variety of ways in which a cybernetic style of thinking characteristic of the digital age has been translated in educational theories, in accounts of pedagogic identities, in the popularization of creativity, in approaches to learning, in re-imagining of the curriculum for the future, and in the reconfiguration of pedagogy. All of this constitutes a set of ways in which the future of education has been made intelligible and thinkable – as a 'better' future, with better learning institutions, which can contribute to the betterment of society. This kind of thinking has turned the persuasive political imaginaries of the globally networked knowledge economy and cool capitalism into a seemingly hegemonic reality to which there is no viable alternative. Within these techno-euphoric dreams of the future, new learning identities have been made up and promoted, not just in school curricula and pedagogies, but in the more seductive imagery of a future learning landscape where learning has been distributed everywhere, learners have attained autonomy for their own pedagogic pathways, and networked digital media has taken over from the school as society's most successful learning institution.

Thinking, however, changes over time, and what we also hope to have highlighted is how dominant ways of thinking today have resulted from a complex genealogy of convergences and combinations, rather than from any single lineage or simple line of descent. Educational technology in schools has changed over 30 years, not only in the policies, devices and applications used, but also in how it is thought and made intelligible, and in the theories of learning that underpin activities and practices, from constructionism to interactionism and connected learning. Educational technology has been thought not only as a mode of delivery of curriculum, but also as a *'toolforthought'* that can shape and bring about changes in knowledge of subject, context, pedagogy and learner identity. In singling out thought as the basis for our explorations, we have aimed to question those things that have been given to us as if they are natural and taken-for-granted, to interrupt the seemingly fluent narratives that encode our own thinking; and by taking up a critical attitude, we have tried to ask what might be amenable to our thought and action, and to 'think of it being made *otherwise*' (Rose 1999b: 20). Other ways of thinking, based on other utopian goals, may be possible.

John Tomlinson, a pioneer of many significant educational ideas, described how our current practice contains our desires and hopes for future generations:

> This is not to suggest that anyone has thought that education was the only or even the most important influence on the next generation, but because the kind of schooling we decide to offer our young is the clearest public statement we can make about the kind of society we want *them* to build.
>
> (Tomlinson, 1993: 62)

In writing this book, we have considered how our thinking for the future of education, technology and creativity is rooted in complex genealogies of past traditions and practices, yet sought to remain alert to emerging alternatives, counter-narratives, and different possible interpretations. This openness to alternative trajectories is important if, following Tomlinson, we want to ensure that the thinking of our young is not fastened down, limited and fixed to our contemporary fantasies of certainty.

Of course, the history of educational technology tells a story that is littered with the broken remains of failed prototypes, discarded pedagogies, discontinued product lines, and disheartened educators. The promised radical transformation of education has not happened. Yet nevertheless there have been encounters in the interstices and margins of formal education, and a recognition of the range of spaces in which dominant learning identities might be creatively disrupted by contingency and improvisation. The prospective pedagogic identities woven through curriculum and pedagogy are not necessarily determined, appropriated and conscripted into participation in the knowledge economy, but contain other encounters and possibilities. Early uses of digital technologies in classrooms focused on immediate learning needs and pedagogical changes to reflect constructivist approaches in active experiences, not necessarily preparation for future vocations which were articulated later. Being 'ready, willing and able' to teach, calls for a reading of the world in which content, context and tools can be orchestrated with skill and purpose which go beyond immediate competence in teaching strategies and offer a deeper sounding of depth, scope and reach. These encounters, moments of practice, alternative readings and interpretations give us some clues to follow in the pursuit of possible other ways of thinking and other ways of doing education in the education systems of tomorrow.

Perhaps, then, we can end on a personal reflection from Avril's experience of different ways of doing things over 30 years as an educator in the 'digital age'. Avril's practices in schools and higher education have been experiences of being bewitched, bothered and bewildered. In the early 1980s, when microcomputers were introduced to English primary schools, we were bewitched by the constructionism of programming with LOGO, and the conjecture of simulations and adventure games. The key to this fascination was how we could make these microcomputers 'do' things. We could solve problems, make other problems, play and fiddle, look for patterns, make connections between ideas and concepts in a range of subjects from displaying dynamic rates of change in maths to analysing census data in history, and find ways of representing them in text and image. Being in control of the technologies enabled us to think about new digital literacies through multimedia and active engagement. Early discussions of 'ICT capability' prefigured later understandings of technological pedagogical content knowledge. We were bewitched by the potential for novel – and legitimated – kinds of activity and play in our classrooms.

In the 1970s, Kemmis, Atkins and Wright described four 'paradigms' for the ways in which we could design and use computer applications in education: instructional, emancipatory, revelatory, and conjectural, and we understood how the software at the time might be used for such active learning, from drill and practice to designing open-ended programs (Kemmis, Atkins and Wright, 1977). Thirty years later we are still bewitched by multimedia, mobility, animation, the internet, email, the World Wide Web, hypertext, location/context aware devices, search engines, virtual spaces, augmented spaces, social software, convergence, apps, games and so on. The technologies have developed rapidly and some of the purposes of delivery and consumption rather than production have dominated, yet the focus on active learning which builds knowledge and makes conceptual connections is still essential to a wider participation, creativity and agency.

As practice developed, however, we were bothered by some of the less welcome outcomes of the uses of digital technologies in education. The promised transformations of pedagogy, of the radical changes in relationships between teachers, learners, environments and knowledge, as heralded by some, did not happen. The layout of classrooms, interactions between teachers and learners, the time and space of teaching and learning remained much the same on an international scale, despite pockets of innovation. In many schools, computer suites were set up with controlled timetables, where – as observed by one student – 'the room was full of technique rather than learning'. The victory narrative of the fairground barkers offering solutions to all our problems and deficiencies as teachers and parents sounded hollow. We were bothered too that the measures of success in the use of digital tools were often linked closely with attainment in high stakes tests rather than indicators of the development of a wider collection of ways of thinking, working, using tools, and living in the world of the demands of the twenty-first century. The research evidence over 20 years indicates that the picture is complex, that the relationships between access to digital technologies and test scores are not straightforward. Purposeful uses of these technologies are related more to context, culture and pedagogy, than to a causal link between access and attainment. The issues beyond access also raised concerns about a digital divide which has implications for social justice and inclusion at local, national and international levels, for people of different ages, socioeconomic groups, languages, learning capabilities and cultures.

Nevertheless, being bewildered – in pathless places – was not necessarily a bad place to find ourselves. It provoked us to search for a vocabulary to help us to describe and explain what we were experiencing and observing both as learners in a new field, and as educators in schools, universities and beyond these boundaries. Relational and communicative approaches drew attention to the theories of tools and contexts in shaping activities and enabling people to think in conjunction with others. The acknowledgement of creativity, contingency and agency in context reminded us of possibilities for learning in ways that went both with and against the grain of mainstream education. Didactic analysis enabled us to ground our pedagogy and design in questions that connect us to wider purposes of education, culture and being human. Such bewilderment raises challenges to teacher education: the articulation of theories of learning which underpin practice; the development of pedagogy rooted in substance, value and the design of learning experiences and environments in which digital technologies are embedded; and the understanding of how teachers and educators are 'made up' which offer opportunities for choices and alternative styles of thinking.

In conclusion, we offer not yet another call for radical reform for education futures, but a more modest reflection on the ways in which education, technology and creativity have been thought, influenced and acted upon. In the 30 years so far collected under the banner of 'a digital age', there have been changes in thinking, changes in practice and changes in vision for pedagogy and curriculum. We would encourage readers – educators, policymakers, researchers – to reflect critically upon the discourses, imaginaries, and visions of the future of education that have influenced their thinking, ways of knowing and ways of acting. In suggesting a type of critical thinking as a modest final thought, we have been drawn to Foucault's comment (cited in Thrift 2005, vi) that:

> … a critique is not a matter of saying that things are not right as they are. It is a matter of pointing out on what kinds of assumptions, on what kinds of familiar, unchallenged, unconsidered modes of thought the practices that we accept rest.

BIBLIOGRAPHY

Alexander, R. (1996) In search of good primary practice, in P. Woods (ed.), *Contemporary Issues in Teaching and Learning*, London & New York: Routledge.

Alexander, R. (ed.) (2010) *Children, their World, their Education: Final Report and Recommendations of the Cambridge Primary Review*, London and New York: Routledge.

Allais, S. (2010) Economics imperialism, education policy, and educational theory. Paper presented at the Education, Work and the Knowledge Economy seminar, School of education, University of the Witwatersrand, 10 September 2010.

Andrejevic, M. (2011) Social Network Exploitation, in Z. Papacharissi, (ed.) *A Networked Self: Identity, Community, and Culture on Social Network Sites*, New York: Routledge.

Angeli, C. & Valanides, N. (2009) Epistemological and Methodological Issues for the Conceptualization, Development, and Assessment of ICT-TPCK. Advances in Technological Pedagogical Content Knowledge (TPCK), *Computers and Education*, 52(1): 154-168.

Apple, M. (2000) *Official Knowledge: Democratic Education in a Conservative Age*, 2nd ed. New York: Routledge

Apple, M. (2006) *Educating the 'Right' Way: Markets, Standards, God, and Inequality*, 2nd ed. New York: Routledge.

Apple, M., Kenway, J. & Singh, M. (eds) (2005) *Globalizing Education: Policies, Pedagogies and Politics*, New York: Peter Lang.

Austin, H., Dwyer, B. & Freebody, P. (2003) *Schooling the Child: The Making of Students in Classrooms*, London: RoutledgeFalmer.

Bache, I. (2003) Governing through Governance: Education Policy Control under New Labour. *Political Studies* 51, no. 2: 300-314

Bacon, N., Brophy, M., Mguni, N., Mulgan, G. & Shandro, A. (2010) *The State of Happiness: Can public policy shape people's wellbeing and resilience?* London: Young Foundation.

Ball, S.J. & Exley, S. (2010) Making policy with 'good ideas': policy networks and the 'intellectuals' of New Labour, *Journal of Education Policy* 25(2): 151-169.

Ball, S.J. & Junemann, C. (2012) *Networks, New Governance and Education*, Bristol: Policy Press.

Ball, S.J. (1990) *Politics and Policy Making in Education: Explorations in Policy Sociology*, London: Routledge.

Ball, S.J. (1994) *Education Reform: A Critical and Post-Structural Approach*, Buckingham: Open University Press.

Ball, S.J. (2007) *Education plc. Understanding Private Sector Participation in Public Sector Education*, Abingdon: Routledge.

Ball, S.J. (2008) *The Education Debate*, Bristol: Policy Press.

Ball, S.J. (2012) *Global Education Inc. New Policy Networks and the Neo-liberal Imaginary.* Abingdon: Routledge.

Ball, S.J., Maguire, M. & Braun, A. (2012) *How Schools Do Policy: Policy Enactments in Secondary Schools.* Abingdon: Routledge.

Banaji, S. (2011) Mapping the rhetorics of creativity, in J. Sefton-Green, P. Thompson, K. Jones & L. Bresler (eds), *The International Handbook of Creative Learning* (36–44), Abingdon and New York: Routledge.

Banaji, S., Burn, A., & Buckingham, D. (2007) *The rhetorics of creativity: a review of the literature*, London: Arts Council England

Barber, B. (2007) *Consumed: How Markets Corrupt Children, Infantilize Adults, and Swallow Citizens Whole*, New York: W.W. Norton & Co.

Barham, N. (2004) *Disconnected: Why Your Kids Are Turning Their Backs on Everything You Thought You Knew*, London: Ebury Press.

Bauman, Z. (2000) *The Individualized Society*, Cambridge: Polity.

Bauman, Z. (2004) *Identity*, Cambridge: Polity.

Bauman, Z. (2005) Education in Liquid Modernity, *Review of Education, Pedagogy and Cultural Studies* 27: 303–317

Bauman, Z. (2007) *Liquid Times*, Cambridge: Polity.

Bauman, Z. (2008) *The Art of Life*, Cambridge: Polity.

Baym, N. (2010) *Personal Connections in the Digital Age*, Cambridge: Polity.

Beck, U. & Beck-Gernsheim, E. (2002) *Individualization: Institutionalized Individualism and its Social and Political Consequences*, Trans.. P. Camiller. London: Sage.

Beck, U. (2006) *The Cosmopolitan Vision*, Trans. C. Cronin. Cambridge: Polity.

Beetham, H. & Sharpe, R. (2007) An introduction to rethinking pedagogy for a digital age, in H. Beetham & R. Sharpe (eds.), *Rethinking Pedagogy for a Digital Age: Designing and delivering e-learning*, Abingdon and New York: Routledge.

Belsey, C. (2002) *Poststructuralism: A Very Short Introduction*, Oxford: Oxford University Press.

Bentley, T. & Gillinson, S. (2008) *A D&R System for Education*, London: Innovation Unit.

Bentley, T. (1998) *Learning Beyond the Classroom*, London: Demos.

Berliner, D.C. & Biddle, B.J. (1995) *The Manufactured Crisis: Myths, Fraud, and the Attack on America's Public Schools*, Reading, MA: Addison-Wesley Publishing Co.

Bernstein, B. (1996) *Pedagogy, Symbolic Control andIidentity*, New York: Rowman and Littlefield.

Bernstein, B. (2000) *Pedagogy, Symbolic Control and Identity*, 2nd edn, Oxford: Rowman & Littlefield.

Bernstein, B. (2004) Social class and pedagogic practice, in S.J. Ball (ed.) *The RoutledgeFalmer Reader in Sociology of Education*, pp. 196–217. Abingdon: RoutldgeFalmer.

Biesta, G. (2006) *Beyond Learning: Democratic Education for a Human Future*, London: Paradigm.

Bijker, W. & Law, J. (1992) *Shaping Technology/Building Society: Studies in Sociotechnical Change*, Cambridge: MA: MIT Press.

Birch, S. (2008) *The Political Promotion of the Experience Economy and the Creative Industries: Cases from UK, New Zealand, Singapore, Norway, Sweden and Denmark,* Fredriksburg, DK: Samfundslitteratur.

Boden, M. (1992) *The Creative Mind,* London: Abacus.

Bogost, I. (2007) *Persuasive Games: The Expressive Power of Videogames,* Cambridge, MA: MIT Press.

Bolstad, R. & Gilbert, J. (2008) *Disciplining and Drafting, or 21ˢᵗ Century Learning: Rethinking the New Zealand senior secondary curriculum for the future,* Wellington: NZCER Press.

Boltanski, L. & Chiapello, E. (2007) *The New Spirit of Capitalism,* Trans. G. Elliott. London: Verso.

Bonal, X. & Rambla, X. (2003) Captured by the Totally Pedagogised Society: teachers and teaching in the knowledge economy, *Globalisation, Societies and Education* 1, no. 2: 169–84.

Boon, S. & Sinclair, C. (2009) A world I don't inhabit: disquiet and identity in Second Life and Facebook, *Educational Media International* 46, no. 2: 99–110.

BOP-Consulting (2006) *Study of the Impact of Creative Partnerships on the Cultural and Creative Economy,* London: BOP.

Boyd, D. (2008) Why youth love social networking sites: The role of networked publics in teenage social life, in D. Buckingham (ed.) *Youth, Identity and Digital Media,* 119–42. Cambridge, MA: The MIT Press.

Boyd, D. (2011) Social network sites as networked publics: affordances, dynamics, and implications, in Z. Papacharissi (ed.) *A Networked Self: Identity, Community, and Culture on Social Network Sites,* 39–58. Abingdon: Routledge.

Brown, P. & Lauder, H. (2001) *Capitalism and Social Progress: The Future of Society in a Global Economy,* Houndmills: Palgrave.

Brown, P., Lauder, H. & Ashton, D. (2011) *The Global Auction: The Broken Promise of Education, Jobs, and Incomes,* New York: Oxford University Press.

Bruner, J. (1990) *Acts of Meaning,* Cambridge, MA: Harvard University Press.

Bruner, J. (1996) *The Culture of Education,* Cambridge, MA: Harvard University Press.

Bruns, A. (2008) *Blogs, Wikipedia, Second Life and Beyond: From production to produsage,* London: Peter Lang.

Bryson, M. & de Castell, S. (1998) Telling tales out of school: modernist, critical, and postmodern 'true stories' about educational computing, in H. Bromley & M.W. Apple (eds) *Education/Technology/Power: Educational Computing as a Social Practice,* 65–84, Albany, NY: State University of New York Press.

Buckingham, D. (2007) *Beyond Technology: Children's learning in the age of digital culture,* Cambridge: Polity.

Buckingham, D. (2008) Introducing Identity, in D. Buckingham (ed.) *Youth, identity and digital media,* 1–24, Cambridge, MA: The MIT Press.

Buckingham, D. (2011) *The Material Child: Growing up in consumer culture,* Cambridge: Polity.

Burn, A. (2009) *Making New Media: Semiotics, culture and digital literacies,* Oxford: Peter Lang.

Byron, T. (2008) *Safer Children in a Digital World: The Report of the Byron Review,* Department for Children, Schools and Families.

Cachia, R., Ferrari, A., Kirsti, A.-M., & Punie, Y. (2010) Creative Learning and Innovative Teaching: Final Report on the Study on Creativity and Innovation in Education in EU Member States. Seville: Institute for Prospective Technological Studies (IPTS).

Candy, S. (2011) Opening minds: A curriculum for the 21st century, *Forum* 53, no. 2: 285–91.

Carolan, B., Natriello, G. & Rennick, M. (2003) *Rethinking the Organization and Effects of Schooling: The Post-Industrial Conundrum,* EdLab research paper, Teachers College, Columbia University, New York.

Carrington, V. & Robinson, M. (eds.) (2009) *Digital Literacies: Social learning and classroom practices,* London, Thousand Oaks, New Delhi, Singapore: SAGE.

Carvin, A. (2002) Literacy and Content; Building a foundation for bridging the digital divide, in A. Loveless & B. Dore (eds) *ICT in the Primary School,* Buckingham, Philadelphia: Open University Press.

Castells, M. (1996) *The Rise of the Network Society: The Information Age, Vol. I.* Oxford: Blackwell.

Castells, M. (1997) *The Power of Identity: The Information Age,* Vol. II, Oxford: Blackwell.

Castells, M. (2009) *Communication Power,* Oxford: Oxford University Press.

Castells, M. (2010) *The Rise of the Network Society,* 2nd edn rev'd, Oxford: Wiley-Blackwell.

Castells, M. (2011) A Network Theory of Power, *International Journal of Communication* 5: 773–87.

Cheney-Lippold, J (2011) A New Algorithmic Identity: Soft biopolitics and the modulation of control, *Theory, Culture & Society,* 28: 164–81.

Claxton, G. (1984) *Live and Learn: An Introduction to the psychology of growth and change in everday life,* London: Harper and Row.

Claxton, G. (2000) The anatomy of intuition, in T. Atkinson & G. Claxton (eds), *The Intuitive Practitioner,* Buckingham, Philadelphia: Open University Press.

Claxton, G. & Lucas, B. (2004) *Be Creative: Essential steps to revitalize your work and life,* London: BBC Books.

Cohen, R. & Kennedy, P. (2007) *Global Sociology,* 2nd edn. Houndmills: Palgrave Macmillan.

Cole, M. (1996) *Cultural Psychology: A once and future discipline.* Cambridge, MA: Harvard University Press.

Cook, D.T. (2008) The missing child in consumption theory, *Journal of Consumer Culture* 8, no. 2: 219–43.

Cook, J., Pachler, N. & Bachmair, B. (2011) Ubiquitous Mobility with Mobile Phones: A cultural ecology for mobile learning, *E-Learning and Digital Media,* 8(3), 181–95.

Countryman, L.W. (1999) *Living on the Border of the Holy: Renewing the Priesthood of All,* Church Publishing, Inc.

Craft, A. (2000) *Creativity Across the Primary Curriculum: Framing and developing practice,* London: Routledge.

Craft, A. (2005). *Creativity in Schools: Tensions and dilemmas.* London: Routledge.

Craft, A. (2011) *Creativity and Education Futures in the Digital Age,* Stoke on Trent: Trentham Books.

Creative-Partnerships. (2002) *What is Creative Partnerships?* Online. Available http://www.creative-partnerships.com/aboutcp/ (accessed 6 April 2012).

Crook, C., Fisher, T., Graber, R., Harrison, C., Lewin, C., Cummings, J., Luckin, R., Logan, K. & Oliver, M. (2008) *Web 2.0 technologies for learning at KS3 and KS4: implementing Web 2.0 in secondary schools,* England: British Educational Communications and Technology Agency.

Csikszentmihalyi, M. (1996) *Creativity: Flow and the Psychology of Discovery and Invention,* New York: HarperCollins.

Daniels, H. (2001) *Vygotsky and Pedagogy,* London: RoutledgeFalmer.

Darras, B. (2011) Creativity, creative class, smart power, social reproduction and symbolic violence, in J. Sefton-Green, P. Thompson, K. Jones & L. Bresler (eds) *The International Handbook of Creative Learning* : 90–98, Abingdon and New York: Routledge.

Davidson, C. & Goldberg, D. (2009) *The Future of Learning Institutions in a Digital Age,* Cambridge, MA: MIT Press.

Davidson, C. (2009) Blamed for Change: Historical Lessons in Youth, Labour, and New Media Futures, *International Journal of Learning and Media* 1, no. 3: 11–18.

Davies, J. & Merchant, G. (2010) *Web 2.0 for Schools: Learning and Social Participation,* Oxford: Peter Lang.

de Lima, J.A. (2010) Thinking more deeply about networks in education, *Journal of Educational Change* 11: 1–21.

Deacon, R. (2006) Michel Foucault on Education: a preliminary theoretical overview, *South African Journal of Education* 26, no. 2: 177–87.

Dean, M. (2010) *Governmentality: Power and Rule in Modern Society*, 2nd edn. London: Sage.

Deleuze, F. (1992) Postscript on the Societies of Control, October, 59: 3–7.

Department of Culture (2001) *Culture and Creativity: The Next Ten Years* London: Department of Culture, Media and Sport.

Department of Culture, Department for Business & Department for Innovation (2008), *Creative Britain: New talents for the creative economy*, London: DCMS.

Dervin, F. & Abbas, Y. (2009) Introduction, in Y. Abbas & F. Dervin (eds) *Digital Technologies of the Self:* 1-15, Newcastle-upon-Tyne: Cambridge Scholars.

Dews, P. (1987) *Logics of Disintegration: Post-structuralist thought and the claims of critical theory,* London: Verso.

Dillon, P. (2008) Creativity, wisdom and trusteeship – niches of cultural production, in A. Craft, H. Gardner & G.Claxton (eds) *Creativity, Wisdom and Trusteeship in Education,* Thousand Oaks, CA: Corwin Press.

Dillon, P., Bayliss, P., Stolpe, I., & Bayliss, L. (2008). What Constitutes 'Context' in Sociocultural Research? How the Mongolian experience challenges theory. *Transtext(e)s Transcultures*, 4 Online. Available HTTP : http://transtexts.revues.org/244 (accessed 15 August 2011).

Drabble, E. (2012) How to teach ... Kony 2012. *The Guardian*. Online. Available HTTP: <www.guardian.co.uk/education/2012/apr/23/kony-2012-teaching-resources> (accessed 25 May 2012).

Dyer-Witheford, N. & de Peuter, G. (2009) *Games of Empire: Global capitalism and video games,* Minneapolis: University of Minnesota Press.

Eagleton, T. (2008) *The Meaning of Life: A very short introduction*, Oxford: Oxford University Press.

Ecclestone, K. & Hayes, D. (2009) *The Dangerous Rise of Therapeutic Education*, Abingdon: Routledge.

Education Queensland (2000) New Basics: Theory into Practice. Brisbane: Queensland State Education.

Edwards, R. & Carmichael, P. (2012) Secret Codes: The Hidden Curriculum of Semantic Web Technologies. *Discourse: Studies in the Cultural Politics of Education*, iFirst: DOI:10.1 080/01596306.2012.692963.

Efland, A. (2004) Emerging visions of art education, in E. Eisner & M. Day (eds), *Handbook of Research and Policy in Art Education:* 691–9, Mahway, NJ: Lawrence Erlbaum Associates.

Egan, K. (2008) *The Future of Education: Reimagining Our Schools from the Ground Up*, New Haven and London: Yale University Press.

Ehrenzweig, A. (1973) *The Hidden Order of Art*, St Albans: Paladin.

Elliott, A. & Lemert, C. (2009) The Global New Individualist Debate: Three theories of individualism and beyond, in A. Elliott & P. du Gay (eds) *Identity in Question*: 37–64, London: Sage.

Elliott, A. & Urry, J. (2010) *Mobile Lives*, Abingdon: Routledge.

Ellis, V. (2001) Analogue clock/Digital display: Continuity and change in debates about literacy, technology and English, in A. Loveless & V. Ellis (eds) *ICT, Pedagogy and the Curriculum: Subject to change*, London: Routledge.

Ellis, V. (2004) Negotiating contrad(ICT)ions: Teachers and students making multimedia in the secondary school, *Technology, Pedagogy and Education,* 13(1), 11–28.

Ellis, V. (2007) Taking subject knowledge seriously: From professional knowledge recipes to complex conceptualizations of teacher development, *The Curriculum Journal*, 18, 4: 447–62.

Ellis, V., Edwards, A., & Smagorinsky, P. (eds) (2010) *Cultural-historical Perspectives on Teacher Education and Development*, London and New York: Routledge.

Engeström, Y. (1999) Activity theory and individual and social transformation, in Y. Engeström, M. Reijo & R.-L. Punamäki (eds) *Perspectives on Activity Theory*, Cambridge: Cambridge University Press.

Erstad, O., Gilje, O., Sefton-Green, J. & Vasbø, K. (2009) Exploring 'learning lives': community, identity, literacy and meaning, *Literacy*, 43(2), 100–6.

Evans, J. & Rich, E. (2011) Body policies and body pedagogies: every child matters in totally pedagogised schools? *Journal of Education Policy*, 26, no. 3: 361–79.

Evans, J., Davies, B. & Rich, E. (2009) The body made flesh: embodied learning and the corporeal device, in *British Journal of Sociology of Education*, 30, no. 4, 391–406.

Facer, K. & Green, H. (2007) Curriculum 2.0: Educating the digital generation, in S. Parker & S. Parker (eds) (2007) *Unlocking Innovation: Why citizens hold the key to public service reform,* London: Demos.

Facer, K. & Pykett, J. (2007) *Developing and Accrediting Personal Skills and Competences: Report and ways forward*, Bristol: Futurelab.

Facer, K. & Sandford, R. (2010) The next 25 years?: future scenarios and future directions for education and technology, *Journal of Computer-Assisted Learning* 26: 74–93.

Facer, K. (2011) *Learning Futures: Education, Technology and Social Change*, Abingdon: Routledge.

Fejes, A. & Nicholl, K. (2008) *Foucault and Lifelong Learning: Governing the subject,* Abingdon: Routledge.

Fendler, L. (2001) Educating flexible souls: The construction of subjectivity through developmentality and interaction, in K. Hultqvist & G. Dahlberg (eds) *Governing the Child in the New Millennium*: 119–42. London: RoutledgeFalmer.

Fenwick, T. & Edwards, R. (2010) *Actor-Network Theory in Education,* Abingdon: Routledge.

Fenwick, T., Edwards, R. & Sawchuk, P. (2011) *Emerging Approaches to Educational Research: Tracing the sociomaterial,* Abingdon: Routledge.

Ferguson, K. & Seddon, T. (2007) Decentred education: suggestions for framing a socio-spatial research agenda, *Critical Studies in Education* 48, no. 1: 111–29.

Fisher, T., Denning, T., Higgins, C. & Loveless, A. (2012) Teachers' knowing how to use technology: exploring a conceptual framework for purposeful learning activity, in *Curriculum Journal.*

Fisher, T., Higgins, C. & Loveless, A. (2006) *Teachers Learning with Digital Technologies: A review of research and projects*, Bristol: Futurelab.

Florida, R. (2003) *The Rise of the Creative Class: And how it's transforming work, leisure, community and everyday life*, Basic Books Inc.

Foucault, M. (1990) *The Will to Knowledge: The history of sexuality*, vol I, Trans. R. Hurley. London: Penguin.

Foucault, M. (2007) *Security, Territory, Population: Lectures at the Collège de France, 1977–1978*, edited by M. Senellart, Trans. G. Burchell, New York: Palgrave Macmillan.

Foucault, M. (2008) *The Birth of Biopolitics: Lectures at the Collège de France, 1978–1979*, edited by M. Senellart, Trans. G. Burchell, New York: Palgrave Macmillan.

Fougere, M. & Solitander, N. (2010) Governmentality and the creative class: harnessing Bohemia, diversity and freedom for competitiveness, in *International Journal of Management Concepts and Philosophy*, 4, no. 1: 41–59.

Francis, R. (2010) *The Decentring of the Traditional University: The Future of (Self)Education in Virtually Figured Worlds*, New York: Routledge.

Frankham, J. (2006) Network utopias and alternative entanglements for educational research and practice, *Journal of Education Policy* 21, no. 6: 661–77.

Gamble, A. (2009) *The Spectre at the Feast: Capitalist crisis and the politics of recession*, Houndmills: Palgrave Macmillan.

Gardner, H. (1988) Creative lives and creative works: A synthetic scientific approach, in R.J. Sternberg (ed.) *The nature of creativity*: 298–321, New York: Cambridge University Press.

Gee, J.P. (2008) Learning and Games, in K. Salen (ed.) *The Ecology of Games: Connecting youth, games, and learning,* Cambridge, MA: MIT Press.

Gee, J.P. (2003) *What Video Games Have to Teach Us about Learning and Literacy*, Houndmills: Palgrave MacMillan.

Gee, J.P. (2004) *Situated Learning and Literacy: A critique of traditional schooling,* London: Routledge.

Geertz, C. (1973) *The interpretation of Cultures*, New York: Basic.

Gewirtz, S. & Cribb, A. (2009) *Understanding Education: A sociological perspective*, Cambridge: Polity.

Gibson, J.J. (1972) A Theory of Direct Visual Perception, in J. Royce & W. Rozenboom (eds) *The Psychology of Knowing*, New York: Gordon & Breach.

Giddens, A. (1991) *Modernity and Self-identity: Self and society in the late modern age*, Cambridge: Polity.

Gilpin, D. (2011) Working the Twittersphere: Microblogging as professional identity construction, in Z. Papacharissi (ed.) *A Networked Self: Identity, community, and culture on social network sites*, 232–50. Abingdon: Routledge.

Giroux, H. (2005) Cultural studies in dark times: Public pedagogy and the challenge of neoliberalism. Fast Capitalism, 1, no. 2. Online. Available HTTP: www.henryagiroux.com/online_articles/DarkTimes.htm (accessed 9 October 2012).

Gladwell, M. (2009) *Outliers: The Story of Success*. London: Penguin.

Goodson, I. & Mangan, J. (1996) Computer literacy as ideology, *British Journal of Sociology of Education* 17, no. 1: 65–80

Goodson, I. (2010) Times of educational change: towards an understanding of patterns of historical and cultural refraction, *Journal of Education Policy* 25, no. 6: 767–75.

Goodson, I.F. & Gill, S. R. (2011) *Narrative Pedagogy: Life history and learning*, New York: Peter Lang.

Goodson, I.F., Biesta, G.J.J., Tedder, M. & Adair, N. (2010) *Narrative Learning*, London: Routledge.

Goodson, I. & Sikes, P. (2001) *Life History Research in Educational Settings*, Buckingham & Philadelphia: Open University Press.

Goodson, I.F. (2005) Long waves of educational reform, in I.F. Goodson (ed.) *Learning, Curriculum and Life Politics: The selected works of Ivor F. Goodson*: 105–29. Abingdon: Routledge.

Goodson, I.F. (2008) Schooling, curriculum, narrative and the social future, in C. Sugrue, (ed.) *The Future of Educational Change: International perspectives*: 123–35. Abingdon: Routledge.

Gough, N. (2002) Voicing Curriculum Visions, in W.E. Doll & N. Gough (eds) *Curriculum Visions*, New York: Peter Lang.

Grant, L. (2011) Life Narratives in Social Media, *DMLcentral.net*. 15 August. Online. Available HTTP: < www.dmlcentral.net/blog/lyndsay-grant/life-narratives-social-media> (accessed 17 July 2012).

Green, C.S., & Bavelier, D. (2003) Action video game modifies visual selective attention, *Nature*, 423:534–37.

Green, H. & Hannon, C. (2007) *Their Space: Education for a digital generation*, London: Demos.

Green, H., Facer, K. & Rudd, T. (2005) *Personalisation and Digital Technologies*, Bristol: Futurelab.

Green, H., Facer, K., Rudd, T., Dillon, P. & Humphreys, P. (2006) *Personalisation and Digital Technologies*. Bristol: Futurelab.

Greenfield, S. (2008) *i.d.: The Quest for Identity in the 21st Century*, London: Sceptre.

Hacking, I. (2006) Making Up People, *Generation Online*. Online. Available HTTP: <www.generation-online.org/c/fcbiopolitics2.htm> (accessed 11 July 2012).

Hague, C. & Williamson, B. (2009). *Digital participation, digital literacy, and school subjects: A review of the policies, literature and evidence*. Bristol: Futurelab.

Hall, C., & Thomson, P. (2007) Creative partnerships? Cultural policy and inclusive arts practice in one primary school, *British Educational Research Journal, 33*(3): 315–29.

Hall, C., Thomson, P. & Russell, L. (2007) Teaching like an artist: the pedagogic identities and practices of artists in schools, *British Journal of Sociology of Education*, 28(5): 605–19.

Hall, R. (2011) *Towards a critique of mobile learning*, Online. Available HTTP: <http://www.richard-hall.org/2011/12/07/towards-a-critique-of-mobile-learning/> (accessed 15 July 2012).

Hall, S. (2000) Who needs 'identity'? in P. du Gay, J. Evans & P. Redman (eds) *Identity: A reader*: 15–30. London: Sage.

Hanke, B. (2011) The Network University in Transition. MIT 7 Conference, 14 May.

Haraway, D.J. (1991) *Simians, Cyborgs and Women: The Reinvention of Nature*, London: Free Association Books.

Hardt, M. (2008) Affective Labour. *Generation Online*. Online. Available HTTP: <http://www.generation-online.org/p/fp_affectivelabour.htm> (accessed 11 July 2012).

Hargeaves, D. (2004) *Education Epidemic*, London: Demos.

Hargreaves, A. (2008) The coming of post-standardization: Three weddings and a funeral, in C. Sugrue (ed.) *The Future of Educational Change: International perspectives*. London: Routledge.

Harris, R. & Burn, K. (2011) Curriculum theory, curriculum policy and the problem of ill-disciplined thinking, *Journal of Education Policy* 26, no. 2: 245–61.

Harris-Hart, C. (2009) Performing Curriculum: Exploring the role of teachers and teacher educators, *Curriculum Inquiry* 39, no. 1: 111–23.

Hartley, D. (1997) *Re-schooling Society*, London: RoutledgeFalmer.

Hartley, D. (1999) Marketing and the 're-enchantment' of school management, *British Journal of Sociology of Education* 20, no. 3: 309–23.

Hartley, D. (2006) The instumentalization of the expressive, in A. Moore (ed.) *Schooling, Society and Curriculum*, London: Routledge.

Hartley, D. (2009) Personalisation: The nostalgic revival of child-centred education? *Journal of Education Policy* 24, no. 4: 423–34.

Hartley, D. (2010) Rhetorics of regulation in education after the global economic crisis, *Journal of Education Policy* 25, no. 6: 785–91.

Harvey, D. (2010) *The Enigma of Capital and the Crises of Capitalism*, London: Profile.

Hawkey, R. (2001) Science beyond school: Representation or re-presentation? in A. Loveless & V. Ellis (eds) *ICT, Pedagogy and the Curriculum: Subject to change*, London: Routledge.

Hay, S. & Kapitzke, C. (2009) 'Smart state' for a knowledge economy: Reconstituting creativity through student subjectivity, *British Journal of Sociology of Education* 30, no. 2: 151–164.

Hayles, N.K. (1999) *How We Became Posthuman: Virtual bodies in cybernetics, literature and informatics*, London: University of Chicago Press.

Hetland, L. (2008) Studio Thinking: a model of artistic mind, in J. Sefton-Green (Ed.), *Creative Learning*, London: Creative Partnerships.

Hetland, L., Winner, E., Veenema, S. & Sheridan, K. M. (2007) *Studio Thinking: The real benefits of visual arts education*, New York: Teachers' College Press.

Hillocks, G. (1999) *Ways of Thinking, Ways of Teaching*, New York and London: Teachers' College Press.

Holland, D., Lachicotte, W., Skinner, D., & Cain, C. (1998) *Identity and Agency in Cultural Worlds*, Cambridge, Massachusetts and London, England: Harvard University Press.

Horne, M. (2008) *Honest Brokers: Brokering innovation in public services*, London: Innovation Unit.

Howker, E. & Malik, S. (2010) *Jilted Generation: How Britain has bankrupted its youth*, London: Icon Books.

Hudson (2007) Comparing different traditions of teaching and learning: what can we learn about teaching and learning? *European Educational Research Journal, 6*, 2: 135–46.

Hudson, B. (2011) Didactical design for technology enhanced learning, in B. Hudson & M. A. Meyer (eds) *Beyond Fragmentation: Didactics, learning and teaching in Europe*, Opladen and Farmington Hills: Verlag Barbara Budrich.

Hudson, B., Buchberger, F., Kansanen, P., & Seel, H. (1999). *Didaktik/Fachdidaktik* as Science(-s) of the Profession? *TNTEE Publications*, 2,1.

Hudson, B. & Meyer, M. A. (eds) (2011). *Beyond Fragmentation: Didactics, learning and teaching in Europe*, Opladen and Farmington Hills: Verlag Barbara Budrich.

Hultqvist, K. & Dahlberg, G. (eds) (2001) *Governing the Child in the New Millennium*, London: RoutledgeFalmer.

Humphreys, M. & Hyland, T. (2002) Theory, Practice and Performance in Teaching: Professionalism, intuition and jazz, *Educational Studies*, 28,1: 5–15.

Ito, M. (2009) *Engineering Play: A cultural history of children's software*. Cambridge, MA: MIT Press.

Ito, M. *et al.* (2010) *Hanging Out, Messing Around, and Geeking Out: Kids living and learning with new media*, Cambridge, MA: MIT Press.

Jared, E. (2008). *The Ask NRICHers: researching the everyday story of virtual folk*. Paper presented at the Information Technology in Teacher Education.

Jarvis, P. (2004) Globalisation, the learning society and comparative education, in S.J. Ball (ed.) *The RoutledgeFalmer Reader in Sociology of Education:* 72–85. Abingdon: RoutledgeFalmer.

Jeffrey, B. & Woods, P. (2003) *The Creative School: A framework for success, quality and effectiveness*, London & New York: RoutledgeFalmer.

Jenkins, H. (2006) *Convergence Culture: Where old and new media collide*, New York: New York University Press.

Jenkins, H. with Purushtoma, R., Clinton, K., Weigel, M. & Robison, A.J. (2007) *Confronting the Challenges of Participatory Culture: Media education for the 21st century*, Chicago: The MacArthur Foundation.

Jensen, C.B. & Lauritsen, P. (2005) 'Digital Denmark': IT Reports as Material-Semiotic Actors, *Science, Technology and Human Values* 30, no. 3: 352–73.

Jessop, B. (2002) *The Future of the Capitalist State*. Cambridge: Polity.

Jessop, B., Brenner, N. & Jones, M. (2008) Theorizing sociospatial relations, *Environment and Planning D: Society and Space*, 26: 389–401.

Johnson, S. (2006) *Everything Bad is Good for You: How popular culture made us smarter*, London: Penguin.

John-Steiner, V. (2000) *Creative Collaboration*. New York: Oxford University Press.

Jonassen, D.H. (2000) *Computers as Mindtools for Schools: Engaging critical thinking*, 2nd edn, Upper Saddle River, New Jersey, Columbus, Ohio: Merrill/Prentice Hall.

Jones, J. (2009) *Culture and Creative Learning: A literature review*, London: Creativity, Culture and Education.

Jones, K. & Thomson, P. (2008) Policy rhetoric and the renovation of English schooling: the case of Creative Partnerships. *Journal of Education Policy*, 23, no. 6: 715–27.

Jones, K. (1989) *Right Turn : The Conservative Revolution in Education*, London: Hutchinson Radius.

Jones, K. (2010) Crisis, what crisis? *Journal of Education Policy* 25, no. 6: 793–798

Jupp, R., Fairly, C. & Bentley, T. (2001) *What Learning Needs: The challenge for a creative nation*, London:Demos.

Kalantzis, M., & Cope, B. (2010) The Teacher as Designer: pedagogy in the new media age, *E-learning and digital media*, 7, 3: 200–22.

Kane, P. (2004) *The Play Ethic: A manifesto for a different way of living*, London: Pan MacMillan.

Kemmis, S., Atkins, R. & Wright, E. (1977) *How do students learn?* (Vol. Occasional Paper 5), Norwich: Centre for Applied Research in Education, University of East Anglia.

Kendall, L., Morrison, J., Yeshanew, T. & Sharp, C. (2008a) *The Longer-Term Impact of Creative Partnerships on the Attainment of Young People: Results from 2005 and 2006*, England: National Foundation for Educational Research.

Kendall, L., Morrison, J., Sharp, C. & Yeshanew, T. (2008b) *The Impact of Creative Partnerships on Pupil Behaviour*, Final report, England: National Foundation for Educational Research.

Kenway, J. & Bullen, E. (2001) *Consuming Children: Entertainment–education–advertising*, Maidenhead: Open University Press.

Kenway, J. & Bullen, E. (2005) Globalizing the Young in the Age of Desire: Some Educational Policy Issues, in M. Apple, J. Kenway & M. Singh (eds) *Globalizing Education: Policies, Pedagogies and Politics*: 31–44, New York: Peter Lang.

Kenway, J. Bullen, E. & Fahey, J. with Robb, S. (2006) *Haunting the Knowledge Economy*, Abingdon: Routledge.

Kinsley, S. (2010) Representing 'things to come': feeling the visions of future technologies, *Environment and Planning A*, 42: 2771–90.

Klafki, W. (2000) Didaktik analysis as the core of preparation of instruction, in I. Westbury, S. Hopmann & K. Riquarts (eds) *Teaching as a Reflective Practice: the German Didaktik tradition*: 197–206, Mahwah: Lawrence Erlbaum Associates.

Kline, S. Dyer-Witheford, N. & de Peuter, G. (2003) *Digital Play: The Interaction of Technology, Culture and Marketing,* Montreal: McGill-Queen's University Press.

Knobel, M. & Lankshear, C. (eds) (2010) *DIY Media: Creating, sharing and learning with new technologies,* Oxford: Peter Lang.

Knox, H. Savage, M. & Harvey, P. (2005) Social networks and the study of relations: networks as method, metaphor and form, *Economy and Society* 35, no. 1, 113–40.

Koehler, M.J. & Mishra, P. (2005) What happens when teachers design educational technology? The development of technological pedagogical content knowledge, *Journal of Educational Computing Research,* 32, 2: 22–152.

Koehler, M.J., Mishra, P. & Yahya, K. (2007) Tracing the Development of Teacher Knowledge in a Design Seminar: Integrating Content, Pedagogy and Technology, *Computers and Education, 49,* 3: 740–62.

Kucklich, J. (2005) Precarious Playbour: Modders and the Digital Games Industry, *The Fibreculture Journal* 5. Online. Available HTTP: <http://five.fibreculturejournal.org/fcj-025-precarious-playbour-modders-and-the-digital-games-industry> (accessed 11 July 2012)

Lachs, V. (2000) *Making Multimedia in the Classroom: A practical guide,* London: Routledge.

Landy, L. (2012) *Making music with sounds,* New York: Routledge.

Lanier, J. (2010a) *You Are Not a Gadget,* London: Penguin.

Lanier, J. (2010b) Does the digital classroom enfeeble the mind? *New York Times,* 16 September, Online. Available HTTP: <www.nytimes.com/2010/09/19/magazine/19fob-essay-t.html?pagewanted=all> (accessed 11 July 2012).

Lash, S. & Urry, J. (1987) *The End of Organized Capitalism,* Cambridge: Polity.

Lash, S. (2002) *Critique of Information,* London: Sage.

Latour, B. (1987) *Science in Action: How to Follow Scientists and Engineers Through Society,* Cambridge, MA: Harvard University Press.

Latour, B. (2005) *Reassembling the Social: An Introduction to Actor-Network-Theory,* Oxford: Oxford University Press.

Latour, B. (2011) Networks, Societies, Spheres: Reflections of an Actor-Network Theorist, *International Journal of Communication* 5: 796–810.

Latour, B., Jensen, P., Venturini, T., Grauwin, S. & Boullier, D. (2012) The whole is always smaller than its parts: A digital test of Gabriel Tarde's Monads, *British Journal of Sociology.* Online. Available HTTP: <www.bruno-latour.fr/sites/default/files/123-WHOLE-PART-FINAL.pdf> (accessed 11 July 2012).

Lauder, H., Young, M. Daniels, H., Balarin, M. & Lowe, J. (eds) (2012) *Educating for the Knowledge Economy? Critical Perspectives,* Abingdon: Routledge.

Laurillard, D. (2012) *Teaching as a Design Science: building pedagogical patterns for learning and technology,* New York & London: Routledge.

Law, J. & Hassard, J. (eds) (1999) *Actor Network Theory and After,* Oxford: Blackwell.

Law, J. (1992) Notes on the theory of the actor-network: Ordering, strategy and heterogeneity, *Systemic Practice and Action Research* 5, no. 4: 379–93.

Law, J. (2010) The Double Social Life of Method, Sixth Annual CRESC conference on the Social Life of Method, St Hugh's College, Oxford. Online. Available HTTP: <http://heterogeneities.net/publications/Law2010DoubleSocialLifeofMethod5.pdf> (accessed 11 July 2012).

Lawler, S. (2008) *Identity: Sociological Perspectives,* Cambridge: Polity.

Leach, J. & Moon, B. (eds) (1999) *Learners and Pedagogy,* London: Paul Chapman Publishing in association with The Open University.

Leadbeater, C. & Wong, A. (2010) *Learning from the Extremes,* San Jose: Cisco Systems.

Leadbeater, C. (2010) *Cloud Culture: The future of global cultural relations,* London: Counterpoint/British Council.

Learning Futures (2010) *Learning Futures: Engaging schools,* London: Paul Hamlyn Foundation/Innovation Unit.

Learning Futures (2012) *Spaced Learning: Making memories stick,* London: Paul Hamlyn Foundation/Innovation Unit.

Lee, N. (2001) *Childhood and Society: Growing up in an age of uncertainty,* Maidenhead: Open University Press.

Lee, N. (2008) How might childhood change over the next 18 years as a result of the development of technology? Report to the Beyond Current Horizons programme, Bristol: Futurelab.

Lemke, T. (2011) *Biopolitics: An Advanced Introduction,* Trans. E.F. Trump. New York: New York University Press.

Little, B. (ed.) (2010) *Radical Future: Politics for the next generation,* Soundings/CompassYouth/ Lawrence Wishart.

Liu, A. (2004) *The Laws of Cool: Knowledge work and the culture of information,* London: University of Chicago Press.

Livingstone, S. (2008) *Theorising the benefits of new technology for youth: controversies of learning and development,* in: ESRC seminar series: The educational and social impact of new technologies on young people in Britain, 12 March 2008, Department of Education, University of Oxford, Oxford, UK. Online. Available HTTP: <http://eprints.lse.ac.uk/33821/ > (accessed 17 July 2012).

Loi, D. & Dillon, P. (2006) Adaptive educational environments as creative spaces, *Cambridge Journal of Education,* 36: 363–81.

Long, S. (2001) What effect will digital technologies have on visual education in school? in A. Loveless & V. Ellis (eds) *ICT, Pedagogy and the Curriculum: Subject to Change,* London: Routledge.

Loveless, A. (1997) Visual Literacy and New Technology in Primary Schools: The Glebe School Project, *Journal of Computing and Childhood Education,* 8(2/3): 98–110.

Loveless, A. (1999) A Digital Big Breakfast: The Glebe School Project, in J. Sefton-Green (ed.), *Young People, Creativity and New Technology: The challenge of digital arts,* London: Routledge.

Loveless, A. (2003a) Making a difference? An Evaluation of Professional Knowledge and pedagogy in Art and ICT, *International Journal of Art and Design Education,* 22(2), 145–54.

Loveless, A. (2003b) The interaction between primary teachers' perceptions of ICT and their pedagogy, *Education and Information Technologies,* 8(4), 313–26.

Loveless, A. (2007) Preparing to teach with ICT: subject knowledge, Didaktik and improvisation, *The Curriculum Journal,* 18, 4: 509–22.

Loveless, A. (2009). Thinking about creativity: developing ideas, making things happen, in A. Wilson (ed.), *Creativity in Primary Education* (2nd edn), Exeter: Learning Matters.

Loveless, A. (2011) Didactic Analysis as a Creative Process: Pedagogy for Creativity with Digital Tools, in B. Hudson & M. A. Meyer (eds) *Beyond Fragmentation: Didactics, Learning and Teaching in Europe,* Opladen and Farmington Hills: Verlag Barbara Budrich.

Loveless, A. & Ellis, V. (eds) (2001) *ICT, Pedagogy and the Curriculum: Subject to Change,* London: Routledge.

Lucas, B. & Claxton, G. (2009) *Wider Skills for Learning: What are they, how can they be cultivated, how could they be measured and why are they important for innovation?* London: NESTA.

Lucas, B. (2007) *New Kinds of Smart: Emerging thinking about what it is to be intelligent today,* Winchester: The Talent Foundation.

Lucas, B. & Claxton, G. (2010) *New Kinds of Smart.* Maidenhead: Open University Press.

Luckin, R. (2008) The learner centric ecology of resources: A framework for using technology to scaffold learning, in *Computers and Education,* 50: 449–62.

Luckin, R. (2010) *Re-Designing Learning Contexts,* London: Routledge.

Luckin, R., Logan, K., Clark, W., Graber, R., Oliver, M. & Mee, A. (2008) *Web 2.0 Technologies for Learning at KS3 and KS4: Learners' use of Web 2.0 technologies in and out of school,* England: British Educational Communications and Technology Agency.

McDonald, C. (2009) The importance of identity in policy: The case for and of children, in *Children and Society* 23: 241–51.

McGuigan, J. (2009) *Cool Capitalism,* London: Pluto Press.

Mackenzie, A. (2006) *Cutting Code: Software and Sociality,* Oxford: Peter Lang.

Mackenzie, A. (2010) *Wirelessness: Radical Empiricism in Network Culture,* London: MIT Press.

Mackenzie, A. (2012) More parts than elements: how databases multiply, *Environment and Planning D: Society and Space* 30: 335–50.

MacKenzie, D. & Wajcman, J. (eds) (1999) *The Social Shaping of Technology,* 2nd edn, Maidenhead: McGraw-Hill.

McLennan, G. (2004) Travelling with vehicular ideas: the case of the Third Way, *Economy and Society* 33, no. 4: 484–99.

Mager, A. (2012) Algorithmic Ideology: How capitalist society shapes search engines, *Information, Communication and Society,* iFirst: DOI:10.1080/1369118X.2012.676056

Mahari, J. (2011) *Digital Tools and Urban Schools: Mediating a Remix of Learning,* University of Michigan Press.

Martens, L. (2005) Learning to Consume—Consuming to Learn: Children at the interface between consumption and education, *British Journal of Sociology of Education* 26, no. 3: 343–57.

Mayes, T. & de Freitas, S. (2007) Learning and e-learning: The role of theory, in H. Beetham & R. Sharp (eds) *Rethinking Pedagogy for a Digital Age: Designing and delivering e-learning,* Abingdon and New York: Routledge.

McCarthy, H., Miller, P. & Skidmore, P. (eds) (2004) *Network Logic: Who governs in an interconnected world?* London: Demos.

McCrea, P (2012) *Capturing learning in digital spaces* Online. Available HTTP: http://www. capturinglearning.com (accessed 6 May 2012).

Menck, P. (1995) Didactics as construction of content, *Journal of Curriculum Studies,* 27,4: 353–63.

Miller, P. & Rose, N. (2008) *Governing the Present: Administering economic, social and personal life,* Cambridge: Polity.

Mitchell, W. (1994) *The Reconfigured Eye,* Cambridge, Mass. and London: MIT Press.

Molnar, A. (2005) *School Commercialism: From democratic ideal to market commodity,* New York: Routledge.

Monahan, T. (2005) *Globalization, Technological Change, and Public Education,* Abingdon: Routledge.

Moore, R. & Young, M.F.D. (2001) Knowledge and the Curriculum in the Sociology of Education: Towards a reconceptualisation, *British Journal of Sociology of Education* 22, no. 4: 445–61.

Moore, R. (2004) *Education and Society: Issues and explanations in the sociology of education,* Cambridge: Polity.

Morgan, J. & Williamson, B. (2008) *Enquiring Minds: Schools, knowledge and educational change,* Bristol: Futurelab.

Morgan, J. (2011) Enquiring Minds: A radical curriculum project? *Forum* 53, no. 2: 261–72.

Morgan, J., Williamson, B., Lee, T. & Facer, K. (2007) *Enquiring Minds: A Guide,* Bristol: Futurelab.

Mulgan, G. & Steinberg, T. (2005) *Wide Open: Open source methods and their future potential,* London: Demos.

Mulgan, G. (2007) *Ready or Not? Taking innovation in the public sector seriously,* London: NESTA.

NACCCE (1999) *All Our Futures: Creativity, culture and education,* Sudbury: National Advisory Committee on Creative and Cultural Education: DfEE and DCMS.

Nachmanovitch, S. (1990) *Free Play: Improvisation in life and art,* New York: Jeremy P. Tarcher/Putnam a member of Penguin/Putnam Inc.

Nardi, B.A. & O'Day, V.L. (1999) *Information Ecologies: Using technology with heart,* London, Cambridge Mass: MIT Press.

Newfield, C. (2010) The structure and silence of the cognitariat, *Globalization, Societies and Education* 8, no. 2: 175–89.

Ofsted (2006) *Creative Partnerships: Initiative and Impact,* London: Ofsted

Osborne, T.S.D. & Rose, N. (1999a) Governing cities: Notes on the spatialisation of virtue, *Environment and Planning D: Society and Space,* 17: 737–60.

Osborne, T.S.D. & Rose, N. (1999b) Do the Social Sciences Create Phenomena? The example of public opinion research, *British Journal of Sociology* 50(3): 367–96.

Osborne, T.S.D. (2003) Against 'creativity': A philistine rant, *Economy and Society* 32, no. 4: 507–25.

Osborne, T.S.D. (2004) On mediators: Intellectuals and the ideas trade in the knowledge society, *Economy and Society* 33, no. 4: 430–47.

Osgerby, B. (2004) *Youth Media.* Abingdon: Routledge.

Owen, M., Grant, L., Sayers, S. & Facer, K. (2006) *Social software and learning,* Bristol: Futurelab.

Pachler, N. (ed.) (2007) *Mobile Learning: towards a research agenda,* London: WLE Centre, Institute of Education.

Pachler, N., & Daly, C. (2011) *Key Issues in e-Learning: Research and practice,* London and New York: Continuum.

Papacharissi, Z. (2011) Conclusion: A Networked Self, in Z. Papacharissi (ed.) *A Networked Self: Identity, Community, and Culture on Social Network Sites,* 304–18, New York: Routledge.

Papert, S. (1980) *Mindstorms: Children, Computers and Powerful Ideas,* New York: Basic Books.

Papert, S. (1993) *The Children's Machine: Rethinking School in the Age of the Computer,* New York, London, Toronto, Sydney, Tokyo & Singapore: Harvester Wheatsheaf.

Parker, D. & Ruthra-Rajan, N. (2011) The challenges of developing system–wide indicators of creativity reform: the case of Creative Partnerships, UK, in J. Sefton-Green, P. Thompson, K. Jones & L. Bresler (eds) *The International Handbook of Creative Learning,* Abingdon and New York: Routledge.

Parker, R. (2007) Networked Governance or Just Networks? Local governance of the knowledge economy in Limerick (Ireland) and Karlskrona (Sweden), *Political Studies* 55, no. 1: 113–32.

Parker, S. & Parker, S. (eds) (2007) *Unlocking Innovation: Why citizens hold the key to public service reform,* London: Demos.

Patten, K. (2004) Neuropedagogy: Imagining the Learning Brain as Emotional Mind, Paper presented at *IERG 2004*, Vancouver, Canada.

Patton, A. (2012) *Work that Matters: The teacher's guide to project-based learning*, London: Paul Hamlyn Foundation.

Pea, R.D. (1993) Practices of distributed intelligence and designs for education, in G. Salomon (ed.) *Distributed cognitions: psychological and educational considerations*, Cambridge: Cambridge University Press.

Peck, J. (2007) The creativity fix, *Eurozine*, 28 June 2007. Online. Available HTTP: <www.eurozine.com> (accessed 11 July 2012)

Peck, J. (2010) *Constructions of Neoliberal Reason*, Oxford: Oxford University Press.

Perkins, D. (1983) *The Mind's Best Work*, Cambridge: Harvard University Press.

Perkins, D. (1993) Person-plus: a distributed view of thinking and learning, in G. Salomon (ed.) *Distributed cognitions: Psychological and educational considerations*, Cambridge: Cambridge University Press.

Perkins, D. (1994) *The Intelligent Eye: Learning to think by looking at art*, Los Angeles J. Paul Getty Center for Education in the Arts.

Peters, M.A. (2012) 'Openness' and the Global Knowledge Commons: An emerging mode of social production for education and science, in *Educating for the Knowledge Economy?: Critical Perspectives*, ed. H. Lauder, M. Young, H. Daniels, M. Balarin & J. Lowe, 66–76. Abingdon: Routledge.

Pinar, W.F. (2004) *What is Curriculum Theory?* Mahwah, NJ: Erlbaum.

Pinar, W.F., Reynolds, W.M., Slattery, P. & Taubman, P.M. (1995) *Understanding Curriculum: An Introduction to the Study of Historical and Contemporary Curriculum Discourses*, New York: Peter Lang.

Pope, R. (2005) *Creativity: Theory, history, practice*, Abingdon: Routledge.

Popkewitz, T.S. (2008) *Cosmopolitanism and the Age of School Reform: Science, education, and making society by making the child*, Abingdon: Routledge.

Popkewitz, T.S. (2012) Numbers in Grids of Intelligibility: making sense of how educational truth is told, in *Educating for the Knowledge Economy? Critical perspectives*, edited by H. Lauder, M. Young, H. Daniels, M. Balarin & J. Lowe, 169–91. Abingdon: Routledge.

Postman, N. (1969) *Bullshit and the Art of Crap-Detection,* talk delivered at the National Convention for the Teachers of English [NCTE], 28 November 1969, Washington, D.C., Online. Available HTTP: < http://criticalsnips.wordpress.com/2007/07/22/neil-postman-bullshit-and-the-art-of-crap-detection/> (accessed 15 July 2012).

Postman, N. (1993) *Technopoly: The surrender of culture to technology*, New York: Vintage.

Price, D. (2010) *Learning Futures: Engaging students*. London: Paul Hamlyn Foundation/Innovation Unit.

Price, D. (2011) Learning Futures: Rebuilding curriculum and pedagogy around student engagement, *Forum* 53, no. 2: 273–84.

Priestley, M. & Humes, W. (2010) The Development of Scotland's Curriculum for Excellence: Amnesia and déjà vu, *Oxford Review of Education* 36, no. 3: 345–61.

Priestley, M. (2011) Whatever Happened to Curriculum Theory? Critical realism and curriculum change, *Pedagogy, Culture and Society* 19, no. 2: 221–37.

Prout, A. (2005) *The Future of Childhood: Towards the interdisciplinary study of children*, Abingdon: RoutledgeFalmer.

Purcell, S. (2002) *Musical Patchwork: The threads of teaching and learning in a Conservatoire*, London: Guildhall School of Music and Drama.

Putnam, R. T. & Borko, H. (2000) What do new views of knowledge and thinking have to say about research on teacher learning? *Educational Researcher, 29*, 1: 4–15.

Pykett, J. (2007) Making citizens Governable? The Crick Report on governmental technology, *Journal of Education Policy* 22, no. 3: 301–19.

QCA (2004) *Creativity: Find it, promote it.* Online. Available HTTP: http://www.ncaction.org.uk/creativity (accessed 22 January 2005).

Queensland Education (2000)

Rheingold, H. (2003) *Smart Mobs: The next social revolution*, Cambridge, MA: Perseus Publishing.

Rizvi, F. & Lingard, B. (2010) *Globalizing Education Policy*, Abingdon: Routledge.

Roberts, P. (2006) *Nurturing Creativity in Young People*, London: Department for Culture, Media and Sport; Department for Education and Skills.

Robertson, S. (2005) Re-imagining and rescripting the future of education: global knowledge economy discourses and the challenge to education systems, *Comparative Education* 41, no. 2: 151–70.

Robinson, K. (2001) *Out of our minds: learning to be creative*, Chichester: Capstone Publishing Ltd.

Robinson, K. (2010) *The Element: How finding your passion changes everything*, London: Penguin.

Rojek, C. (2006) *Cultural Studies*, Cambridge: Polity.

Rose, N. (1996) *Inventing Our Selves: Psychology, Power, and Personhood,* Cambridge: Cambridge University Press.

Rose, N. (1999a) *Governing the Soul: The shaping of the private self*, 2nd edn. London: Free Association Books.

Rose, N. (1999b) *Powers of Freedom: Reframing political thought,* Cambridge: Cambridge University Press.

Rose, N. (2007) *The Politics of Life Itself: Biomedicine, power, and subjectivity in the twenty-first century,* Princeton, NJ: Princeton University Press.

Rosenberg, D. & Harding, S. (eds) (2005) *Histories of the Future*, London: Duke University Press.

Rudd, T., Sutch, D. & Facer, K. (2006) *Towards New Learning Networks*, Bristol: Futurelab

Ruppert, E. & Savage, M. (2012) Transactional Politics. *Measure and Value: Sociological Review Monographs Series*, 59, supp. no. 2: 73–92.

Ryan, J. (2010) *A History of the Internet and the Digital Future*, London: Reaktion.

Salen, K. (2008) Toward an Ecology of Gaming, in K. Salen (ed.) *The Ecology of Games: Connecting Youth, Games, and Learning*: 1-20. Cambridge, MA: MIT Press.

Salen, K., Torres, R., Wolozin, L., Rufo-Tepper, R. & Shapiro, A. (2011) *Quest to Learn: Developing the school for digital kids*, Cambridge, MA: MIT Press.

Saljo, R. (2004) Learning and technologies, people and tools in co-ordinated activities, *International Journal of Educational Research,* 41: 489–494.

Saljo, R. (2010) Digital tools and challenges to institutional traditions of learning: technologies, social memory and the performative nature of learning, *Journal of Computer Assisted Learning,* 26(1), 53–64.

Salomon, G. (1993) *Distributed Cognitions – psychological and educational considerations,* Cambridge: Cambridge University Press.

Salomon, G. & Perkins, D. (2005) Do Technologies Make Us Smarter? Intellectual amplification *with, of* and *through* technology, in R.J. Sternberg & D.D. Preiss (eds) *Intelligence and Technology*: 71–86, Mahweh New Jersey and London: Lawrence Erlbaum Associates.

Sandlin, J. & McLaren, P. (2010) Introduction: Exploring Consumption's Pedagogy and Envisioning a Critical Pedagogy of Consumption—Living and learning in the shadow of the 'shopocalypse', in J. Sandlin & P. McLaren (eds) *Critical Pedagogies of Consumption: Living and learning in the shadow of the 'shopocalypse'*, Abingdon: Routledge.

Savage, M., Ruppert, E. & Law, J. (2010) Digital Devices: nine theses, CRESC Working Paper Series No. 86. Milton Keynes: The Open University.

Scholz, R. T. (2010b) Facebook as Playground and Factory, in D.E. Wittkower (ed.) *Facebook and Philosophy*, Chicago: Open Court/Carus Publishing.

Scholz, R. T. (ed.) (2010a) *Learning through Digital Media: Experiments in Technology and Pedagogy*, Institute for Distributed Creativity.

Scott, D. (2008) *Critical Essays on Major Curriculum Theorists*, Abingdon: Routledge.

Sefton-Green, J. (ed.) (2008) *Creative Learning*, London: Creative Partnerships.

Sefton-Green, J. & Sinker, R. (1999) *Evaluating Creativity: Making and Learning by Young People*, London: Routledge.

Seiter, E. (1993) *Sold Separately: Parents and Children in Consumer Culture*, Bloomington: Indiana University Press.

Seiter, E. (2005) *The Internet Playground: Children's access, entertainment, and mis-education*, New York: Peter Lang.

Seldon, A. (2010) *An End to Factory Schools: A Manifesto for Education 2010–2020,* London: Centre for Policy Studies.

Selinger, M. (2001) Information and communication technologies and representation of mathematics, in A. Loveless & V. Ellis (eds) *ICT, Pedagogy and the Curriculum: Subject to change*, London: RoutledgeFalmer.

Seltzer, K. & Bentley, T. (1999) *The Creative Age: Knowledge and skills for the New Economy*, Buckingham: Demos.

Selwyn, N. & Brown, P. (2007) Education, Nation States and the Globalization of Information Networks, in B. Lingard & J. Ozga (eds) *The RoutledgeFalmer Reader in Education Policy and Politics*, 154–77. Abingdon: Routledge.

Selwyn, N. (2010) Looking beyond learning: notes towards the critical study of educational technology, *Journal of Computer Assisted Learning* 26: 65–72.

Selwyn, N. (2011a) *Schools and Schooling in the Digital Age: A Critical Analysis*, Abingdon: Routledge.

Selwyn, N. (2011b) *Education and Technology: Key Issues and Debates*, London: Continuum.

Selwyn, N., & Facer, K. (2007) *Beyond the Digital Divide: Rethinking digital inclusion for the 21st century*, Bristol: Futurelab.

Shaffer, D.W. & Clinton, K.A. (2006) Toolforthoughts: Re-examining Thinking in the Digital Age, *Mind, Culture and Society*, 13(4), 283–300.

Shaffer, D.W. (2006) *How Computer Games Help Children Learn*. Houndmills: Palgrave MacMillan.

Shallcross, D.J. (1981) *Teaching creative behaviour: how to teach creativity to children of all ages*, Englewood Cliffs, NJ: Prentice Hall.

Sharp, C., Pye, D., Blackmore, J., Brown, E., Eames, A., Easton, C., Filmer-Sankey, C., Tabary, A., Whitby, K., Wilson, R. and Benton, T. (2006) *National evaluation of Creative Partnerships*, England: Arts Council of Great Britain Creative Partnerships.

Shulman, L. S. (1987) Knowledge and Teaching: Foundations of the New Reform, *Harvard Educational Review, 57*,1: 1–22.

Shulman, L. S., & Shulman, J. H. (2004) How and what teachers learn: a shifting perspective, *Journal of Curriculum Studies, 36*, 2: 257–71.

Siemens, G. (2005) Connectivism: A learning theory for the digital age, *International Journal of Instructional Technology and Distance Learning 2*, 10. Online. Available HTTP: <http://www.elearnspace.org/Articles/connectivism.htm> (accessed 31 July 2011).

Snyder, I. (1997) *Page to Screen: Taking Literacy into the Electronic Era*, Sydney: Allen and Unwin.

Somekh, B. (2001) Methodological Issues in Identifying and Describing the Way Knowledge is Constructed With and Without Information and Communications Technology, *Journal of Information Technology for Teacher Education,* 10, 1 & 2: 157–78.

Somekh, B. (2007) *Pedagogy and learning with ICT: researching the art of innovation*, London and New York: Routledge.

Spring, J. (2009) *Globalization of Education: An Introduction*. New York: Routledge.

Sternberg, R.J. & Lubart, T.I. (1999) The concept of creativity: prospects and paradigms, in R.J. Sternberg (ed.) *Handbook of Creativity*, Cambridge, UK: Cambridge University Press.

Stevenson, N. (2010) Education, neoliberalism and cultural citizenship: Living in 'X Factor' Britain, *European Journal of Cultural Studies* 13, no. 3: 341–58.

Suoranta, J. & Vadén, T. (2010) *Wikiworld*, London: Pluto Press.

Terranova, T. (2000) Free Labour: Producing Culture for the Digital Economy, *Social Text* 18, no. 2: 33–58.

Thomson, P., Jones, K. & Hall, C. (2009a) *Creative School Change Research Project: Final Report*, Creative Partnerships, University of Nottingham, University of Keele.

Thomson, P., McGregor, J., Sanders, E., & Alexiadou, N. (2009b) Changing Schools: More than a lick of paint and a well-orchestrated performance? *Improving Schools, 12*(1), 15–57.

Thrift, N. (2005) *Knowing Capitalism*, London: Sage.

Tomlinson, J. (1993) *The Control of Education*, London: Cassell.

Trifonas, P.P. (ed.) (2012) *Learning the Virtual Life: Public Pedagogy in a Digital World*, New York and London: Routledge.

Turkle, S. (1995) *Life on the Screen: Identity in the age of the internet*, London: Phoenix.

Turvey, K. (2010) Pedagogical-research designs to capture the symbiotic nature of professional knowledge and learning about e-learning in initial teacher education in the UK, *Computers and Education,* 54: 783–90.

Turvey, K. (2013) *Narrative Ecologies: Teachers as Pedagogical Toolmakers,* London, New York: Routledge.

Underwood, J. D. M. & Underwood, G. (1990) *Computers and Learning: Helping children acquire thinking skills*, Oxford: Blackwell.

Usher, R. (2009) Consuming learning, in Sandlin, J. & McLaren, P. (eds.) *Critical Pedagogies of Consumption: Living and learning in the shadow of the 'shopocalypse'*. Abingdon: Routledge.

Valtonen, T., Pontinen, S., Kukkonen, J., Dillon, P., Vaisanen, P. & Hacklin, S. (2011) Confronting the technological pedagogical knowledge of Finnish net generation student teachers, *Technology, Pedagogy and Education, 20*, 1: 3–18.

Veen, W. & Vrakking, B. (2004) *Homo Zappiens: Growing up in the digital age*, London: Network Continuum Education.

Voogt, J., Fisser, P., Pareja Roblin, N., Tondeur, J. & Van Braak, J. (2012) Technological pedagogical content knowledge, A review of the literature, *Journal of Computer Assisted Learning*, Article first published online: 16 March 2012.

Warwick, P., Hennessy, S., & Mercer, N. (2011) Promoting teaching and school development through co-enquiry: Developing interactive whiteboard use in a 'dialogic classroom', *Teachers and Teaching: Theory and Practice, 17*, 3: 303–24.

Watkins, C. & Mortimore, P. (1999) Pedagogy: What do we know? in P. Mortimore (ed.) *Understanding Pedagogy and its impact on learning*, London: Paul Chapman Publishing.

Webb, M. (2011) Changing models for researching pedagogy with information and communications technologies, *Journal of Computer Assisted Learning,* Article first published online: 2 December 2011 DOI: 10.1111/j.1365-2729.2011.00465.x.

Webb, M. & Cox, M. (2004) A Review of Pedagogy Related to Information and Communications Technology, *Technology Pedagogy and Education*, 13(3), 52–286.

Weber, S. & Mitchell, C. (2008) Imagining, Keyboarding, and Posting Identities: Young People and New Media Technologies, in D. Buckingham (ed.) *Youth, Identity and Digital Media*: 25–48. Cambridge, MA: The MIT Press.

Webster, F. (2006) *Theories of the Information Society*, 3rd edn, Abingdon: Routledge.

Weigel, M., James, C. & Gardner, H. (2009) Learning: Peering backward and looking forward in the digital era, *International Journal of Learning and Media* 1, no.1: 1–18.

Wenger, E. (1998) *Communities of Practice: Learning, meaning and identity,* Cambridge: Cambridge University Press.

Wertsch, J.V. (1998) *Mind as Action*, New York: Oxford University Press.

Wertsch, J.V. (2002) *Voices of Collective Remembering*, Cambridge: Cambridge University Press.

Wheelahan, L. (2012) The problem with competency-based training, in H. Lauder, M. Young, H. Daniels, M. Balarin & J. Lowe (eds) *Educating for the Knowledge Economy? Critical perspectives*: 152-165. Abingdon: Routledge.

Whitty, G. (2012) Social class and school knowledge: Revisiting the sociology and politics of the curriculum in the 21st century, in H. Lauder, M. Young, H. Daniels, M. Balarin & J. Lowe (eds) *Educating for the Knowledge Economy? Critical perspectives*: 224–38. Abingdon: Routledge.

Williamson, B. (2012) Centrifugal schooling: Third sector policy networks and the reassembling of curriculum policy in England, *Journal of Education Policy*, iFirst: http://dx.doi.org/10.1080/02680939.2011.653405

Woolgar, S. (1991) Configuring the user: The case of usability trials, in J. Law (ed.) *A Sociology of Monsters: Essays on Power, Technology and Domination*: 57–102. London: Routledge.

Woolgar, S. (2002) Five Rules of Virtuality, in S. Woolgar (ed.) *Virtual Society? Technology, Cyberbole, Reality*: 1–22, Oxford: Oxford University Press.

World Economic Forum (2011) Personal Data: the Emergence of a New Economic Asset Class, Geneva: World Economic Forum.

Young, M.F.D. & Muller, J. (2010) Three Educational Scenarios for the Future: Lessons from the sociology of knowledge, *European Journal of Education* 45, no. 1: 11–27.

Young, M.F.D. (1998) *The Curriculum of the Future: From the 'New Sociology of Education' to a Critical Theory of Learning,* London: Falmer Press.

Young, M.F.D. (2008) *Bringing Knowledge Back In: From social constructivism to social realism in the sociology of education,* Abingdon: Routledge.

Young, M.F.D. (2012) Education, Globalization and the 'Voice of Knowledge', in H. Lauder, M. Young, H. Daniels, M. Balarin & J. Lowe (eds) *Educating for the Knowledge Economy? Critical perspectives*: 139–51. Abingdon: Routledge.

Yowell, C.M. (2012) Connected Learning: Designed to mine the new, social, digital domain. *DMLcentral.net*, 1 March 2012. Online. Available HTTP: <www.dmlcentral. net/blog/constance-m-yowell-phd/connected-learning-designed-mine-new-social-digital-domain> (accessed 11 July 2012).

Yusuf, S. (2007) From Creativity to Innovation, World Bank Policy Research Working Paper 4262, Washington, D.C.: World Bank.

Žižek, S. (2008) *Violence*, London: Profile.

INDEX